Other Books and Series by Jeff Bowen

Crow Agency Montana 1898-1905 Census Volume I 1898-1901 with Illustrations
Crow Agency Montana 1898-1905 Census Volume II 1902-1905 with Illustrations

COMPLIMENT THIS SERIES WITH A FANTASTIC MEMOIR OF A WHITE MAN WHO BECAME A CROW INDIAN!

Memoirs of a White Crow Indian (Thomas H. Leforge) As told by Thomas B. Marquis with Full Index and Illustrations

➢ Hardback ISBN: 978-1-64968-171-3

Other Books and Series by Jeff Bowen

Cherokee Granted Enrollment Cards & Dawes Packets 1900 - 1907 Volumes I, II & III

COMPLIMENT ALL CHEROKEE SERIES WITH THE GREATEST CHEROKEE HISTORY AND GENEALOGICAL BOOK PUBLISHED!

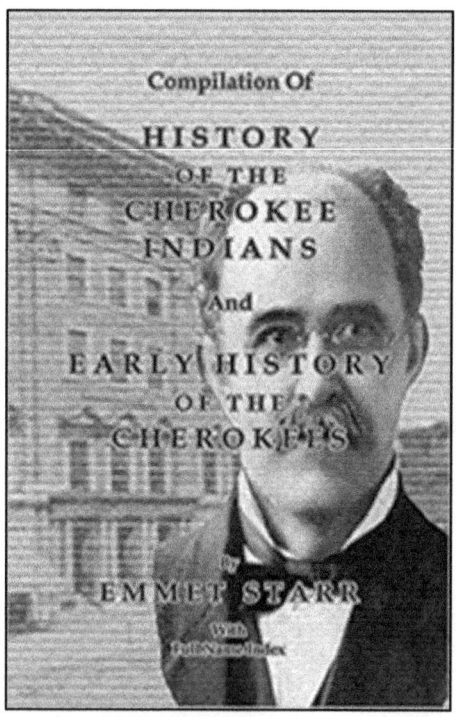

- ➤ Softback ISBN: 978-1-64968-119-5
- ➤ Hardback ISBN: 978-1-64968-127-0

Other Cherokee Publications You May Not Know About

- *Compilation of History of the Cherokee Indians and Early History of the Cherokees* by Emmet Starr *with Combined Full Name Index* (Hardbound & Softbound)

Other Books and Series by Jeff Bowen

Compilation of History of the Cherokee Indians and Early History of the Cherokees by Emmet Starr with Combined Full Name Index (Hardbound & Softbound)

1901-1907 Native American Census Seneca, Eastern Shawnee, Miami, Modoc, Ottawa, Peoria, Quapaw, and Wyandotte Indians (Under Seneca School, Indian Territory)

1932 Census of the Standing Rock Sioux Reservation with Births and Deaths 1924-1932

Kiowa, Comanche, Apache, Fort Sill Apache, Wichita, Caddo and Delaware Indians Birth and Death Rolls 1924-1932

Census of The Blackfeet, Montana, 1897- 1901 Expanded Edition

Eastern Cherokee by Blood, 1906-1910, Volumes I thru XIII

Choctaw of Mississippi Indian Census 1929-1932 with Births and Deaths 1924-1931 Volume I
Choctaw of Mississippi Indian Census 1933, 1934 & 1937, Supplemental Rolls to 1934 & 1935 with Births and Deaths 1932-1938, and Marriages 1936-1938 Volume II

Eastern Cherokee Census Cherokee, North Carolina 1930-1939 Census 1930-1931 with Births And Deaths 1924-1931 Taken By Agent L. W. Page Volume I
Eastern Cherokee Census Cherokee, North Carolina 1930-1939 Census 1932-1933 with Births And Deaths 1930-1932 Taken By Agent R. L. Spalsbury Volume II
Eastern Cherokee Census Cherokee, North Carolina 1930-1939 Census 1934-1937 with Births and Deaths 1925-1938 and Marriages 1936 & 1938 Taken by Agents R. L. Spalsbury And Harold W. Foght Volume III

Seminole of Florida Indian Census, 1930-1940 with Birth and Death Records, 1930-1938

Texas Cherokees 1820-1839 A Document For Litigation 1921

Starr Roll 1894 (Cherokee Payment Rolls) Districts: Canadian, Cooweescoowee, and Delaware Volume One
Starr Roll 1894 (Cherokee Payment Rolls) Districts: Flint, Going Snake, and Illinois Volume Two
Starr Roll 1894 (Cherokee Payment Rolls) Districts: Saline, Sequoyah, and Tahlequah; Including Orphan Roll Volume Three

Cherokee Intruder Cases Dockets of Hearings 1901-1909 Volumes I & II

Indian Wills, 1911-1921 Records of the Bureau of Indian Affairs Books One thru Seven
Native American Wills & Probate Records 1911-1921

Other Books and Series by Jeff Bowen

Turtle Mountain Reservation Chippewa Indians 1932 Census with Births & Deaths, 1924-1932

Chickasaw By Blood Enrollment Cards 1898-1914 Volume I thru V

Cherokee Descendants East an Index to the Guion Miller Applications Volume I
Cherokee Descendants West an Index to the Guion Miller Applications Volume II (A-M)
Cherokee Descendants West an Index to the Guion Miller Applications Volume III (N-Z)

Applications for Enrollment of Seminole Newborn Freedmen, Act of 1905

Eastern Cherokee Census, Cherokee, North Carolina, 1915-1922, Taken by Agent James E. Henderson   Volume I (1915-1916)
Volume II (1917-1918)
Volume III (1919-1920)
Volume IV (1921-1922)

Eastern Cherokee Census, Cherokee, North Carolina, 1923-1929, Taken by Agent James E. Henderson   Volume I (1923-1924)
Volume II (1925-1926)
Volume III (1927-1929)

Complete Delaware Roll of 1898

Applications for Enrollment of Seminole Newborn Act of 1905 Volumes I & II

North Carolina Eastern Cherokee Indian Census 1898-1899, 1904, 1906, 1909-1912, 1914   Revised and Expanded Edition

1932 Hopi and Navajo Native American Census with Birth & Death Rolls (1925-1931) Volume 1 - Hopi
1932 Hopi and Navajo Native American Census with Birth & Death Rolls (1930-1932) Volume 2 - Navajo

Western Navajo Reservation Navajo, Hopi and Paiute 1933 Census with Birth & Death Rolls 1925-1933

Cherokee Citizenship Commission Dockets 1880-1884 and 1887-1889 Volumes I thru V

Applications for Enrollment of Chickasaw Newborn Act of 1905 Volumes I thru VII

Cherokee Intermarried White 1906 Volume I thru X

Applications for Enrollment of Creek Newborn Act of 1905 Volumes I thru XIV

Other Books and Series by Jeff Bowen

Applications for Enrollment of Choctaw Newborn Act of 1905 Volumes I thru XX

Choctaw By Blood Enrollment Cards 1898-1914 Volumes I thru XX

Oglala Sioux Indians Pine Ridge Reservation 1932 Census Book I
Oglala Sioux Indians Pine Ridge Reservation Birth and Death Rolls 1924-1932 Book II

Census of the Sioux and Cheyenne Indians of Pine Ridge Agency 1896 - 1897 Book I
Census of the Sioux and Cheyenne Indians of Pine Ridge Agency 1898 - 1899 Book II

Northern Cheyenne Tongue River, Montana 1904 - 1932 Census 1904-1916 Volume I
Northern Cheyenne Tongue River, Montana 1904 - 1932 Census 1917-1926 Volume II
Northern Cheyenne Tongue River, Montana 1904 - 1932 Census 1927-1932 Volume III

Sac & Fox - Shawnee Estates 1885-1910 (Under Sac & Fox Agency) Volumes I-VIII
Sac & Fox - Shawnee Estates 1920-1924 (Under The Sac & Fox Agency, Oklahoma) & Wills 1889-1924 Volume IX
Sac & Fox - Shawnee Deaths, Cemetery, Births, & Marriage Cards (Under The Sac & Fox Agency, Oklahoma) 1853-1933 Volume X
Sac & Fox - Shawnee Marriages, Divorces, Estates Log Books Volumes 1 & 2, Log Book Births & Deaths (Under Sac & Fox Agency, Oklahoma)1846-1924 Volume XI
Sac & Fox - Shawnee Guardianships Part 1 (Under Sac & Fox Agency, Oklahoma) 1892-1909 Volume XII
Sac & Fox - Shawnee Guardianships, Part 2 (Under The Sac & Fox Agency, Oklahoma) 1902-1910 Volume XIII
Sac & Fox - Shawnee Guardianships, Part 3 (Under The Sac & Fox Agency, Oklahoma) 1906-1914 Volume XIV

Census of the Pima, Tohono O'odham (Papago), and Maricopa Indians of the Gila River, Ak Chin & Gila Bend Reservations 1932 with Birth and Death Rolls 1924-1932

Identified Mississippi Choctaw Enrollment Cards 1902-1909 Volumes I, II, III
Identified Mississippi Choctaw Enrollment Cards' Dawes Packets 1902-1909 Volumes IV, V, VI & VII

Census of the Northern Navajo, Navajo Reservation, New Mexico, 1930 Volume I
Census of the Northern Navajo, Navajo Reservation, New Mexico, 1931 Volume II

Other Books and Series by Jeff Bowen

History of the Osage Nation, Its People, Resources, and Prospects, The Last Reservation to Open in the New State by Philip Dickerson, M.A.

COMPLIMENT *THE HISTORY OF THE OSAGE NATION* WITH THE *CENSUS OF THE OSAGE INDIANS OF OSAGE AGENCY, OKLAHOMA, 1906 – 1929* starting with *1906-1911 Volume I*

(More volumes to come, soon)

➢ Softback ISBN: 978-1-64968-176-8

Other Books and Series by Jeff Bowen

- *Eastern Cherokee by Blood, 1906-1910, Volumes I thru XIII*

- *Eastern Cherokee Census Cherokee, North Carolina 1930-1939 Census 1930-1931 with Births And Deaths 1924-1931 Taken By Agent L. W. Page   Volume I*
- *Eastern Cherokee Census Cherokee, North Carolina 1930-1939 Census 1932-1933 with Births And Deaths 1930-1932 Taken By Agent R. L. Spalsbury   Volume II*
- *Eastern Cherokee Census Cherokee, North Carolina 1930-1939 Census 1934-1937 with Births and Deaths 1925-1938 and Marriages 1936 & 1938 Taken by Agents R. L. Spalsbury And Harold W. Foght   Volume III*

- *Texas Cherokees 1820-1839 A Document For Litigation 1921*

- *Starr Roll 1894   (Cherokee Payment Rolls) Districts: Canadian, Cooweescoowee, and Delaware   Volume One*
- *Starr Roll 1894 (Cherokee Payment Rolls) Districts: Flint, Going Snake, and Illinois   Volume Two*
- *Starr Roll 1894 (Cherokee Payment Rolls) Districts: Saline, Sequoyah, and Tahlequah; Including Orphan Roll Volume Three*

- *Cherokee Descendants East An Index to the Guion Miller Applications Volume I*
- *Cherokee Descendants West An Index to the Guion Miller Applications   Volume II (A-M)*
- *Cherokee Descendants West An Index to the Guion Miller Applications   Volume III (N-Z)*
- *Cherokee Intruder Cases Dockets of Hearings 1901-1909 Volumes I & II*

- *Eastern Cherokee Census, Cherokee, North Carolina, 1915-1922, Taken by Agent James E. Henderson   Volume I (1915-1916)*
  - *Volume II (1917-1918)*
  - *Volume III (1919-1920)*
  - *Volume IV (1921-1922)*

Other Books and Series by Jeff Bowen

- *Eastern Cherokee Census, Cherokee, North Carolina, 1923-1929, Taken by Agent James E. Henderson   Volume I (1923-1924)*
  - *Volume II (1925-1926)*
  - *Volume III (1927-1929)*

- *North Carolina Eastern Cherokee Indian Census 1898-1899, 1904, 1906, 1909-1912, 1914   Revised and Expanded Edition*

- *Cherokee Citizenship Commission Dockets 1880-1884 and 1887-1889   Volumes I thru V*

- *Cherokee Intermarried White 1906 Volume I thru X*

- *Cherokee Granted Enrollment Cards & Dawes Packets 1900 - 1907   Volumes I, II & III*

Visit our website at *www.nativestudy.com* to learn more about these other books and series by Jeff Bowen

HISTORY OF THE OSAGE NATION

Its People, Resources, and Prospects
The Last Reservation to Open in the New State
by PHILIP DICKERSON, M.A.

TRANSCRIBED BY
JEFF BOWEN

NATIVE STUDY
Gallipolis, Ohio
USA

Copyright © 2025
by Jeff Bowen

ALL RIGHTS RESERVED
No part of this publication may be reproduced,
distributed, or transmitted in any form or by any means,
without the prior written permission of the publisher.

Native Study LLC
Gallipolis, OH
www.nativestudy.com

Library of Congress Control Number: 2025905902

ISBN: 978-1-64968-178-2

Made in the United States of America.

This book is dedicated to

the Osage People

both past and present.

INTRODUCTION

This *History of the Osage Nation* isn't just a reproduction copy like a Xerox that's unreadable and so small you need a magnifying glass to read it. It is a fully transcribed and indexed copy of the original old Osage history from 1906 where you can actually comprehend who the Osage of old were. Philip J. Dickerson was to the Osage Nation what Emmet Starr was to the Cherokee; historian and keeper of their tribal culture and traditions.

He filled his text with not just their history, but gave names and backgrounds. Even at one point later he began to make an attempt at describing the deceptions of what the Osage dealt with in early times though unsuccessfully; likely with a fear of oppression from, to us unawares. But he spoke of the people, their stature and connections to a civilized world, their origins whether newcomer or an established tribal member; also their intelligence, capabilities and productiveness.

This is a history that most never imagined, and for some never wanted in print. This volume will not only help many to find their family connections but from firsthand experience will give you an exacting history from the roots of a people struggling to build their world.

At some point Dickerson points out he had difficulties in getting this piece published and that some of the business world there seemed to not want his work completed. He has a great deal of typographical mistakes within the text itself but it also makes you wonder why when he seems to get so much right. There were some forces at odds to the Osage because of their riches so it seems only natural that he wasn't going to have an easy time promoting the Osage. The opposition likely wanted as little attention as possible and his book wasn't going to help that. But reading the material will help you understand or almost feel his frustrations. You can almost feel his distractions at times. Maybe even see with your own eyes the sabotage of a written work rather than celebration of a people. Yet Dickerson seemed to fight the good fight.

You will enjoy reading this piece of Native American history from the land of where David Grann pursued the truths of an Indian Nation, the Osage. By reading their history the reflection of a peaceful people's nature and their peaceful homes sprang horrendous crimes, then years later the creation of a novel, *Killers of the Flower Moon*; along with a movie titled the same as recently as 2023.

Through this research you will learn about the sorted tale of an innocent people who at times wished the blessing bestowed upon them had never come. The little flowers that came in May on their prairie lands eventually found its simple beauty labeled with a sad terrible truth, deception and fear. But this book gives a complete understanding of a noble people who at times seem to have been forgotten until they found themselves under a flood of greed from others. This is their story before it got really bad or started to....

Jeff Bowen
Gallipolis, OH
NativeStudy.com

BELIEF IN CREATION—IN THE GREAT GOD AND A MESSIAH.

One day the Osage while hunting saw a beaver sitting on a beaver hut. Mr. beaver asked him what he was looking for. The Osage answered: "I am thirsty and came for a drink." The beaver then asked him who he was and when he came. The Osage replied that he had no place of residence. "Well, then said the beaver, "as you appear to be a reasonable man I wish you to come and live with me. I have many daughters and if any of them should be agreeabel[sic] to you, you may marry." The Osage, as the legend goes, accepted his offer and married one of his daughters, by whom he had many children. The Osage ancestors gave this as their reason for not killing the beaver, as their offspring were believed to be Osage "people."

[This is an abridged version of Dickerson's explanation of the Osage creation to explain the image of a beaver on the book cover.]

[Though the transcription is exactly as Dickerson finalized his text the pictures or what he called a "cut" in many instances were arranged to make the text as comfortable as possible for the reader. In some cases either he or the printer of the original would develop a story and then drop the story within an insertion of some form with another subject and then pick up that story again either a page or more later.]

History of the Osage Nation
Its People, Resources and Prospects.
The Last Reservation to Open in the New State

(1) Pawhuska, looking Northwest, with M. V. Railway Bridge to the right. (2) Residence section, from National School Heights. (3) Main Street, looking east from M. V. Railroad.

Pawhuska, the capital and Osage county seat.
Skiatook, Wynona, Hominy, Osage Junction, Fairfax, Remington, Burbank.
[3,000 Edition]
By PHILIP DICKERSON, M. A.

(Indian Agent's Office) FIRST NATIONAL BANK OF PAWHUSKA
H. H. Brenner, Pres. W. T. Leahy, V-Pres. A. N. Ruble, Cash. T. E. Gibson, Asst. Cash. Other shareholders—C. N. Purdom, T. J. Leahy, P. J. Monk, Julian Trumbly, Pawhuska. A. C. Miller, H. C. Hanson, DesMoines, Ia. W. M. Wilson, C. M. Smith, Kansas City, Mo. Capital, Surplus and Profits $50,000. Deposits $150,000.

PHILIP DICKERSON, M. A.
Author and Publisher.

INTRODUCTION.

As all wish to know something of those with whom they have any dealings it will not be egotistical first to give a brief sketch of the writer and his purpose. A native of the "Old Dominion," Virginia, he spent part of his boyhood on the farm, and in the public schools there, then traveled extensively before entering upon a higher course of study which he took in some of the best literary institutions in the "North" and "East" for over twelve years. Graduating from Keystone University and Bucknell University, (Pa.) and taking special studies in philosophy and four languages in Richmond College (Va.) one year, he pursued higher studies in languages, sociology, poetics and pedegogy for three years in the University of Chicago, receiving the B. A. and M. A. degrees in the courses of study, since which years he has traveled much, preached as an evangelist, taught, lectured, wrote, read broadly in law, which he has practiced some, but all the time with the purpose, sooner or later, to establish a well located Industrial, Literary, and Scientific college, largely benevolent in work and aim.

Perhaps the first thought of the reader who scans this book will be that it is an "ad." of the country. In one sense it does adertise, but in a much broader sense, it can be as literary, historical and true as any other history. The writer's purpose is to give in a literary brief, in plain style, the true facts of the resources and opportunities of the Osage, in book form so that all may have a brief history of all that interests any class of people, and worth keeping in the home. In this hustling stage of life, all things from the kindergarten to the philosophic grades of university lore, from the humble cot to the Fifth Avenue Palace from the district school and county church, to the city temple, must be kept before the people if we aspire to success. His secondary purpose is to lay the foundation of the college which has been planned through twenty years of study and hopes soon to find a people or benevolently inclined individual who will aid in beginning an institution of self help for the many poorer boys and girls who desire an opportunity to acquire a practical with a thorough literary course. It would be a great benefit to the territory to begin an institution that might soon be self supporting and growing through all time. Nothing could more interest, socially, commercially, and religiously than an unsectarian school rightly conducted on the broader methods and more practical principles of education for both Indians and whites.

Among the many anxious to get at every bit of information from the territory just unfoulding to the world, some are interested in the condition of the churches and schools, where they may make homes, others seeking health in the climate, some in making city homes, wish to know of the town and beauty of location, society, commercial progress, people and the value of property. And the majority looking for country homes, are most interested in the soil, climate, rainfall, temperature, and products of the soil. To all the classes this book comes as a true history and descriptive greeting. Being written by a neutral observer, you may know its contents are true to the best of his knowledge. It does not illustrate or name all of the best of the Osage country and people, which would make a ten fold volume could the writer have taken time to travel it all over, but sufficient to show how well prepared the last reservation in Oklahoma is for statehood and the Osage for allotment and countyhood. Hoping this volume will accomplish its purpose, in its education, ethical and commercial influence for the good of all, for all time and with much gratitude to those interested in and supporting this and all higher grades of publications, the Author is at

All copyrights reserved.   Your Further Service.

HISTORY OF THE OSAGE NATION

Pawhuska residence of Judge Thos. L. Rogers, Main St., and small sketch of Family, children, and grand-children in group.

(Photo by Hargis)

EARLY HISTORY OF OSAGE—THE CIGEHA.

From tribal traditions, according to Dorsey, the ancestors of the Omaha, Ponka, Kwapa, Kansa, and Osage were at first one family dwelling on the Ohio and Wabash rivers, but gradually wandered westward. They first separated at the mouth of the Ohio river. Those going down the Mississippi became the Kwapa, or down-stream people, those ascending the Mississippi, the Omaha or Nomaha, up-stream people. This separation occurring before De Sota's discovery of the Mississippi must have been in the 15th century. The Omahas, including the Osage, Ponka and Kansa group, ascended as far as the Missouri river where after a time the Omahas ascended the Missouri, leaving behind successively the Osage and Kansa families in the present territory of Missouri and Kansas, where the Omahas settles between the Platte and Niobrara, south of the Missouri, and the Ponkas continued into the Black Hills country where Lewis and Clark found them late in the 18th century reduced by smallpox from 3,500 to 300.

The Osage and Kansa ancestors seemed to have separated from the main Omaha group at the mouth of what was known as "White Creek," Grand Tuc (Grandes Eaux, according to Mooney) or Great Osage, which name it afterwards bore instead of referring to the Mississippi, as some claim. In 1673 Marquette refers to them as the "Ouchage" and "Autrechaha." In 1791 Penicaut designates them "Huzzau," "Ous," and "Wawha."

According to Croghan they were found on the Osage river in 1759 but in wending their way westward late in that century they encountered the Comanches and other Shoshonean peoples and turned southward toward the Arkansas river, and held the country between that stream and the Missouri till the immigration of the Cherokees westwward. They lived mainly along the Arkansas and Osage rivers early in the last century. In 1829 Procter estimated their number at 5,000. Schoolcraft April 1853 reckoned them at 3,758 after the removal of Black Dog's band to a new location lower down the Verdigris. In 1860 they composed seven large villages besides many smaller ones along Neosho and Verdigras rivers. In 1904 the full bloods numbered 808. Early in the 18th century the Missouri (Ouemessourit) Indians

HISTORY OF THE OSAGE NATION

being greatly reduced by the Sac and Fox wars, dispersed, and five or six lodges joined the Osages, three the Kansa and the rest amalgamated with the Oto and are now mixed with the blood of these people. It is said by an old Osage that the name Kahsah, Kansa or Kaw, was a term of ridicule given by the Osages to the Kaw band because they would not help the Osage in war against their common enemy, the Cherokee and other tribes, the term in Osage meaning coward. Mr. Wisemeyer, one of the Grey Horse merchants for years and now at Fairfax, and many years among the Osages, in speaking with the Omaha and Sioux Indians, found that they could speak the Osage language, all using the same dialect, showing that they belonged to the same or closely allied tribes. Rev. J. Owen Dorsey, an Episcopalian, who was connected with the Bureau of Ethnology at the Smithsonian institute at Washington, D. C., wrote an alphabet of the Sioux band, and discovered on meeting the Osage, Kaw and allied tribes, that it was applicable to these whose dialect he could speak fluently on first meeting them.

The Osage never had a written language, completed. A priest of Neosho, Kansas, once wrote a dictionary of the language, but dies before it was printed and

The St. Louis Boarding School, Sister Mary Gerard, Superior.

somehow got destroyed before publication. Elex Tall Chief a highly educated young Osage, of the Tall Chief family near Fairfax, is said to be now compiling an Osage dictionary, but the writer has not yet gotten any part of it, nor met this lexicographer. Nor does he consider it of sufficient importance to publish one now, as it will be only a generation till all Osages will know English, the universal language of the future. There is such a thing as dialectic economy of time and energy in educating the world as in other things.

The first record of the Osage yet found is a silver medal dated 1800 with Thomas Jefferson engraved on one side and two claspeh hands on the other over the word "Friendship," perhaps given to them by Uncle Sam to remind them of his desire.

We find but little record of these people till the treaty of 1804 at St. Louis as the colonies had not needed to that time the trans-Mississippi lands. Here we find the French traders and explorers first marrying into the Osage Tribes. Choteau, after whom Choteau Avenue is named, was a part blood Osage. They once held the whole territory which later formed the states of Missouri, Arkansas and Kansas. By treaty and the press of white immigration, they retired along the Missouri river to the present site of Kansas City, Mo., where they established trading posts.

The Osages and allied French were thus the first settlers of St. Louis and Kansas City, Mo., where they still have not a few distant relatives. What marevlous developments have followed in their former path; not more so however than will still come in their present country in two decades. In the West Bottoms of Kansas City, and on the banks of Turkey Creek, near its mouth lived a woman, the material ancestor of many of the mixed blood Osages, whose leading families are nearly all related by consanguinity or marriage, the wife of a "Canadian French-Alsatian" trapper, trader and interpreter, who died about the '50s, Monsieur Lessart. His wife lived here till Saucy Chief visited there in the '50s. Many of her descendants took up again her maiden name of Roy, of whom more elsewhere in a sketch of the Lessart family. Here lived the Choteaus from St. Louis, Revars (Revards from New Orleans,) Clairmot-Lessarts from Canada or Alsatis, Plomondons, (Prudhommes,) Del Oriers, Pappans, Pappins, Perriers, Tayrians, Raveletts, Mongrains, Soldanis, DeNoyas, Mon Cravies, ets., etc. The French mostly formed marriage alliances with the Osage,

THE ST. LOUIS BOARDING SCHOOL

This school located on a beautiful quarter section of land joining Pawhuska on the west, was the first to be built on the new reservation for the Osage children after the osage came from Kansas. It is a fine four story native stone building facing north. It can room and board from 150 to 200 girls of all ages with the best accommodations. The preceeding cut shows some of the beauties of the building and improved grounds, with the happy little Osage girls, mostly under 16 years of age, and the Sisters who teach them all the arts of domestic life and literature and music, for which they have the very best facilities for studying under the kind and efficient instruction of the Sisters. Many of the Osage ladies can look back to the St. Louis school as their first, and often only school of their girlhood,. and send their daughters to their Alma Mater. Here you see many bright little faces and feel the refining, educating influence that prevails in the recitation rooms, dormitories, dining hall, and rectory, all neat, clean, and cosy, surrounded by a broad campus. Music is made a specialty, as many of the Osage girls take readily and naturally to the art of harmony. The school is conducted under contract with the U. S. government to board and educate the children who choose to attend the school, at a stated sum per month.

The land was donated the Catholic people for school purposes and is well improved, with increasing attractiveness as the orchards, ornamental trees and flowers grow more beautiful. The children are under much better influence here than in many of their homes, where the habits of their young lives are moulded in the old modes of living. Some of the best wives and housekeepers in the Osage have been trained in the St. Louis School.

St. John's school for boys on Hominy Creek, near Grey Horse, is a model after the St. Louis, and furnishes equal advantages for the boys. Both were build through the benevolence of Walter Kalhirise, (or Kathrine Drexel,) of Philadelphia. These schools have only begun well their educational work for the Osage with their bright future.

HISTORY OF THE OSAGE NATION

CAN YOU THINK?

THE LITTLE PHILOSOPHER.
A Twentieth Century Thinker.

A Typical Osage Indian Girl.
The Wife of Arthur Bounicastle.

Quapaws, Wyandottes, and Kansas (Kaws.) But as the colonies stretched their bounds westward from the Mississippi, the Osage and their foreign allies receded west and south. They had another trading post some miles west of Missouri's present line, in the county of Linn. Their first school was esttablished in Neosho county, Kansas, by Father Shoemaker, about 1836, now known as St. Paul Misison. They have always been allied with some of the best whites in their territory, but scorning any alliance with the African race except in one case of adoption, one by Prince Albert, (Osage.) Hence they might be termed the royal tribe of American aborigines.

In the summer of 1868 after many peaceable retreats to different points in their successively limited reservations, they ceded by treaty at Drum Creek in present Montgomery county, all eastern Kansas, retaining some lands in west Kansas. For 100 years or more these people have been in close relation with the whites and have shown great shrewdness in making their treaties. Their traditions claim that the first two white men they ever saw came across a great stream (Grandes Eaux) in a boat, were captured, a council held and the two whites released on condition that they recross the water and never return.

Another says that the Osage first met the explorers of America upon the Gulf coast (or Atlantic) as they refer to the great water (the ocean perhaps,) then shoved their way up the Mississippi to the site of Napoleon, at Arkansas river mouth, there separated into the Great and Little Bone bands, and the Kaws and Poncas, the former taking up said river, the latter toward the headwaters of the Missouri and Kaw which retained the latter's name. But this is variance in vague history and given only to show the uncertainty of individual tradition. The great waters might have been the Pacific, or Great Lakes, or Ohio, or Mississippi rivers, as all the aborigines first emigrated from the northwest coast. The Dakota confederates, like the Wichitas, were a large tribe of Indians that were supposed to have migrated south from the far northern regions, from which direction ethnologists claim or believe, all the aboriigines of

HISTORY OF THE OSAGE NATION

America came. From north Asia the human race may have first found its way across the narrows of the Behring Sea, into what is now known as Alaska. All the historic legends of the various tribes seem to bear out this theory, and the bronze color and characteristics of the Indians are circumstancial evidence that these people were branches or offspring of the Asiatic races.

The tradition of the older ones of a battle against whites led by a general on a white horse signifies that their ancestors may have participated in a fight against Gen. Babcock, on Braddock's Field, now a park in the midst of the town by that name, a suberb of Greater Pittsburg (Pa.) 12 miles from its center, which historic field the writer has frequently viewed, in thoughts of the Red men and French who won that victory, but finally realized that the westward march of a commercial, scientific and semi-Christian civilization could never be turned eastward again, till it has circumscribed the globe and with its primitive Asiatic cradle clasps one such unbroken belt of mother earth. Fort Duquesne finally fell, where still the log barricade marks the center of the world's greatest iron, coal, and oil markets, the unceasing hum of a thousand productive trades. Every temporary victory was but the prelude to a Tippecanoe, Custer's last charge but the funeral knell of the wild buffalo, wild horse unborken plains, unfelled forests and barbaric life.

WHEN FIRST CALLED OSAGE INDIANS

They first lived in Kansas. They called themselves "Wa-sa-s(a)h" (?) the name of the tribe. There were three divisions, the Big Hills, the Little Osages and Kaws. The latter the Osages once refused to own, as the Kaws drifted away as a band of Osages but were not received back after their long absence. They speak about the same dialect and can understand each other. The Kaws have already allotted their lands in 1902 and occupy the Kaw (from which Kansas is derived) country, the northwest part of the Osage.

When the Cherokees moved from North Carolina and Tennessee across the Mississippi river, and were assigned territory west of Arkansas, the Osages felt that the Cherokees were intruding upon Osage country and this circumstance brought the two tribes into conflict and resulted in the battle of Claremore Hills, near the present town of Claremore, I. T., in which the Cherokees won a victory over the Osages, capturing some and driving the rest west to their Kansas country. When the Osages ceded their Kansas land to the United States government "Uncle Sam" gave them by treaty the present Osage country, to have and hold as long as "water glows, grass grows and fire burns."

ORIGIN OF THE TERM OSAGE.

The Great and Little Osages so named by the government authorities were once called the Big Bone and Little Bone Indians, a term applied to each other even in their councils at Pawhuska. of a few years ago. The above names have perhaps been latinized through the English from the term Bone people to Osage, from the Latin Ossa (?) meaning bone. Hence Little Bone (Little Osage) and Big Bone (Great Osage). But this is only a probability. From the report of the Bureau of American Ethnology the director, J. W. Powell, or rather Mr. James Mooney, a man of great research in Indian Territory lore and language, says: "The popular name 'Osage' is a corruption of Wasash, the name used by themselves. The Osage being the principal southern Souan tribe, claiming at one time the whole territory from the Missouri to the

HISTORY OF THE OSAGE NATION

Arkansas and from the Mississippi far into the plains, were geographically brought equally into contact with the agricultural and sedentary tribes of the eastern country, and the roving hunters of the prairie, and in tribal habit and custom they formed a connecting link between the two."

They were once a strong band but have been greatly decreased by war before coming to their present home, and many are said to have fallen by dissipation, but this the writer is unabel to confirm from his own personal knowledge.

W. J. McGee, in referring to the transformation of the Indian names into English says:

"Most of the names are simply corruptions of the original terms though frequently the modification is so complete as to render identification and interpretation difficult—it is not easy to find Wa-cace in 'Osage' (so spelled by the French) whose orthography was adopted and mispronounced by English speaking pioneers."

The meaning of most of the eastern names are lost. The Osage or Wa-ca-ce ("People" 'We are the people' if McGee is correct,) were comprised of several bands herein named.

The nomenclature of the Osage is difficult. Like that of Souan peoples and the great Dakota confederacy, they seem to have had a general term meaning only the "People." The Osages perhaps once belonged to the powerful aboriginal organization, the Dakotas, who had only descriptive terms of the allied tribes, as a greeting or countersign, and an alternate proper descriptive term—"Seven Council Fires" from which the Osage Seven Fire-places in their charmed circle were derived, thus indicating the antiquity of their ancestors as it was applied before the separation of the Asiniboin (a Canadian band.) The Cigeha group (a probabel branch of the Dakotas) was a term applied to the allied Omaha, Osage, Ponka, Kansas, Oto, etc., before their separation, who were without denotive designations, but proudly styled themselves "Local People," (a separate peculiar people.) "Men," "Inhabitants," and with still more pride "People of the Parent Speech," bearing an air of the first people, first families, of the world, lords in all their realm. too much "men," to distinguished a "people," for special titles, just as the terms "men" and "women" in sacred history language means the greatest work of God in creation. They felt the need of no other honor than the term "People." There is much variance in their names and spelling by different writers as in opinions and figures, but we can from the forms of Wa-sa-sah (or sha), Wasash, Wa-ca-ce and Wa-wha draw this conclusion: Wa, meaning great, and sash, sha, cace, wha, etc., meaning bone or people. Their own term is "Great Bone" (English slang, "Great Backbone,") a "Great People."

According to Dorsey, Shahan was a synonym of Osage, Wak, Otto, etc.

THE BANKS OF PAWHUSKA.

THE FIRST NATIONAL BANK

The First National Bank was the first to be established, October 1901, before which date the money affairs had been handled mostly by the Indian traders. This bank began with a capital stock, and under the direction of men of large means, that

HISTORY OF THE OSAGE NATION

assures its success and growth. The officers and share holders whose names appear under the cut, are some of the financial pillars of the Osage country. They stand high

socially as well as in finance. A statement at the close of business August 25, 1905, speaks much for the bank and town. The banking business of a community is the criterion by which its resources and progress are estimated by the commercial world. Mr. Brenner, the president, is a man of extensive business experience and is well known thoughout the Osage nation, having lived there many years, engaged in the mercantile, cattle and other business enterprises, prior to organizing the bank. He is largely interested in real estate and the oil and gas development here, has a beautiful cottage home on Main Street. and is ever ready to advance the interests of his town. With Mr. W. T. Leahy, A. W. Ruble, T. E. Gibson, and assistants, they are doing a large banking business. They occupy a stone building south of the park square on the triangle, and will gladly welcome and aid every new enterprise for Pawhuska and substantial individual.

THE CITIZENS' NATIONAL BANK

Was established October 1, 1903, as a state bank with $15.000 capital stock but such was its volume and increase of business that in June 1905, the capital stock was increased to $25,000 and on August 26, 1906, the institution was converted into a national bank. Its last statement issued September 1, 1905, showed the total resources to be $84,509.98; deposits to exceed $50,000 surplus and individual profits over $5,000 and increasing rapidly. Mr. W. S. Mathews who has been its president since organization, is of Osage ancestry, born and reared among them, and for many years honored and prominent in their tribal affairs. He is now a member of the Osage council. His family is one of the oldest and most prominent citizen families. His children are enjoying the best literary schools of the states. Mr. Mathews is an unassuming man, but of broad knowledge of national affairs, and Osage history, and excellent business experience and judgment; a congenial lodge man, a K. P. and a most trusted and excellent man too steer a financial house. He has very able efficient officers in Mr. R. E. Trammell, vice-president, and Mr. D. H. Spruill, cashier, both young men well fitted for their responsibility, worth of your trust, and most obliging in their business. At present the bank occupies a central buliding of Messrs. Beck and Hunt, by the Pawhuska hotel and council house south of the Triangle but has purchased a corner lot opposite at $5,000, the highest price paid during the sale.

HISTORY OF THE OSAGE NATION

THE BANK OF COMMERCE

Has lately been organized (October 1, 1905) under the official management of J. D. Scarborough, president; Clifton George, vice-president, Ethan Allen, cashier, M. O. Garrett, assistant cashier. Mr. Scarborough, formerly of Texas, has for many years run the Waujomis bank, Oklahoma. They have chartered at $10,000 capital stock, but expect to increase to $20,000. The best make of a Mangenes steel safe has been placed in their office on the east side of the triangle. Mr. Scarborough and his assistants will add much to the progressive influence of the town, do a general banking business, and make a specialty of collections, and welcome new patrons.

THE GENTILE SYSTEM AMONG THE OSAGE.

Among the Osages there were formerly three primary divisions or tribes composed of what was termed seven fire places each, Tsicu-utse-pecu-da A(A*), the Seven Tsicu fireplaces, Hanka, fireplaces, and Wacace-utse-pe-cuda, the Seven Osage Fireplaces.

The Hankas were the last to join the nation. When this occurred the first seven were reckoned as five, and the Osage as two gentes in order to keep the number of gentes on the right side of the tribal circle. Thus we find the Hebrew idea of the sacredness of the number seven and in their ceremonies they used seven pipes each. The circle was divided into halves the right side representing war, the left side peace. According as the children of one or the other side of the gens circle are sick they apply for food from the other side for them. To the peace or war side belong all the fireplaces or families of the tribe. Each family could trace his lineage back according to the side of the circle and names adopted from animals and plants. In this system were involved methods of choosing chiefs, warriors, officers, voting upon measures to be pursued in war, peace, punishment, treaties, etc., a system too much involved, vague and too obsolete to be given in detail in a brief historical sketch.

NAMING OF THEIR CHILDREN.

According to Saucy Chief, the care and naming of Osage children was a privilege conferred upon the Tsciu wactake (chief) and Pah-ka-wactake, who proceed with as much ceremony as some of the churches in confirmation. When a child of the Tsicu is named a certain old man sang songs without the camp, dropping tobacco from his pipe on his left toes as he sings each song. On the first day he (the Tsicu wactake) takes four grains of corn, a black, red, blue and white, after the four grains of corn dropped by four buffalo in the Osage tradition. After chewing the grains he passes them between the lips of the babe to be named. Four stones, pointing to the four points of the compass were put into the fire. The Tsicu called for some cedar and a special kind of grass that dies not in winter for use on the second day, on which, before sunrise, the old man says of the cedar tree and branches "It shall be for the children." Likewise he mentions the river, its deep holes and tributarie, as future medicine for the children. Upon the heated stones placed in a pile, is put the cedar and grass. Water is then poured on them making a steam in which the child is held. Then four names are given by the head man of the father's gens, who chooses one for the child. Meantime the men of the other gens bring stones, cedar water, etc., each performing his distinctive ceremonies. The old Tsicu putting cedar into some of the water, gives the child four

Pawhuska, Hotel,
Miss Jennie Larson, Proprietress.   W. S. Mathews, Pres.; R. E. Trammel, vice-Pres.; D. H. Spruill, Cash.
The Citizens' National Bank.

(Photo by Hargis)

sips. Then dipping his left hand in the water rubs the child down the left side from head to foot. Then repeats the process on the left, right an back side of the child. And all the women of his gens are invited to come forward and receive the same sign of blessing as the child, while all the women of the other gens are similarly treated by the head men of their respective gentes. All these tokens of stones, cedar, grass, water, fire, steam and corn and sips of water plainly signify, "May the world (all lands) with its forests, plains, rivers, streams or creeks, be the heritage of the child, to eat, drink and be merry, his whole being rendering glory to the woman who gave it birth." So deep are these principles inculcated in mothers and children that perhaps no mothers and fathers of the world idolize their children more, nor any children reverence more their parents, till this Israelitish virtue is handed down through part blood posterity, till among the Osage descendants it is often beautiful to behold a quiet Caucasian father or mother, with scarce enough Osage blood to darken their hair and eyes, which are frequently blond, gather a little flock of still more beautiful children about them in ideal parental love. No money too valuable, no time too precious to spend with the little folks, at morn or noon or night, even at times to extreme indulgence in their childish wishes and imitative language, far from baby brogue. How different is the scene, if any at all, in may of the blue blood Caucasian homes (?) where no stork ever comes with her burden of blessing, and when she does bring her proffered gifts, how frequently the so-called "Queen of the Home" is too bound to her social clubs and social rounds, to welcome tht little strangers. And this maternal trait or trend among the Osage and their descendants is not explained as some would have us believe " by the fact that each child is born heir to a common estate of $15,000 or $20,000 each." though this fact may be a favorable, assuring condition. But how many of the better fixed and wealthier classes of Caucusians welcome not the little, but bighter stars of every home, worth the name of "Home, Home, Sweet Home!" The orphan sighs: "What is home without a mother?" The true parent asks: "what is home without children and their happy glee?"

HISTORY OF THE OSAGE NATION

* The letters k, c, and t were reversed in their dialectic characters, and c crossed, but could not be linotyped.

BELIEF IN CREATION—IN THE GREAT GOD AND A MESSIAH.

In the mythological legends as to the creation of certain lands the beaver, otter, and muskrat hold the role of formation. The Iroquois narrated that their primitive female ancestor was kicked from the sky by her enrager spouse when there was yet no land for her habitation, but that it "suddenly bubbled up under her feet, and waxed bigger till a whole country was in her possession." Others claim that the beaver, otter and muskrat, seeing her fall rushed to the bottom of the deep to bring up mud sufficient to construct an island for her residence.

Among the Osages, Takahlis, and Algonkin of the northwest tribes the muskrat was their simple, cosmogonic machinery of land formation. These latter tribes were philosophic enough to see no real creation in such an account, but only formation by the action of these amphibious animals. The earth was there but hidden by boundless waters, and heaved up for dry land by the muskrat, as a formation only, logically distinguishing between the terms formation and creation, not assuming to know anything of creation, and considered any questions concerning it nonsense. Their amphibians were not considered creative constructors, but merely reconstructors, a very judicious and important corollary. It supposed a previous existance of matter on earth anterior to ours, but one without light or human inhabitants. A lake they said, burst it bounds, and submerbed all lands (note some similarity to the Bible deluge) and became the primeval ocean. We find among all primitive peoples some marvelous parallels of beiief in the mythic epochs of nature, the catastrophies, calamities and deluges of fire and water, which have held and swayed all human fancy in every land in every age. But all fancies have been lost in the dilemma of an explanation of a creation of matter from nothing on the one hand, and the "eternity of matter" on the other. **"Ex nihilo nihil"** (est) is an apothem indorsed alike by the profoundest metaphysicians and the most uncultured of primeval man.

Frances S. Drake, in his "Indian History for Young People" gives the following fabulous legend as the Osage metaphysician's natural philisophy for the origin of his "people." Many Osages believe that the first man of their nation came out of a sheel; that while he was walking on earth he met the Great Spirit, who gave him a bow and arrow and told him to go a hunting. After he had killed a deer the Great Spirit gave him fire and told him to cook and eat his meat and told him also to take the skin and cover himself wih it, and with the skins of other animals that he should kill. One day the Osage while hunting saw a beaver sitting on a beaver hut. Mr. Beaver asked him what he was looking for. The Osage answered: "I am thirsty and came for a drink." The beaver then asked him who he was and when he came. The Osage replied that he had no place of residence. "Well, then said the beaver, "as you appear to be a reasonable man I wish you to come and live with me. I have many daughters and if any of them should be agreeabel to you, you may marry." The Osage, as the legend goes, accepted his offer and married one of his daughters, by whom he had many children. The Osage ancestors gave this as their reason for not killing the beaver, as their offspring were believed to be the Osage "people." Such were their former traditions, not present.

HISTORY OF THE OSAGE NATION

Mr. and Mrs. Davis Fronkier, a cut of whose Pawhuska home and Milland Hotel appear with this sketch, are citizens of the Osage and Kaw country. He is of the Kaw, she of the Osage Nation. Mrs. Fronkier's father, Gasso Chouteau, was half Osaage and half French, and was the government interpreter for several years. His grandmother Chouteau was a full blood. They have a beautiful cottage home in Pawhuska and two good farms in the Osage and Kaw. They had four children, two

The Old Home of Mr. and Mrs. David Fronkier.
(Photo by Hargis)

are living, a boy, Arthur, and Rose, the wife of Jasper Rogers, one of the most beautiful brides of the Osage descendants, showing prominently the French features and beauty. Their beautiful home is no less striking than the life of the inmates, being a characteristic, happy, Osage citizen home, with his young son and attractive little wife dwelling with them. The Midland Hotel is centrally located and valuable property which they lease to proprietors.

THE OSAGE TELEPHONE COMPANY

MR. R. S. HARRIS, Mgr.

HISTORY OF THE OSAGE NATION

Mr. R. S. Harris, the successful manager of the Osage Telephone Co., is a native of Missouri, but spent some years in Texas in the cattle business. He has been in the Osage since 1889, ten years of which time he was devoted to the Mercantile business under the firm name of Leahy (W. T.) & Harris. But seeing a fine opportunity in the great convenience of the times, put in a telephone system of 60 phones, and now has nearly 200 installed, and one of the best systems in the territory, operated day and night, with about 100 miles of wire and 2000 feet of cable in town, and long distance connections to all points. He owns some valuable property in Pawhuska, and is a far sighted business man, and a good citizen wide awake to all advancement. He married a Miss Yoacum, whose sister, Miss Dora, is his chief operator. She is a most typical Kansas and western girl, with a combination of business qualities rarely found. She has been in the Osage for ten years and is a successful operator.

OSAGE TREE OF LIFE AND HEAVEN MYTHOLOGY.

Rev. J. Owen Dorsey, refers to a chart that was accompanied by chanting a tradition by the members of a secret society of Osages drawn by an Osage, Hada—cutse, Red Corn, early adopted by a white man named Matthews. Hence Rer Corn was named Wm. P. Matthews, or "Bill Nix," becoming one of the tribal lawyers. He belongs to the Sadekice gens. Other versions were given by Pahuska (present Pawhuska. While Hair, chief of the Bald Eagle sub-gens of the Tsicu gens, and from Saucy Chief, from the Wa-ca-ce gens, and from Good Voice of the Miki gens. The chart represents the tree of life, by a flowing river, both described in conferring the order. When a woman is initiated she was required by the head of her gens to take four sips of water (symbolizing the river). Then rubs cedar on the palms of his hands with which he rubs her from head to foot. If she belongs to the left side of the tribal circle he first strokes the left side of her head, making three passes, pronounciing the sacred name of the Great Spirit three times, repeating the process on her forehead, right side and back part of her head making twelve strokes in all (a perfect number).

Beneath the river were the following objects: The Watsetuka male slaying animal, or morning, (red), star, (2) six stars ("Elm Rod"), (3) the evening star (4), the little star. Beneath these are the moon, seven stars and sun. Under the seven stars the peace pipe and war hatchet which is close to the sun. The moon and seven stars are on the same side of the chart. Four parallel lines across the chart represent the four degrees through which the ancestors of the Tsicu people passed from the upper heavens to the earth. The lowest heavens rest on a red oak tree (Pusuku). The Sadekice tradition begins below the lowest heavens on the left side under the peace pipe. The stanza of the chant point to the different periods of evolution, first when the children of the first period ("former end") of the race were without human bodies and human souls. Then birds over the arch denote the evolution of human souls in bird bodies. Then the progress from the fourth to the first heavens, followed by descent to the earth. The ascent to four and ddescent to three make up the sacred number seven. When they alighted, as the legend runs, it was on a beautiful day, when the earth was clothed in luxuritant vegetation. From this time the path of the Osages diverged, the war gens marching to the right, the peace gens to the left, including the Tsicu, who originated the chart. Then conflict and the question of rights begun. The Tsicu, peace gens, met the messenger and they sent him off to the different stars for aid. According to the chart he approached in order the morning star (Watse-tuka), sun (Hapata

HISTORY OF THE OSAGE NATION

Wakanta—the God of day, the sun), moon (Watantaka—the God of night), seven stars (Mikake-pecuda), (Ta-adxi Three deer?), Big Star (Mikake-tanka), and Little Star (Mikake-cinka). Then Black Bear went to the Wacinka-cutse, a female red bird sitting on her nest. This grandmother granted his request giving them human bodies, made from her own body. The Hankaucantsi, the most warlike people; made a treaty of peace with the Waccace and Tsico gems and from the union of the three resulted in the last Osage nation but not including the allied races. A somewhat different version is given by the other gens, but all showing more or less the Darwinian theory of man's evolution, or ascent—almost as plausible in reason, when we link to this the first man's marriage with the beaver's daughter.

THE GHOST DANCE, RELIGION AND MESSIAH.

The Ghost-dance that is so potent in the religious life and belief of the Arapahos and Cheyennes of the west made but little impression and progress, among the Osages, who seem to have had a more philosophic premises of religious belief and practice. This dance was practiced by a majority of the Pawnees in full anticipation of the early coming of the Messiah and the buffalo, becoming as devoted to the belief and dance as the Arapahos who introducd and propagated the method of worship, but stenuously opposed by the agency authorities because of the spirit of unrest, conquest and conquering it engendered among its adherents. Yet it was but the inherent idea and feeling of all humanity from the most untutored savage of Africa's dismal jungles to the learned "Bard of Avon" that somewhere the human paradise has been lost to be regained by reverential approach to the Great God of Cristianity, the Great Spirit, or many gods of pagan minds. And the "Restoration idea" is the stronger in those whose life is proportionately hard to bear—a universal truth. Thus, perhaps, explains why the Osages being the most opulent, wealthiest tribe of America and the world, felt less need of a redeeming Messiah than those less fortunate. And being long under the influence and teaching of the Catholic church, many are firm believers in, and worshipers of the Christian Messiah, Jesus. Yet all belief in a Messiah is virtually the same though vested in moral, ethical, philosophy or in silken robes, or in simple nude pagan imagination. "Paradise lost" and Messianic return and restoration; though one be to John's revealed Heaven of the Spirit, the other to the happy hunting and fishing grounds. It is mainly a difference in comprehension of what is the ideality and perfection of life and its ultimate purpose and reward. "The belief and teachings as to the Hebrew Messiah, the Christian's millennium, the Hindu Avator and the Hesunanin

FOURTH JUDICIAL DISTRICT UNITED STATES COURT.

Composed of Noble, Kay and Pawnee counties, and the Osage Reservation, with the following officers: Bayard, judge and Jay E. Pickard, clerk, of Perry, O. T.; Judge E. N. Yates, deputy, and U. S. Commissioner, and Mrs. Mary B. Yates, deputy, Pawhuska. Judge Yates is a native of Putnam county, Indiana, but has been in Kansas and Oklahoma seven years. He is also deputy clerk of the District court. His commissioner's court is always in session. Hon. Horace Speed, U. S. attorney, and Jno. H. Scothorn, his assistant, practice here.

HISTORY OF THE OSAGE NATION

THE OSAGE COUNCIL HOUSE.

In this historic building is Council Hall and the offices of Judge E. N. Yates; U. S. Commissioner, Mr. J. N. Coulter, E. W. Kind and Jos. B. Mitchell, lawyers, Dr. F. C. Gale, Dentist, W. M. Dial, and Geo. B. Mellotte, Real Estate and Insurance. The Blue Point Restaurant and young Mr. Blanc's Barber-shop in the basement. The Osage Council meets in Council Chamber every three months about quarterly payments or oftener at the call of the chief, O-lo-ho-wal-la or the assistant chief, Bacon Rind.

(Photo by Hargis)

("Our Father") of the Indian ghost-dance are in essence the same and are born in the hopes and longings cherished by all human beings.

Quoting Mr. Mooney, the compiler of Indian lore and legend, the following is worthy of reprint: "There are hours, long departed, which memory brings like blossoms of Edden to twine around the heart."—Moore.

"The wise men tell us that the world is growing happier—that we live longer than did our fathers, have more of comfort and less of toil, fewer wars and discords, and higher hopes and aspirations. So say the wise men, but deep in our hearts we know they are wrong. For were not we, too, born in Arcadia and have we not each one of us in that May of life, when the world was young, started out lightly and airly along the pathway that led through green meadows to the blue mountains on the distant horizon, beyond which lay the great world we were to conquer? And through others dropped behind, have we not gone on through morning brightness and noonday heat, with eyes always steadily forwward until the fresh grass begun to be parched and withered, and the way grew hard and stony, and the blue mountains resolved into gray rocks and thorny cliffs? And when at last we reached the toilsome summits we found the glory that had lured us onward was only the sunset glow that fades into darkness while we look, and leaves us at the very goal to sink down tired in body and sick at heart, with strength and courage gone, to close our eyes and drem again, not of the fame and fortune that were to be ours, but only of the old time happiness that we have left so far behind."

As with men so it is with nations. The lost paradise is the world's dreamland of youth. What tribe and people has not had its golden age, before Pandora's box was loosed, when women were nymphs and dryads and men were gods and heroes? And when the race lies crushed and groaning beneath an alien yoke, how natural is the ddream of a redeemer, an Arthur, who shall return from exile or awake from some long sleep to drive out the usurper and win back for his people what they have lost. (The hope become a faith and the faith becomes the creed of priests and prophets (preachers), until the hero is a god and the dream a religion, looking to some miracle of nature for its culmination and accomplshment.

> Say, shall not I at last attain some height from whence the past is clear?
> In whose immortal atmosphere I shall behold by dead again?—**Bayard Taylor**.
> For the fires grow cold and the dances fail,
> And the songs in their echoes die;
> And what have we left but the grave beneath,
> And above the waiting sky?—**The Song of the Ancient People**.
> My father, have pity on me! I have nothing to eat,
> I am dying of thirst—everything is gone!—**Arapaho Ghost Dance**.

The Family reunion of the descedants of Julia Roy and Clemont Lessert, represeting four generations, from Mrs. Martha Dunham, the elderly lady sitting in the center of the group to the youngest baby.. Moses Shaw, son of Frank and Rosa Shaw.

(Photo by Hargis)

DOCTRINE OF THE GHOST DANCE—BY THE PROPHET OR MESSIAH —WOVOKA.

"When the sun died, I went up to heaven and saw God and all the people who had died a long time ago. God told me to come back and tell all my people they must be good and love one another and not to fight, steal or lie. He gave me this dance to give to my people. * * * You must not fight, do no harm to any one. Do right always. It will give satisfaction in life. The Revelation of Wovoka, the son of Tavibo, the prohet of Mason Valley, Nev., who died about 1870. Wovoka (meaning

HISTORY OF THE OSAGE NATION

cutter) was an industrious boy working till 30 years of age, when he announced this revelation that made him famous. He was reared in a narrow valley of the Sierras, 30 miles long, walled in by convulsively torn volcanic mountain walls, towering to perpetual snows, sparkling with diamond icycles, with a background of pine forests, the whole under the canopy of a cloudless, infinite, blue sky, through which the mind is called in thought to far off worlds above. Rasselas-like, a valley apart from the rushing world beyond, a favorable home for the contemplative mind of a dreamer whose instinctive spiritual power is producing a religious code that needed no human assistance. The doctrine anticipates that the whole Indian race, dead or alive, will be reunited upon some regenerated abode, or planet to live again in their aboriginal happiness "forever free from death, disease and misery." And these fundamental beliefs are common to all Indian peoples with only the mythological differences attributed by each apostle or prohet according to his traditions or his mental trend or ideas of happiness as characterize each tribe; but scarcely more variations of interpretation than are found in Christianity with hundreds of sects and creeds and innumerable shades of individual opinions that divide the ranks of Christianity and with, perhaps, as much sound reason. For our differences are mostly those of interpretation or definition that converge when followed out to the same fundamental points and premises leaving only a difference in imagination or practice, if any vital difference.

The writer treats this subject of religious life among American aborigines, to show how little Jamestown and Plymouth Rock colonies subsequently added to these principles except to teach them how to live the "Great Father's" teachings in precept and practice. And the Indian and Christianized Caucasian, too, sometimes doubt that even these have been accomplished except in a smattering of science among them.

All Indian believers were exhorted to make themselves worthy of the rewards of the promised happiness, conditioned upon discarding cruelty and war and practicing honesty, peace and good will not only among each other, but toward the pale-faced alien, among them. Many believed that the white races were of secondary importance, spiritually unreal and would have no part in the Red Man's plan of regeneration, would be left behind as other earthly things, and perhaps case entirely to exist after the coming of the Indian Messiah and the regenerative dawn, which some even nixed on certain days or years, as has often been done by religious enthusiasts among Christian adherents.

A PARAGRAPH OF THE MESSIANIC LETTER.

"Do not tell the white people about this. Jesus is now like a cloud. The dead are all alive again. I do not know when they will be there. May be this fall or in the spring. When the time comes there will be no more sickness and everyone will be young again."

"Do not refuse to work for the whites, and do not make any trouble with them until you leave them. When the earth shakes, (at the coming of the new world) do not be afraid. It will not hurt you.

"I want you to dance every six weeks. Make a feast at the dance and have food that everybody may eat. Then bathe in the water. That is all. You will receive gods words again from me sometime. Do not tell lies."

It is evident that these people have either a system of ethics, mytholigy, and ceremonial observance, skeletons of which were brought from eastern Asia, and the first from Western Asia, some thousands of years ago or gathered from the earliest missionary colonists from the old world, or it shows that all aborigines had an intuitive inherent religious belief and standard, as the birth-right of man, given by the creator, from his own image. Both may be true. Comparing the old prophecies, Christ's sermon on the mount, the two comprehensive laws of supreme love to God and fellowman (our neighbors) upon which two fundamental commandmments hang all the laws and prophets, and then add the interpretations of the apostles in their acts and letters, the above Indian code falls but little short of our Christian code in theory at least; and, we dare say, practice too, by the masses. The return of the Messiah to take up all Indians high upon the mountains where all kinds of game roam in abundance, while a flood comes to drown the bad (white man), then nobody but Indians live and game of all kinds thick, is only another interpretation of Mt. Ararat, and all the unworthy drowned.

"All Indians must dance, everywhere, and keep on dancing till their year of jubilee, is but the continuation of the ancient religious dance, as Meriam, David and others, danced before the Arkansas of God or the thousands in religious festivals, dancing only to the glory of god, till the practice of dancing was introduced upon the Greek and Roman pulpita or stage by men and women dacing together for show and pleasure. The full blood Indian knows no dance but by men alone and that partakig of a religious nature. Few, if any, of the part bloods take part in these dances, but manifest their love of music and dancing by frequently participating in the reel, two-step and waltz.

It was recently the writer's privilege to witness a full blood dance, to their four guests, men, from the Pueblos of New Mexico, in the Round House (a dancng, feasting and council buildding, similar in shape to a round circus tent, or locomotive round house) that stands in the midst of the Indian village, one mile northeast of Pawhuska. Four corpulent braves seated in a circle with drum sticks, beat a large one-headed kettle drum, with the same regular stroke and beat, making a thundering roar. One began the three others following what appearedd to the ear untrained to such music a doleful song or chant with equal time to the drum beats, which sounded to the writer's ear thus: Doom, Doom, doom. doomity-doom, doom, doom, doom, doomity-doom, or giving the a a broad Latin or Italian sound something like this: Dam, dam, dam, dam'pol, dam, dam, dam, dam, dam'ool, dam. But this is not the white man's swearing expletives, for the Osages have no swear words, and whenever using one which is seldom, they must adopt or transfer the language of his enlightened, civilized white cousin.

A charm of a small stone image is carried by some, as is the custom of the Ute also.

The following incident related to the writer by a most excellent devoted Christian girl, Miss Hilton, shows the susceptibility of the full bloods to Christian teachings.

The Family Reunion of Mr. Moses and Mrs. Clementine Plomondon in the accompanying cut shows four generations, all descendants of Martha Durham, who appears in the group. She was the daughter of Julia Roy and Clemont Lessart, of French Canadian descent. Julia Roy was a half blood Osage, who came from Kansas in 1872. After death she was buried near Silver Lake. Mrs. Clementine Plomondon was the oldest daughter of Martha Dunham, now 75 years old, and her first husband, Francis DeNoya. She had no children by her second husband, but six were born to her

HISTORY OF THE OSAGE NATION

in her first marriage, three girls and three boys, Martha, Mary, and Rosa, and Frank, Lewis, and Clemont DeNoya. Clementine married Moses Plomondon, and was blessed with twelve childdren, ten of whom are living, and five married. Their names were Barney, Martha, (now Mrs. John Palmer), Mary, (now Mrs. Anthony Carlton), Frances, Rosa (Mrs. Frank Shaw), and Stella, Agnes and Louise, the three last still single, and Louis and Dan. The other brothers and sisters of Mrs. Plomondon have from two to thirteen children. Frank married a Miss Carpenter, to whom were born seven children. Frank then married a Miss Mary Long who had seven children. Mary first married Steve Belleiu. To her were born two children Ora and Thomas. She later married Wm. Lewis, Lewis DeNoya married Josephine Revard, who had four children. She met a sad death January 23, 1905, by being dragged to death by a runaway team. She was said to have been one of the most beautiful women of Osage descent. Rosa married Joseph Pearson, and is the mother of eight children and lives next door to Mrs. Plomondon. Clement married a Miss Emma Ross, to whom was born seven children. There are forty-seven grand-children, and twenty-seven great-grand-children, of Mrs. Dunham, the great-grand-mother of this family reunion, ranging in decree of Osage blood from one-quarter, in Mrs. Dunham, (whose grandmother was a full blood) down to the thirty-second degree, in the great-grand-children.

The oldest great-grand-child is now sixteen, miss Mabel Palmer, the eldest daughter of Hon. John Palmer; and the youngest is at this writing an eleven-month-old boy, Moses Shaw, the son of Frank and Rosa Shaw (nee Plomondon.)

The writer gives a brief sketch of this family reunion, because it represents, to some degree of consanguinity, a large part of the Osage citizens, and by intermarriage many of the most prominent families now and for generations to come. The cut does not include many who were absent at the time the photo was taken by Mr. Hargis in September. 1905, when many had come for the quarterly payment.

PAWHUSKA HOTELS

The Midland (Photo by Hargis)

Pawhuska is well supplied with hotel, lodging and boarding facilities. Three hotels afford ample accomodations. The Midland Hotel, owned by David Fronkier, and the Pawhuska Hotel, owned by Messrs. Beck and Hunt, are as first class hotels for their rates as can be found in the two territories. They are both centrally located and well patronized and well conducted by experienced managers. Miss Jennie Larson, who is proprietress of the Pawhuska Hotel, is a native Missourian but need not be shown how to run a hotel. After coming to the Osage Nation with her sisters she conducted a dressmaking parlor for two years, but leasing the Pawhuska hotel and the rooms adjacent over the Citizens National Bank, a building also owned by Messrs. Beck and Hunt, she has, with unusual success, conducted a first class hotel business and has many patrons in and outside of town. Her sister assists her in the business and Mr. Dounce, familiarly called "Uncle Jimmy," for his congenial and obliging manner, is her clerk.

After a young Missionary of the Southern Board had taught a rather troublesome old fellow, L. M., even wicked in beatings his squaws, that if he did not live better and cease beating his wives he would go to the bad place, having consigned two or three wives to the Osage stone covered tomb, he married another, a Christian, who tried to influence him to be better. He came to Miss Emily Cottrelle and said "I want to be a good Indian; my squaw says if I don't do better me will go to the Devil and I don't want to go to the Devil, me fant to be good Indian."

Most of them believe in a good and a bad spirit, that the bad live in a lower place of happiness than the good who continue in spirit life and are rewarded according to good or bad one here, worshipped idols, pictures, or other emblems that signifies the Great Spirit; believed in self torture or self sacrifice in order to obtain forgiveness of wrong doing. At times they marched in solemn prosession bowing to the ground in prayer. and at other times congregations or as individuals asking the Great Spirit for present desires and future favors, in an earnest devout manner. Their emblem is a cooing dove, signifying peace and love.

The elegant and costly residence of Frank Tinker, Park Row, Pawhuska. Built by A. V. Linscott. (Photo by Harris)

But there are many who believe that the white man's religion and ceremonies are no better than their own.

HISTORY OF THE OSAGE NATION

One Osage, Angie P., after marrying two braves, whom she said went crazyz, having ran away from her, she was going to wed another man who desired her to go to Pawnee to get a license to marry in white folks' way. After much persuasion, she was induced to go and have the act sealed by getting a roll of paper, which she was led to believe was the magnet or charm of the Great Father at Washington, to hold this third time her man with her. Soon the third ran away and she said "he got crazy too." Lamenting over the fact that she had married white folks' way and could not again take a man till "Uncle Sam" took back her sham, (charm) said, "Me no marry white folks way again. No good. He ran away too. Roll of paper do no good. Me no like it." And it seems that this Indian woman was not far from being right in her estimate of the charm value of the roll of paper. It is recorded that out of 5,424 court cases docketed in Oklahoma county, one-fifth or over one thousand were divorce cases who did not like the roll of paper, praying the court to take back or annul what it gave. When society learns again that true marriage is an inseparable attachment formed by natural affinity, intelligence, heart devotion, love (meaning true affection without dissimilation,) and not a mere legal and social ceremony for convenience, there will be thousands of more happy homes, and legal separations the exception. There would be according to full-blood Angie P. few "runaways," or run-abouts after marriage.

THE OSAGE MARRIAGE CEREMONY.

Their ideals of virtue are strenuous and exacting in demeanor. They have no courtship. The younger women are constantly under the keenest vigilance of the older married ones. This is their custom. All ancestors are looked upon as mothers, fathers or guardians of the girls till married, which is early in life. Then she becomes the ward of the husband's parents, who feed them both the first year. The parents arrange the match by consent or gift. The boy and girl perhaps never see each other till their wedding hour, even though he ties his ponies in her yard to be received if accepted, or cut loose if rejected.

In marriage the girl was bought by the groom or his father for an agreed sum, or gifts paid to the girl's father, and her relation. It is said the full-bloods still practice this after the official recognition of such marriage by the agent and councils. When the gifts are first brought to the bride to be, time is given for the relatives to be consulted, or called together. The gifts are generally accepted on the second day. Then two days are given for the preparation for the wedding. Some food is sent by the groom each day to his expected bride, to let her know what kind of fare she may expect after marriage, whether it be good. A fine test if it is not only taffy but plain "grub," or "chuck." She is not so liable to be disappointed after marriage. Many "pale face" lads and lassies have all the sweets of well stocked confectionaries, chocolates, bon-bons, angel puffs, grape richey, ice cream socials, taffy, etc., and the finest livery rigs, at any cost before marriage, who often seem unable to get plenty of corn bread and butter milk for food and even a goat cart to ride in after marriage. The Osage young people are consistant. They start in as they expect to go through.

On the fourth day a beautiful, perhaps costly, American flag is raised by the families interested. After this the bride is prepared by putting on all of her best clothes, or all personal effects, often consisting of several fine robes, dresses, or blankets. Then she is taken to the groom's house on the best pony, or in a fine buggy, usually a pony, while another is led near her side. Now the race by the squaws from the grooms house or tent begins. The one reaching her first gets the pony that is led,

HISTORY OF THE OSAGE NATION

The Catholic Church—In the Channel of Bird Creek—Being Moved by Mr. Will Bradshaw, the House Mover, Pawhuska.

Mr. J. W. Bradshaw whose house moving appears herewith, lives in West Pawhuska. He has been a resident of the Osage Country for some years. He is a young man of good business ability and energy, and has spent much time on the farm, but has been engaged in moving houses in Pawhuska since the new railroad cut a swath through the town and made some rearrangement of the streets. He is progressive in idea as to what Pawhuska is and will be. He married Mrs. Zoah Revard, the widow of

Joseph Revard, Jr., the eldest son of "Uncle Joe" Revard. They had six children, Elnora, Margurite, Kert, May, Odel and Carl. Margurite is married to a Mr. Ebert Fenton, Elnora married Mr. Lou Hays. The others are still single. Mr. and Mrs. Bradshay have no children of their own but a pleasant cottage home where they live and good farms for themselves and children. Mrs. Bradshaw is of the Pappin family of historical interest. She is a bright, vivacious woman, much interested in the education of her children. Mr. Bradshaw moved this church across the deep channel of Bird Creek, over one-half mile. (Photo by Hargis)

while those second in the race divide the brides robes among them, leaving her only one scant poorest robe, taking her ribbons, jewelry, etc. When she reaches the groom's home the other women lift her off her pony, put her on a blanket, and take her in, not letting her touch the ground, she is lifted from the blanket to a white spread or table cloth where the wedding supper is spread. Then the groom is called from his hiding place, for he never appears till called, being much more bashful than the white grooms. He seats himself beside her and if both are happy in their parental choice they eat and drink together. If not pleased they may sit moody, solemn, or sullen for hours. In one case a young boy, being a graduate of Carlisle, and imbued with young America's ideas of courtship, did not care to take the girl his parents selceted, and forced him to wed, nor did the girl like the choice better. Both cried and could not be persuaded to eat at first. He was 21 and his bride 16 and educated in the National Government School. After weeping for long hours, they finally smiled at each other, and ate and drank together the Osage marriage ceremony. Oh, ye little "banty sparkers," how would you like the ceremony of "daddy" or "mammy" boxing your ears and making you wed in the Osage way? But Angie P. preferred it. Miss Hilton also deserves credit for the above observation and narration.

SLAVES AMONG INDIANS

It appears that while the Osages never captured members from other tribes for slaves, they themselves were sometimes made slaves by the northern tribes, either by capture or purchase.

Quoting Mr. Augustin Grignon, "The Menominees," "Wisconsins," and other Indian tribes, purchased Pawnee slaves from the Ottawas, Sioux's and other who captured them. Most of the slaves were called Pawnees, though some of them were from other Missouri tribes. He knew three Osages among the Menominees. The slaves were mostly females captured while young. No special pecuniary value was set upon these servants, but he relates where two females were sold at different times for $100 each. Regarding their treatment he remarks: The Pawnee slaves and others were generally treated with great severity. A female slave owned by a Menominee woman while sick, was directed by her unfeeling mistress to take off her over-dress and she then deliberately stabbed and killed her. and this without cause or provocation, and not in the least attributed to liquor.

The dog, among the Osages, as with all Indian people, is a favorite animal, at first being used for burden, before the capture and domesticating of the horse, which was introduced among the prairie tribes about the middle of the seventeenth century. "Long's Naturalist found the horse, ass and mule in use among the Kansas and other tribes, and described the mode of capture of wild horses by the Osage." In the Dakota and Souan dialects, to which the Osage belong the word suk-ton-ka, or sun-ka-wa-kan is a compound work sun-ka, (dog), and an affix tan-ka, and wa-kan, meaning great mysterious or sacred ancient dog, indicating that the dog among the Souan tribes was domesticated before the horse. Whether the Osage ever used canine flesh for food like other Indians, the writer is unable to say, but finds no record of such usage.

The Osage weapons of war were a bent spear, knife, bow and arrow, and tomahawk. The Osages were at war with the Kiowa and their confederated allies, the Comanche and Apache till 1834, for whom the Osage appeared to have a special dislike.

In the summer of 1833, significantly called by the Kiowa, "Summer that they cut off their heads," there was a great massacre in which the Osages cut off the heads of the Kiowas and put them in buckets upon the field of slaughter, just west of Saddle mountain, 25 miles northwest of Ft. Sill, known to Kiowas as, "Beheading mountain," near the headwaters of Otter creek. The Osages were on a western hunt and raid. The Kiowa warriors had gone against the Ute, leaving few except old men, women and children in camp at the mouth of Rainy Mountain creek, near the present site of Mountain View, O. T. Young Kiowa hunters found an Osage arrow sticking in a buffalo near by, gave alarm, the camp broke and fled in four bands, one east, another west and two south to the Wichita mountains. Three escaped. The fourth under A'date (Island Man) thinking all pursuit over, halted on Otter creek, where at the following dawn, a young pony hunter saw the Osages creeping up on foot, the general custom of the Osage and Pawnee, when going into battle with the hope of returning mounted, capturing their horses, a wise, Spartan like forethought, banking on bravery. They were designated by the Kiowas, Domankiago, "walkers." in marauding, but generally returning well mounted, going to social dances on foot, returning on generously donated ponies. At dawn above mentioned, all were asleep in camp save the young man, and the wife of Chief A'date, preparing to dress a hide. She aroused her brave, who rushed out shouting, "Tso batso! Tso batso—To the rocks, to the rocks!" They threw off morbid sleep, some sprang to flee, others upon the blood-thirsty knives of their fleet-footed foe, now slashing right and left. A'date was wounded, but escaped, his faithful wife, Sematma, (Apache Woman), captured, later to escape. One mother fleeing with a baby girl on her back, and a larger one by hand saw the older girl seized, with throat about to receive the cruel beheading knife, rushed at her captor, and beat him off, receiving only a slight scalp wound. Little Aza was rescued by his father by like daring and became an old man to tell the marvelous

(Photo by Hargis)

escape; how his father held him in his teeth while shooting arrows at his pursuers, then taking him in arms again to run. Other women escaped through the brave fight of a Pawnee in camp. The Kiowa warriors being absent it was only a Kiowa run for life.

HISTORY OF THE OSAGE NATION

Many were beheaded by the Osage lance or knife as it was their custom to behead instead of scalp in battle.

It was a wild, panic-stricken fight of old men, women and children in which every one caught, mostly women and children, were beheaded where they fell, and heads placed in brass buckets, bought of the Pawnee by he Kiowas. After the tepes were burned the Osages left the place. For the Kiowa flight and massacre Chief A'date was deposed. The Osages captured the taime medicine, killing the wife of its keeper while untying it from the tepee pole, also both taime images were captured in thir case and kept till peace was made between the Osage and Kiowa who had no sun dance for two years because of the loss of the taime. This massacre of 1833 led to the first dragoon expedition in 1834; the return of the head men of the more western tribes, including fifteen Kiowas with Col. Dodge to Ft. Gibson, where all the territory bands were called together in counsel and treaty of friendship that resulted a year later in an agreement by the southern tribes that all Indians should have equal hunting rights on the southern prairies as far as the western boundary of the United States and all American citizen travelers free pass through Indian hunting grounds, etc. This treaty was never broken, though the Osages served as U. S. scouts against the allied plain tribes later, Chief Clermont of the Osages signed this treaty.

When the Kiowa visited, in friendship, the Osages on the Cimarron, or Salt Fork of the Arkansas, they redeemed it by offering a pinto pony and other ponies, but they brought it from their home and delivered the taime, and as an evidence of friendship accepting only one pony in return. The Osages were strong enemies in war, merciless in battle and generous victors and friends.

Among the Osages, as well as other northern tribes, their brave deeds and numbers of enemy slain were indicated by styles of dress, ornaments and body paint.

THE OSAGE BURIAL AND MOURNING.

When Osage (full bloods) die he is immediately dressed in the best new robes, and blankets are put upon the corpse and prepared for burial by placing the body in a half-reclining position as if the body was calmly seated in a rocking chair. In this attitude the body was buried, by placing it on the ground and building a tomb of rough stones but skillfully constructed to resist beasts of prey and often stood for ages. The dead's personal effects are placed in the tomb with him and his gest and favorite pony was often led to the tomb and shot, that all might pass to the happy hunting ground together. No coffin was used, or desired. One family took its child from the grave and coffin in the cemeterp and placing it on a high rocky point after kind hands from the government school where it had died before the parents could reach their child, had tenderly buried the little body.

But this mode of burial is seldom followed of late years. Professional mourners were hired to bewail the death of the departed and for some days the mourners goes to a lonely wigwam and fasts day and night while he, (as only men can be professional mourners), mourns. But the beloved companion, or parents, mourn for a year. The first duty on each morning, a man is to smear his forehead with smoot, but the women use mud on one side of the head, all wearing the poorest, dirtiest and scantiest clothing, and often fast till they become emaciated and physically exhausted before the year ends. It is similar to the idea of mourning in sack-cloth and ashes in Bible times. This mourning was often kept up for the more prominent deceased till a scalp was obtained from a destroyed enemy of a different tribe, and brought into camp at full speed, after being announced by a runner from the war band, and placed in the hands of the nearest relative who after weeping and prayer to the Great Spirit would wash, or be washed, by a committee, and cleanly dressed and well fed by a feast and his mourning was at an end. The last real scalp for this purpose was a Wichita chief, A-sah-a-wa, about '73 or '74, which came near creating a war between the two nations.

The Wichitas came to Pawhuska with their agent and United States marshal and interpreter, McClusky, but after a few days the difficulty was settled after a week's counciling. The authorities realized the danger of pushing their demand for the slayers of the Wichita chief, withdrew with the understanding that if they settled it in their own way that that scalping should be the last between the two tribes and give the United States a mutual pledge to stop that ancient custom, and cruel sacrificing. The Osages, being sad over the deed of their number killing a good chief of a tribe with whom they were not at war, caught the tears of the widowed Wichita Princess, in a golden cup and dried them up in a silver urn by paying the whole Wichita tribe $2.00 per capita, about $4,000 and hunddreds of dollars value in merchandise of every kind to A-sah-a-wah's bereaved widow. Peace was concluded by all the peace council smoking from the same pipe. Then the chiefs arose, followed by their warriors, clasped right hands in silence for a moment, then warmly embraced each one in turn and in tears and peace and friendship forever was proclaimed in the midst of a grove of giant oaks that still sing the requiem of the dead chief on the beautiful banks of Bird creek, just above where the Pawhuska steel bridge spans that creek that widens at this point into a most beautiful expanse of water for a mile.

An amusing incident occurred in the life time of Saucy Chief, who had lost by death his most beloved daughter, Nellie, 1894. During his mourning some years later a war party started out pretensively to secure a real scalp but only in pretense, as the

HISTORY OF THE OSAGE NATION

government of the Osages, as well as of the United States had stopped the practice of human scalping after the killing of the Wichita chief, as a sacrifice to the departed girl, and as a propitiatory offering for the mourning chief and father.

In the northern part of the Osage was a man mowing hay. The war band conceived the idea of playing their game with this man, but a messenger forwarned him of their prank. Yet when they reached him and encircled him in the old manner of approaching the individual enemy the poor fellow was almost scared out of his senses. He soon understood that the band would not hurt him but wanted to buy a lock of his hair that they might carry out their fictitious drama or tragical comedy to gratify their chief and tribe. By much persuasion the trembling mower at last consented, on condition that they might have the lock of hair if they did not clip too much and too close, and in true brave manner, with scalping knife in hand the warrior approached and with barbaric swing clipped the lock from the dodging "paleface" and with triumphant march returned to camp and placed the lock in Saucy Chief's hand. He facing the setting sun that now buried all his sorrows and sadness beneath the great waters of the Pacific sea, holds long in solemn reverence the supposed scalp of his human offering while the little braves marched in circle to stroke the hand that held the propitiation to the Great Spirit, guardian of his cherished daughter.

Saucy Chief was the first chief to come to an Indian Agent, Laban J. Miles at that time, and declared that he wanted to walk in the way of the white man and desired to have a house built for him. Such was the general antagonism to his action, that his band split up, and one faction elected a chief over them during the '70's. But when they did become reconciled to have houses nearly all wanted the best house, best land, best horses instead of mules. They never used oxen. They manifest much pride in having the best of everything. But the houses were generally rented to the whites while they live in their tents or wigwams.

The primary and Intermediate Grades of the Public Schools—Miss Milne and Miss Pratt, Teachers—Pawhuska. (Photo by Hargis)

HISTORY OF THE OSAGE NATION

Thir religious belief holds in their hopes and aspirations the theory that everybody enjoys in the future world the same things that they enjoy here, only in a greater degree, but that the bad and wicked have no enjoyment. With their quiet, stolid manner the casual observer would think them stocial in nature; but among themselves they are humorous, jollying and merry.

The Osages since that time have lived in peace and without trouble with any people except the trouble about 1875 they fell into on the regular hunt in the Cherokee Strip, when the Kansas militia attached and slaughtered some of them, apparently without just provocation, except to keep them from hunting buffalo on the Western Plains. The Osages never went west more than twice afterwards, and then under United States guards. The government began to issue rations to them as soon as the order was given them not to leave their reservation for fear that the trouble might be repeated.

OSAGES AND CHEROKEES.

From the first emigration of the Cherokees westward to Arkansas after 1785, and early in the 18th century, the Osages looked upon them as intruders. Though they conceded their Arkansas lands to settle the Cherokees in treaty at St. Louis, 1818, trouble continued, as the Osages had not receaved all their prisoners taken by the Cherokees and sent to the Eastern Cherokees. An attempted treaty by Governor Miller, of Arkansas, in 1820, and later at Fort Smith failing to bring peace availing but little to check hostilities till the United States interposed in the fall of 1822. But for some years afterwards the Osages were harassed by Texan bands of Cherokees under the bold leadership of a fearless chief, Tohabee (Tatsi), or Dutch, an early emigrant to Arkansas, but who refusing to abide by the treaty of 1828, had crossed to Texas-Mexican territory. He frequently raided the Osages till General Arbuckle offered a reward of $500 for his capture. In deliberate defiance of the reward he returned to Fort Gibson, attacked an Osage trading post, and scalped one of them. Jumping a precipice, with the bleeding, warm scalp in one hand and rifle in the other, he escaped, within hearing of the drum beats of the Fort. He gave himself up only after promise of amnesty and withdrawal of reward.

The Osage, who were a strong predatory tribe when the Cherokees first began to come in independent squads to Osage territory because of the Hopewell, S. C., treaty, displeasing to many Cherokees, opposed the newcomers who numbered two or three thousand in 1817. They called the Osage, Ani-Wasa-si, from their name Wasash. Hostility grew stronger between the two after the Osage refused to join the general peace conference in 1768, concluded between the Cherokee and Iroquois, the latter sending a delegation to the Cherokees to propose a general alliance of the southern and western tribes. The Cherokees accepted and asked all other to join them. All complied except the Osage, who according to Stand Watie and Cherokee tradition, refused alliance, and of whom the rest said they should be henceforth like a wild fruit on the prairie, at which every bird should pick, and from this incident arose the accusation that the "Osage were a predatory people without friends or allies," and faithless to other neighboring nations. But the charge is not sustained by the quiet peaceful manner of these people and their friendly relations with their friends, the whites and the United States government.

The Osage have a secret organization called Wah-ho-pe, to which only few belong, something like Free Masonry and as costly to enter this Wah-ho-pe, lodge, or taking the Dove which is the symbol of their God and Order. It costs from $100 top

HISTORY OF THE OSAGE NATION

$150 admission. When a brave wishes to become a member of this lodge he brings his costly gifts, premium of cattle or beeves not less than five, to be slaughtered, or merchandise to be divided among the lodge members on initiation, amounting to over $100. Then the dove which is a real dove, skinned and spread out in attitude of living with many other pelts of various birds, with the dove is brought from its sacred keeping in the hands of the new member of the lodge, and spread out before the candidate for initiation who is placed between two lines of members, who perform the ceremony just as the sun is rising in the morning. He is put through a trying test of some kind. Then while their lodge song is chanted his wife and babies or children are brought into the circle and the newly initiated member in tearful solemnity passes his open hand back over their forehead and heads in the manner of blessing them, while the anthem is being sung. Then the gifts or fee is divided among the members of the Order.

Among the Osages we find many full bloods who have not stopped with the National school at Pawhuska, but have aspired to higher education and have gone through Lawrence or Carlisle Indian schools, and some went to the best American colleges. Mr. Michelle was among this number. He speaks English fluently and is employed as a clerk in the Osage agents he fills with credi to himself and people. The rules. applied in the agencies offices and is a good scribe. He is well educated and merits the position give a preference of employment to Indian young men and women who may be found competent to fill the positions in the Indian service. Several of the full bloods fill positions here. Mr. Michelle has a comfortable cottage home in Pawhuska where he spends much of his time with his wife and little daughter. To be

CHARLES S. MICHELLE, WIFE AND LITTLE DAUGHTER.
(Photo by Hargis)

and stay at home after night is a characteristic custom of all Indians. Whether it be induced by mere custom or an awe inspired by darkness is a question the writer cannot answer. Many of the whites might be benefitted by following such a custom. To appreciate the life of any people we must put ourselves in their shoes and view rights and wrongs and customs from their standpoint. On coming to the Osage do not fail to meet and know the better full bloods, whom you will appreciate the more by acquaintance.

ROBERT BOLTWOOD, The Cigar Manufacturer.

Is the first to establish a cigar factory in the Osage country, and the only one at present. He is from Massachusetts and New York where he was connected with some of the largest tobacco factories. He opened business here in September, 1905, under the district of Kansas, factory No. 52. All U. S. licenses in Oklahoma and Indian Territory in the liquor and tobacco business or internal revenue stamps come under this district and receive license from the U. S. office at Leavenworth, Kansas. Mr. Boltwood has the qualifications of an energetic New Englander and does a wholesale business. He was in Wichita, Kansas, during the making of that town, the city of today, and sees a great future for Powhuska and the Osage country. He being first on the field deserves the full patronage of the Osage retailers for his copyright brands, "Something Good" and "Doctors' Prescrip- [paragraph and story not completed]

The dove is then carefully wrapped and tied up in a certain way and turned over to the new member who now being fully installed keeps the dove for the next new member thus handing the emblm down through gnerations of Osages. Then have lodges in various bands or families.

From Judge Rodgers the writer gathered many interesting incidents of later Osage history and merits a full sketch of his own live.

Judge Thomas Louis Rogers, whose beautiful home appears in an accompanying cut, won his title by serving in Osage National Supreme Court two terms, or four years, from '82 to '86, and the first supreme judge elected under the written code of Osage constitution and laws, of which he was former and signer. He served with two full blood Associate Justices, O-ke-sah and Tsa-mah-hah. He was a strong disciplinarian in holding his people to obedience to the law. They were unaccustomed to a written law and code and thought their judge was too strict as he ordered punishment of the "unruly" ones by whipping on two for larceny and one for rape, a remarkable record for four years. They were great raiders of horses and stock in early days, but they dreaded the whipping post much as death and soon became law abiding.

Judge Rogers is one-quarter Cherokee. His father, T. L. Rogers, Sr., was half Cherokee, half Scotch. His mother was half Osage, half French; from whom he inherited an Osage right. He was born near the old Grand Saline District, but has lived among the Osages since first they came to Indian Territory in 1870. He served all through the Civil War as a confederate soldier under command of Col. Stand Watie, a Cherokee volunteer taking part in the battles of Honey Springs against Gen. Brunt, and Cabin Creek battle, and he helped to capture a 300-wagon train and engaged in other fights. Mr. Thomas Leahy, the father-in-law of one of his amiable daughters, cast his lot on the Federal side and was in the same fight with Judge Rogers and escaped capture. But true patriotism and love settles all differences and the two men living opposite each other are co-veterans, friends and united in the marriage of their daughter and son, only one of many examples in the Territory, a union of the Gray and Blue in nuptial bonds. Judge Rogers married February 26, 1869, the daughter, Martha, of Judge John Martin. She also is a quarter Cherokee, but an adopted daughter of the Osages. Her father was of Irish nationality from whom she inherited some of her strongest characteristics and as one of the most cultured and typical mothers and grandmothers among the Osage. She has three children, daughters, Bertha, Martha, and Ellen, all happily married.

Judge Rogers first married Miss Coody, also of Osage descent of the Cherokees by whom he had two sons, Arthur, and Lewis who died in babyhood. Arthur, a most excellent man, lived in Pawhuska where he has a beautiful home and has a well improved farm 12 miles south, near Wynona.

Judge Rogers has also served three years in the Osage National Council and was its chairman for two years, till the amendment of the constitution making the chief chairman by virtue of his office.

Judge Rogers has one of the most beautiful farm homes of the country a large stone building just seven miles east of Pawhuska, half way between Nelogany and Hominy, but he has retired to Pawhuska and has built a fine large dwelling shown in the cut. He, with his children, all near him in Pawhuska, present one of the most cultured and ideal and wealthy families among the Osage citizens. Scarcely would you find more refinement and certainly not mere happiness in any of the best homes of the East or West. He, himself, has more of the appearance and features of a well bred Hindoo of British India than he does Osage or Cherokee; dark complexioned, dark hair and beard, but classical Shakespearan features, with finely modulated voice and a bright, intelligence and memory far beyoud the average Caucasian gentleman. He is known among the Osage full bloods by the name Ehe-sah-pe (Ehe, meaning beard, and sah-pe, black Blackbeard, which they called him because of this striking feature on first coming among them, for the Osages have no beard,) or if they do it is all pulled out with tweezers). The older ones even now pull out all their eyebrows. Some of the older ones shave the head instead of the face, leaving only the top of the head from the forehead to the crown with long hair somewhat similar to the Chinese. A long cue is left on the crown, but the front part is left about two or three inches long and roached back with a striking resemblance to the pompadours the young ladies used to wear. As to why these customs are followed the writer is unable to say, but from the modes of hair dressing prevalent among the various bands it seems to be a tribal mark of the differential characteristic. The deaf and dumb among them refer to

the different tribes by sign language, pointing out their chief characteristics. For example, they would pass the hand around the forehead indicating Cherokee, the tribe that formerly wore a band or handkerchief around the head, so often seen among that people. The Osages were indicated by the motion of pulling out the eye-brows, their general custom; the Creeks a motion of the fingers as if combing the long locks which that tribe left on the temples, cutting all the rest short except these ear-locks; and the Delewares by passing the open hand perpendicularly to the sides of their legens, indicating a wide flap on the outside. The Osages call the whites the Muh-he- (knife) ton-kah (big), meaning big knife people from first meeting the United States soldiers with their swords and bayonets. They refer to the Indian Agent now as Big Knife Chief.

The Home of Chester Jake, the Painter and Paperhanger and U. S. Licensed Trader with the Osage.

Mr. Yake has lived in Chicago, Kansas City, and Independence, Kan., prior to coming to the Osage, but from Canada in 1883, and of German nationality. He has followed the painting trade for 25 years, which has fitted him well for his contracting business in which he employs from three to seven men, and does the best grade of work. He has lived 17 years in Pawhuska, and has done most of the painting in the town, and reservation, for 40 miles distant. Mr. Yake is a skilled artisan and a pleasant gentleman in his business transactions. He married Miss Helen Payne of Independence, in '84, and has a happy family of seven children. His dwelling and paint shop is in the north part of town. He will brighten up your house and mind.

HISTORY OF THE OSAGE NATION

Mr. J. R. Pearson, whose large Pawhuska home appears herewith, came to the Osage twenty-seven years ago, from Kansas, but formerly from the northern part of Missouri. He has been a most successful farmer, and stock raiser during these years, having 800 acres under cultivation, and fine orchards of 16 years' growth, which the writer had the pleasure of visiting on Salt Creek. He is a man of broad experience, most practical ideas and sound judgment. His fine residence shows his ideal of life.

The Commodious Residence of Mr. and Mrs. J. R. Pearson, West Pawhuska is largely interested in the town and a stockholder in the Pawhuska Oil and Gas Co. He married Miss Rosa DeNoya, July, 1873, and has a family of bright, strong, rosy children. His oldest son, October, Married Miss Trumbly and his eldest daughter is now in one of the best schools in Kansas. Their second daughter has the distinction of being the tallest girl of her age in Pawhuska, and perhaps the Osage. Mr. and Mrs. Pearson take great pride in their children, and aspire to their greatest success, socially financially, and in culture and have located them fine farms.

HARDIN EBEY.
Attorney at Law.

HISTORY OF THE OSAGE NATION

Hon. Hardin Ebey was raised at Wichita, Kansas, and went through the schools there and later graduated Christian Church College, but now Friends University. He was well prepared by his broad training to enter the profession of law which next to the ministry demands men of education, studious habits and sound unbiased judgment, and above all, true honesty of purpose and principles which characterize him. Judge Hardin Ebey, as he is known, opened a law office at Pawhuska but was admitted to the bar at Wichita, Kan., in .91'. He served as clerk of the Court at Wichita, also as Deputy Probate Judge there. Though of broad experience in his profession he is still quite a young man and one of high ambitions and fine habits, a student of law and of thoughtful common sense the basis of all true law. He practiced law four years at Oklahoma City and is thoroughly conversant wit Oklahoma laws, and will be a power for good in the Osage.

THE OSAGE TREATIES AND LAWS.

As far back as the year 1804, November 3, we find the Sac, (Sauk) and Fox tribes were in a bloody war with the Great and Little Osages in the country along the Mississippi and Missouri rivers, and a treaty was made with the former tribes at St. Louis, then in the district of Louisiana, binding the tribes to cease their wars and come under the protection of the United States, and make a firm and lasting treaty between themselves and the Osages, under the Indian Commissioner, William Henry Harrison, then governor of Indian affairs and plenipotentiary of the United States to make ay treaties found to be necessary with the Osages.

The chiefs of the respective tribes mentioned above met in friendly treaty of release made at Ft. Clark on right bank of the Missouri river, five miles above Fire Prairie in 1808 in which Peter Choteau, agent to the Osages and the chiefs and warriors of the latter, a large extent of territory was ceded to the United States east of a boundary line running from Fort Clark directly south to the Arkansas river and down the same to the Mississippi for a consideration of $800 cash and $1,000 in merchandise to the Great Osages, and $400 cash and $500 in merchandise to the Little Osages.

In the treaty of August 31, 1822, the Osages released the "Uncle Sam" from the obligation of establishing a well assorted store for the purpose of bartering with them on moderate terms for their peltries and furs at all seasons of the year, for a payment of $2,329.40, paid in merchandise out of of the United States factory by Richard Graham, agent of Indian Affairs.

Again in the treaty of January 11, 1839, at Fort Gibson, Brigadier General M. Arbucle, U. S. Commissioner to the Osages renounced all titles or interests in any reservation previously claimed by them within the limits of any other tribe and all interests under the treaties of November 10, 1818. June 3, 1825, (except contents of art. 6), the Osages bound themselves to remove from all lands of other tribes and to remain within their own boundaries, and in consideration for above concession the United States paid them for a term of twenty years an annuity of $20,000 to be paid in their nation, $12,000 in money and $8,000 in goods, stock, provisions as the president might direct, to furnish them with blacksmiths, grist mill, saw mill, and all necessary stock and utensils for beginning to farm for 1000 families, farming agricultural districts. To give some idea of the Osage dialect the writer would gladly insert the names of the 72 chiefs, hedmen, and warriors of the Osages. (See Vol. II, Treaties, 2nd Edition, page 527.) but cannot in this synopsis.

HISTORY OF THE OSAGE NATION

In the treaty of June 2, 1825, all their right, title and claims to all land in Missouri and territory of Arkansas and westward, as far as a line drawn from the head sources of the Kansas river southwardly through Rock Saline, and all south of Kansas river, except a strip of 50 miles beginning 25 miles west of the Missouri state line, at a point called White Hair's Village, and extending to the said west line of this treaty concession; the United States reserving the right to navigate all navigable streams in that reservation, and in consideration of these concessions paid the Osages $7,000 yearly for twenty years, (from the date of treaty) at their village or at St. Louis, at their option, in money, merchandise, provisions, or domestic animals, as they might elect, at first cost of goods at St. Louis, and free transportation, etc., and many provisions for the tribes in the efforts to farm; and reservations of one section each to all the half-bloods, whose names are mentioned, and from whom have sprung many of the more cultured, educated and wealthy families of Southwest Missouri, Kansas and the present Osage citizens as the Rivards, Chouteaus and others. And all the debts of the Osages due the Delawares, Indian Traders. and for all destroyed property not to exceed $6,000. The treaty of August 10, 1825, called Council Grove Treaty, 160 miles southwest of Ft. Osage, was made for the sole purpose of opening a public public road from the Missouri frontier to New Mexico, and to obtain consent of the Osages for right of way through their reservation and their friendly protection of travelers on the road. to promote friendly and commercial relations with the Republic of Mexico and as a consideration paid to the Osages $500 cash or merchandise.

The Frank and Susan Lessart Family of Three Generations.

Mr. Benjamin, Frank and Edward, Charley's brothers, and Mrs. Laura Lessart, a sister-in-law, all of Ponca City, compose the immediate descendants. The writer would gladly give a sketch of each family of Frank and Susan Lessart, and their children, but has not the facts at hand to do so. Julia Roy, their maternal ancestor, was a historical personage of whom a short sketch might be more appreciated by these families and her many offspring than a sketch of their own families so well and favorably known to many. Going back nearly a century we are told a young woman, Miss Julia Roy, married a man of linguistic genius, a "Canadian-French-Alsatian named Lessart, a trapper and interpreter" of several of the modern languages, also Kaw and Osage. About this time, during, the westward treck of the latter from St. Louis to Kansas City, as stated in the history of that time, many Seneca, Kuapaw, Wyandotte, Kaw and Osage women won French husbands and traders. Miss Julia accepted the traditional scholar, Mr. Lessart, for her masculine half. She lived among the Kaws about where now a million wheels and hammers, both day and night, sound the retreat of the Osage to the Neosho, where fair Mrs. Lessart, with her blond-headed brood later came after the loss of Sir. Lessart. She, it is reported, was denied an Osage right at first by the council because of their blond appearance, but later proved her Osage blood and adoption by Kansas City friends. She was said to be a woman of stately appearance, refered to by the Indians as "Big Woman." With aspiration for the education of her twelve children she came to the Catholic mission, and at last was permitted to enter them in school. "Kihekah-Tun-Kah," the chief of all the Osages, and young Saucy Chief are said to have championed her right, the latter rendering valuable service forty years later in fixing Roy family rights. To settle all dispute Claremore, of royal kin, adopted her into the Nation, hence she was termed at times "Madame Claremore," "Madame Lessart," and "Julia Roy," a large, handsome

HISTORY OF THE OSAGE NATION

woman, good wife, and devoted mother,—the most prominent female character in Osake history. She had three sisters, all of whom wed Canadian-Frenchmen, Revellette, Prue, and Lessarge, whose children inherited Osage rights of citizenship, hence the numerous family of the house of Roy, all coming to the present home, except one boy, who went far northwest with a Sioux wife, only one or two of whose children ever came back to the Osage. "A daughter of the Dakotah Lessart was received by the Council in 1888. Later her father, a son of Julia Roy, was denied because of alien residence. A U. S. Commissioner was dispatched to try the case. Near two hundred of Roy descent were about to be disinherited by testimony when Aged Saucy Chief took the stand and testified to seeing the letters of proof used by Julia Roy some 40 years before. The full bloods failed to exclude the increasing Roys, that they might hold full sway. Now nearly 250 claim lineage, of Julia Roy, who died at the age of sixty (?) soon after coming to this reservation and was buried near the confluence of the Caneys, or Silver Lake, in the memory of her children honored and beloved. And in the faces and physique of the Lessart families in the group, and othher kin, you can see the better, nobler qualities of strong lineage. These brothers all have fine homes in Ponca City and excellent farms in the Osage. Mrs. Laura Lessart, an amiable woman of Kiowa linage, a widow of one brother, deceased, has her bright children in her cottage home here also, and some fine farms in the reservation. While Julia Roy Lessart came to the Neosho Mission with her full brood of little ones in sore need of help and sympathy, her 250 offspring are in aggregate now worth perhaps between four and five million dollars, and many excellent people.

HARGIS AND HARGIS.
Lawyers—General Practice.

The brothers in this firm are men of ability, honor and integrity, formerly from Missouri, but have lived in Winfield, Kansas, since 1887, whence they came to Pawhuska a year ago. Mrs. Gladys or (D. C.) Hargis is a photographer of extraordinary art and skill, and Geo. W. Hargis, her brother-in-law, is also a successful photographer as well as a lawyer. They opened a photo gallery on coming to Pawhuska and are making many fine photos and views of which many appear in this book.

In the treaty of Camp Holmes in the Grand Prairie near the Canadian river in the Muscogee Nation, Aug. 24, 1835, for a similar purpose with the Comanche and Associated Bands including the Osages, over two hundred of the chiefs and head men signed (made their X mark) the treaty to keep peace with the Republic of Mexico. Again in May 26, 1857, a similar treaty was made with the Kiowas, Kakakas, and Ta-wa-ha-ros tribes, to keep peace with Mexico, Texas, and with the Muscogee and Osage Nations of Indians. Mr. Stokes and A. P. Chouteau, commissioner Indian treaties at Ft. Gibson, negotiated the treaty   The informal treaty at Ft. Smith, Arkansas, Sept. 13, 1865, (unratified and not filed in the Indian office but found in Indian Territory Commissioner's reports for 1865) was an agreement by and between ten tribes of Indians, including the Osages in Indian Territory, or country, to re-establish their treaties, etc., and friendly relations with the Federal government, after having entered into treaty stipulations with the Confederated States. thereby forfeiting all rights of treaties and protection by the United States. The Osages, like the other tribes of Indians, were divided in their sympathies between the two above named warring powers and hence the need of this agreement to be restored to all former treaty rights. They were represented by White Hair, principal chief; Po-ne-no-pah-she, second chief; Big Hill Bands, and Wah-dah-ne-gah, counsellors.

By the treaty with the Osages at Canville Trading post, Osage Nation, within the state of Kansas, Sept. 29, 1865, most of their lands in Kansas were ceded to the United States, the Osages having more lands than they could occupy for their greatest good, and for which concession the United States agreed to pay the sum, and place to the credit of the Great and Little Osages, $300,000 to be held in the treasury of the United States and five per cent per annum interest to be paid the Osages semi-annually in money, clothing, provisions, or such articles of utility, as the Secretary of the Interior may from time to time direct. Article 2 also makes provision for the holding in trust a twenty-five mile strip of the reserve left, and sold at a price not less than $1.25 per acre, all moneys from such sales to be placed to their credit and 5 per cent used to aid them in beginning agricultural pursuits under favorable circumstances and "Uncle Sam's" direction.

Twenty-five per cent of the net proceeds of such trust land sales were to be set apart till $80,000 should be accumulated, and placed to the credit of the school fund of the Osages, and the interest thereon, at the rate of five per cent per annum, should be expended semi-annually for the boardidg, clothing and education of the Osage children. In this treaty the Osage people showed their appreciation of the Catholic missionaries among them by granting to John Shoemaker in trust one section of land for their mission, with the privilege to buy two other sections at $1.25 per acre for the use and sutsaining of the Catholic mission located in the ceded territory and the like privilege in the new field.

In this treaty provision is made for the cession of all their Kansas land, at the option of the Osages and seelection of land in Indian Territory, or affiliating with some tribe in said territory and sharing equally all privileges and annuities. Provisions are made for their just debts to James N. Coffey, and A. B. Canville, traders through the Secretary of the Interior, not, however, to exceed $5,000. Charles Mongram, a chief of the Great Osages is remembered for his faithful services by a grant to his heirs of a section of land in fee simple. Also Darius Rogers for his great services to the Osages was granted a patent of 160 acres, and the privilege to purchas 160 more adjoining, subject to the Secretary's approval. They declare against war and desire to establish peace with all men, and declare against the introduction of and use of ardent spirits among them. Should their home be selected in Indian Territory, 50 per cent of the diminnshed Kansas reservation funds were to be used to buy the new home, the rest placed to their credit with similar trust funds.

By the articles of a treaty concluded at the Osage Council Ground on Drum Creek, Osage Nation, state of Kansas, May 27, 1868, through the consent of the United States and according to the desires of the Osages, to remove from Kansas to a new and permanent home in Indian Territory, all their lands in Kansas were sold to (or the company granted the privilege of buying it) the Leavenworth, Lawrence and Galveston Railroad Company in consideration that this company within three months after ratification of the treaty, pay to the Secretary of the Interior $100,000 cash, and duly executed bonds for a further sum of $1,500,000 with interest payable semi-annually at 5 per cent per annum, beginning from a date fixed for the removal of the Osages from these Kansas lands, and $100,000 each year for 15 years, and that said company should build 20 miles of track toward Indian Territory each year, until it

HISTORY OF THE OSAGE NATION

reached the south line of Kansas, and on other conditions not essential to mention here, but fully protecting all rights of the Osages.

THE LIVERIES, WAGONS, AND FEED YARDS.

Next to caring for himself man should give all possible care and kindness to the animals that serve him, even more care might be due, as the animal servant is at his mercy. Pawhuska has four large liveries and three feed yards to board your teams.

The A. M. Davis Wagon and Feed Yard is centrally located near the Osage Mills on the bank of Bird Creek, with free camp house, shady grounds, and abundance of good water, and box stalls for boarding your horses at reasonable rates. Mr. Davis, the proprietor, came from Wichita, Kansas, to Grant County, Oklahoma, whence he came to Pawhuska, March 1905.

Geo. H. Grady, V. S., A VETERINARY SURGEON.

Is from the State Veterinary College of Des Moines, Iowa. He came to Pawhuska from Kansas City, where he practiced for five years with fine success, and now becomes practitioner in Pawhuska, and will welcome all who need his skillful services. Some of the best talent of the country is coming to this new country, which promises great future development. Many fine breed horses and other stock are found in the Osage which is a favorable field for a veterinary surgeon. Dr. Grady offices at the Red Store Wagon and Feed Yard as shown in the cut, with his horses in the

Old Red Store Wagon and Feed Yard.

Of the three yards in town this yard was the first in Pawhuska, located just in the rear of the famous Old Red Store, one-half block from the Council House and Mildand Hotel. It was first built by Mr. N. K. Akers of Roanoke, Va. This feed yard has not only the honor of age, but the days one horse's dinner was a 65c bill of fare; but the present proprietor, C. R. Hare, will feed our horses at 30c a team and groom your vehicle in modern style, at moderate prices and welcome old and new patrons to a free camp house, free water, and free gas.

HISTORY OF THE OSAGE NATION

In Article 6 of this Treaty $20,000 were to be paid by the United States for its failure to furnish in full all the farming utensils agreed upon, and $10,000 for failure to run a saw and grist mill longer than five of the fifteen years agreed upon in the treaty of January 11, 1839. (Art. 2.) Of the $20,000, $12,000 were to be expended in building an agency building in their new home, and also a warehouse, and blacksmith shop, etc., and the remaining $18,000 were to be used in building a school, church and the purchase of a saw and grist mill, which mill was to be managed and controlled by the Catholic Mission, for the benefit of the Osages. In Article 9, the Osages, grateful for the benefits of the Catholic Mission, gave in trust and fee simple to John Shoemaker, two sections of land to be selected at or near the new agency, with right to use all necessary timber to sustain such Mission, and school, for the purpose of educating and civilizing of the Osages. But if the Catholic Mission should fail to avail itself of the provisions of this treaty, within twelve months after the removal of the Osages to their new home, it should forfeit all the rights, privileges and immunities therein conferred; and the same rights should inare to any other Christian society, willing to assume the duties and responsibilities enjoined on such a mission, with the period of two years after settlement in their new home. If no Christian society should avail themselves of these benefits as provided, then all such funds should be used under the direction of the Commissioner of Indian Affairs, as in his judgment would best promote the moral, intellectual, and industrial interests of the Osage Nation not to exceed $5000 a year, to be deducted from their annuities.

In order to be free from all just debts on removing to their new homes $40,000 were voted to settle all debts.

It was also provided that if any head of a family desired to commence farming he was privileged to select 300 acres or less, under the direction of the agent in charge within their new reservation, which selection, when recorded, certified, etc., should cease to be held in common and be individual land, so lang as the accupant cultivated it. Any person over 18 years of age, not being the head of a family, could select 80 acres and hold it as his own, in the same manner, and duly entered upon the "Osage Land Book" with all the rights of improvements of deeded lands, subject to the Federal laws of alienation and descent of property.

In Article 14 of this treaty it is stipulated that the United States agreed to sell to the Great and Little Osage Indians, for their future home, the country they now occupy, at a price not to exceed 25c, (twenty-five cents) per acre, bounded on the east by the 96th meridian west from Greenwich, south to the Creek country, thence by the north line of the Creeks to where that line crosses the Arkansas river, thence along its middle main channel to south line of Kansas, and east to the 96th meridian, composing 1,570,195 acres of land.

The above price of twenty-five cents per acre must be a mistake as the former treaties stipulated the price at $1.25 per acre. There seems to be some discrepancy in the different statements concerning the cost of these lands. H. B. Freeman, reporting to the Indian department in 1895 said: "The Osages own 1,600,195 acres of land which they purchased from the Cherokees at 70 cents per acre cash, including the 100,000 acres of the Kaws purchased from the Osages at the same rate." He further says that at that time the part bloods were unanimously in favor of the allotment of the lands, and full bloods as strenuously opposed, for reasons that will be given later on.

HISTORY OF THE OSAGE NATION

THE PAWHUSKA RINK AND OPERA HOUSE.
R. J. Woodring, Owner, E. H. Mahon, Mgr.

In these days of business rush and nervous tension there is a corresponding desire for physical and mental recreation and past time. With each care, worry and strain of life arises a need, at least a longing, for some intoxicating or restful counteraction. With the increase of wealth on the one hand or ardent toil on the other comes a demand for gratifying entertainment to keep them pace. In no period of the history of nations was the arena or play house more patronized than today. Millions are spent monthly for these classes of entertainments. Scarcely does a town put off her swaddling clothes when the opera robe is donned. Shrewd men seeing this tendency invest fortunes in theatres and operas. Mr. R. J. Woodring was the first in Pawhuska to erect skating ring, dancing hall and opera house combined. He is a clerk in the Osage Mercantile company's store, and a citizen by marriage to Miss Tina Herrard of Osage lineage. His energetic business qualities are manifest by the erection of this play house. Mr. Claud Conway was formerly a partner but now Mr. Woodring alone conducts the enterprise. Stage decorations of beautiful and costly scenery have been ordered from Chicago at $25 a scene, and hung in place. Scenes robes and paraphanalia, often make one-half the shows, in any house. The first show here occurred October 17, 1905, with full house inspite of rain, and several popular plays since. The photo failing to come, a cut could not be shown as ordered.

FEDERAL AND OSAGE LAWS

In the act admitting the state of Kansas, Jan 29, 1861, it specially provided that the Indian Reservation in that state should not be alienable for any purpose except with the consent of the Indians in such Reservation, and then in accordance with the treaty authorizing such alienation.

On January 21, 1867, a treaty with the Great and Little Osages was proclaimed and a trust created to dispose of their lands by the government at "a price not less than $1.25 per acre and the funds placed to the credit of these tribes, as the proceeds accrued from such sales in the United States Treasury." The Secretary of the Interior was by this bill authorized to make a correct accounting of the exact acreage of the Osage lands in the state of Kansas and draw upon the United States Treasury for all moneys not correctly credited from their land sales, and to be held by the Secretary of the Interior as custodian of their trust funds to be invested and distributed according to existing treaties. Here begun the great financial wealth of the Osages, widely heralded as the richest people per capita in the world. The term per capita is rightly used because each one born into the Osage tribe has equal financial rights with every other, with exceptions that will be discussed later.

A similar accounting and settlement was made with the Indian Civilization Fund for the 16 and 32 sections given by the United States to the state of Kansas, within the limits of the Osage lands ceded by the aforesaid treaty.

HISTORY OF THE OSAGE NATION

HON. JOHN T. LEAHY.

Mr. J. T. Leahy, the Senior partner of the law firm of Leahy and Scott (E. F.) is by virtue of his ability, profession and marriage in a most prominent family of Osage descent, one of th leading personages of the civil social and political life of these people He is a citizen by marriage to Miss Bertha Rogers, one of the accomplished daughters of Judge T. L. Rogers and a sister of Mrs. Will Leahy. John and Will are cousins. He is the son of Edward Leahy, a brother of Thomas Leahy. His father lived among the Osages in Kansas but died in '69, four years before their removal here. He has been associated with the Osage Interests most of his life, and has lived in Pawhuska for 13 years. He is a graduate of the Kansas Normal College at Ft. Scott, and has practiced law ever since coming to Pawhuska in 1892. He has represented the Osage delegations in Washington as advisory counsel to two committee or allotment delegations in 1903 and 1904-5, and is now a delegate to Washington. In 1896 during the investigation of the Osage rolls he represented a large number of citizens whose rights were questioned and succeeded in keeping most of them on the rolls after 90 days testimony. He is a young man of fine ability and has a profitable, successful practice. He is a man of fine discretion and broad knowledge in general as well as his profession. He has a pretty cottage home opposite Judge Rogers, has four fine specimens of children, and a most devoted husband and father. He has a large law library costing about $3,000. He will be a representative citizen of Osage county and the new state of Oklahoma. There will be no necessity of importing men for high positions when the new state is admitted. He was assistant attorney for two years, before the Court of Claims. He is on ardent Knight of Pythias, having organized the lodge No. 11 of Pawhuska in 1894, and was its first "C. C." He was Supreme Representative one term from Oklahoma, having previously served as grand chancellor of the territory. Being well versed in Osage history the writer gathered from him some information along this line.

His law partner Mr. E. F. Scott is also a young man of ability and an intermarried citizen. His wife was a Miss Johnson, one of the leading families of the Osage, and a sister of Mrs. Thomas, whose parents have long lived on their well improved farm two miles northeast of Pawhuska and active members of the M. E. church, and excellent people.

HISTORY OF THE OSAGE NATION

Fine Home of Chas. Leech—Built by Mr. A. V. Linscott.

Mr. A. V. Linscott, the contractor who appears on the fore ground of this building is one of the first builders and contractors ever established in the Osage nation. He was formerly from Texas, but has resided in the Osage for twenty years and applied his trade all over the Osage country. Some of the finest types of architectural buildings have been erected by himself. The cut represents one of his latest buildings, put up for Mr. Chas. Leech, a surveyor. Mr. Frank Tinker's beautiful cottage home is also one of his best in Pawhuska, and others equally fine. He is an expert at his trade and is satisfied with only the best work, and will gladly give you estimates. He is still a bachelor, and ready for any engagements in contracting, if not nuptially inclined.

One Source of Osage Wealth.

One of Pawhuska Oil & Gas Co's. wells. Natural gas flow of this section said to be 15,000,000 cubic feet every twenty-four hours.

CURTIS BROS., MEAT MARKET & BAKERY.
and Hon. Jno. Palmer's Home and Summer Pavilian on National Heights.

Fresh, Salt and Cured Meats, Pure Lard, Fresh Fish and Oysters in Season, and all kinds of Fine Bakery Goods at Wholesale and Retail.

Curtis Bros., (C. W. and H. K.,) formerly of Illinois, have been residents of the Osage six years in the cattle business. In Nov., 1904, they bought the old market of Mr. Simcix, and have since bought out Geo. Saxon's and H. T. Leahy's bakery business and now run both, and doing a flourishing business. They also run a ranch three miles from town and slaughter all their cattle fresh from the pasture and feeding stalls, thus furnishing the best meats that grass and grain produces. With the zeal characteristic of their native state, Pawhuska will feel their progressive force and citizenship.

HISTORY OF THE OSAGE NATION

AN ACT TO LEALIZE INTERMARRIAGE WITH WHITE MEN

Art. IX. (Para. 99.) Section 1 of the Laws of the Osage reads: "Whereas the peace and prosperity of the Osage people require that in the enforcement of the laws, jurisdiction of the civil law should be exercised over all persons whosoever who may from time to time be privileged to reside within the limits of the Osage Nation, therefore any white man or citizen of the United States who may hereafter come into the country to marry an Osage woman shall first be required to make known his intentions to the Nation Council by applying for a license and such license may under the authority of the National Council, to be issued by the clerk thereof. Any person so obtaining a license shall pay to the clerk the sum of twenty dollars ($20.00) for such license, and take an oath to support the constitution and abide by the laws of the Osage Nation, which oath may be administered by the President of the National Council or the clerk of the body, authorized for that purpose, and it shall be the duty of the clerk to record the same in the Journals of the National Council. But if any such white man or citizen of the United States shall refuse to subscribe to the oath, he shall not be entitled to the rights of citizenship, and shall forthwith be removed without the limits of the Osage Nation as an intruder. The Osage laws relating to man's and woman's conduct to each other, and for the protection of woman's virtue and offspring, sections 23 to 33, holds as high a standard of morals as the most advanced people of any age of civilization.

For more than a half century they have had all the modern privileges of a literary education. They have had schools in their midst for many decades and all who have desired to go, have been sent to Carlisle, Penn., or Lawrence, Kan., to graduate, or to other institutions equally famous. In January (12), 1884, the Osage Council passed a practically compulsory education law for the children of their nation.

"That every child of school age (from 7 to 14 years of age) who has not been in school four months out of the six months preceeding an annuity payment, shall be enrolled, and payment withheld, unless the child was sick and unable to attend school, which fact shall be certified to by the agency physician, and the annuity paid.

It is not the object of this short synopsis to give a digest of all the laws of this people, but only such as indicate the high degree of self-government, and civic and educational development.

Their Constitution and laws published in 1895, under the authority of the National Council of the Osage Nation, and certified to by Thomas Mosier, their National Secretary, show a close following of the constitution of the Federal government and States:—"We the people of the Osage Nation in National Council assembled, in order to establish justice, insure tranquility, promote the common welfare, to secure to ourselves and posterity the blessing of freedom—acknowledge with humility and gratitude the goodness of the Sovereign ruler of the universe in permitting us to do, and implore his aid and guidance in its accomplishment, do ordain and establish this constitution for the government of the Osage Nation."

Any people that can, with the spirit and purpose of such a preamble legislatively formulate and judiciously execute the laws following this preamble, were, or are, or ought to be as capable of self government and as competent and well fitted to protect the weaker ones of their nation as any community on the face of the American continent. They are certainly able to organize immediately, and govern well and judiciously the County of Osage in the new state of Oklahoma, which we all hope to greet this winter. The Osages have long exercised the Legislative, Executie, and Judicial functions of a well formulated government, under the authority of "citizens" or part Osages with as bright minds, and noble qualities as can be found in any county or state. Such men as Judge T. L. Rogers, Judge J. W. Pettit, Hon. John Palmer, Hon. Jno. T. Leaky, C. N. Prudom, Mathews, J. W. Trumbly, and others who have served years in the judicial departments and many other strong men from the citizens, and the best and shrewdest of the "fullbloods" have represented their districts in the Osage National Council, composed of three members from each of the five districts into which the whole Nation was divided. The councilmen are elected for two years, vica voce, by the qualified voters, all male citizens over 18 years of age. Only Osage male citizens can be elected, and not before 25 years of age. No one convicted of a felony was or is eligible to office, appointment of honor, profit or trust in the nation. And each member on being seated in the Nation Council took the following oath or affirmation:

"I, A. B., do solemnly swear or affirm, (as the case may be,) that I have not obtained my election by bribery, treat, or any undue and unlawful means, used by myself, or others, by my desire or approbation for that purpose, that I consider myself constitutionally qualified as a member of the Osage Council, etc., and that all questions and measures which may come before me, I will give my vote and so conduct myself, as in my judgment shall appear most conductive to the interest and prosperity of this nation, and that I will bear true faith and allegiance to the same, and to the utmost of my ability and power, observe, conform to, support, and defend the Constitution thereof."

Such an oath would certainly make many a state politician tremble, and turn pale, at such a stunner for pure government.

The supreme executive power was vested in a Principal Chief, called "The Principal Chief of the Osage Nation" elected by popular vote of the qualified electors on the general election day. He must be a natural born citizen and 35 years of age. In the same manner is elected an Assistant Chief under the same conditions, and both hold office for two years subject to impeachment by the Council. But the Chief's oath of office is not a searching as the oath of the Councilmen. He says: "I do solemnly swear (or affirm) that I will faithfully execute the duties of Principal Chief and defend the Constitution of the Osage Nation."

The Assistant is to aid and advise the Principal Chief, a more important relationship in this respect than the Vice President is to the President of the United States. The Constitution provides for supreme and circuit courts presided over by Judges elected by the National Assembly or Council, who have complete criminal jurisdiction in all cases and manners as might be provided by law. And all indictments conclude thus: "Against the peace, and dignity of the Osage Nation."

There seems to be no provision of trial by jury, but that all civil cases should be tried by a supreme court composed of one Chief Justice and two Associate Judges and in criminal cases these three should select two other persons of good character and knowledge, to constitute with them, a court to decide all criminal cases. In all other respects the Constitution provided for similar laws, and manner of procedure as found in the most of states, and unnecessary to repeat here.

The Osage Executive Council was composed of the Principal and Assistant chief and three other men appointed by the National Council, on the recommendation of the

HISTORY OF THE OSAGE NATION

Chief whom with the Assistant Chief he called together from time to time for directing the affairs of the Nation according to law.

The Salaries of the Osage National Officers were not of such amounts as would entice the average politician to spend hundreds or thousands of dollars, or even many cents, in their elaborate campaigns. The Principal Chief was allowed a salary of only $450 per annum; Assictant Chief, $350; Justice of the Supreme Court, $250; Associate Justice in addition to legal fees, $150 per annum; Prosecuting Attorney $300; National Secretary $350; each member of the National Council $250; High Sheriff, $250; each District Sheriff, $200; each member of Executive $100; Principal Chief's Private Secretary $150; his Private Interpreter $150 per annum; making a total of $3,459, less than $4,000 per year expenses for running the government—a good example for future use.

HON. J. N. COULTER
Attorney-at-law.

Mr. J. N. Coulter, the subject of this sketch was born in the mountain region of Pennsylvania. His parents moved to Indiana when he was yet a boy, where he lived and grew up to manhood, receiving a liberal education at Wabash college. The western fever struck him at the time of the opening of old Oklahoma in 1889. Entering the territoriy on the 22d day of April as one of the boomers, he located in Guthrie, where he lived till September 1893. When the strip opened he came to Pawnee, Pawnee county, where he lived until the first of May, 1905, removing at that time to Pawhuska, where he now lives with his family, consisting of his wife and little daughter, seven years old, a happy trio. Mr. Coulter is successful and enjoys a good practice of the best clientage of the Osage Nation.

HISTORY OF THE OSAGE NATION

The Pretty Park Home of John Conway, Park Row.

Mr. Conway is a native of New York state, born in Albany, where he lived as a boy, but lived at Syracuse after he was sixteen. He enlisted in the Federal army in the Fourteenth N. Y. Volunteers and served three months. Discharges Aug. 2,'61 for disability, re-enlisted Dec. 22, '61 for three years in Battery F, 3rd N. Y. L. Art. Helped to capture Fort Sumpter and as a sergeant volunteered to carry the colors to a Gabion, midway the trenches and the Fort, and was promoted to a lieutenant for this deed of bravery. He was a prisoner in Petersburg, Livy, and Bells Isle, from which he escaped through the indulgence of the officers because of his clerical services, and rejoined his battery. He came to the Osage Nation in 1884, and married Mrs. Jane Wilson, nee Miss Revard, the sister of Joseph Revard. They now live in their Pawhuska cottage home amid flowers and trees, a happy, aged couple, retired for a golden sunset of life. They take much pride in their quiet home, and its flowers and pets. Notice a large snail or sea shell found in Beech Creek on his farm. It is a prehistoric specimen and weighs about fifty pounds.

(Photo by Hargis)

BAKER- CERNEY COMPANY.

These Hardware, Furniture, Harness and Vehicle Dealers have one of the largest department stores in Pawhuska, furnishing all kinds of hardware, stoves, tinware and tinship, of which they have the finest in the territory. Their various lines cannot be excelled. They carry also the best of **carpets and drapery. Axminister rugs, and lace Curtains.** Their business being established in 1904, on a much smaller basis has grown to large proportions, with a number of rooms stored full of high grade goods andd the best make of implements and vehicles. Mr. Adolph Cerney supervises the hardware department. He is broadly experienced in his line and ably assisted by well qualified clerks.

Mr. O. M. Baker gives his special attention to the furniture and carpet sales, stocks and rooms, and their successful business proves his fine qualifications for his

HISTORY OF THE OSAGE NATION

department. Mr. A. W. McCoy, conducts the book-keeping and heavy office work. Their present building has a 115 foot front, by 80 deep, stored full from centre to circumference. They incorporated at $100,000, and now doing a $125,000 business per year. Mr. Baker is president, Mr. A. S. Sands, (of Iowa), vice president; Mr. McCoy, secretary; Mr. Cerney treasurer and one of the managers. They were formerly from Nebraska and Iowa, and of broad generous principles.

ENACTMENT PROHIBITING INTOXICATING DRINKS

From the earliest history of the Osage people they have encouraged the United States to prohibit and embodied in treaties provisions to prohibit the introduction and sale of intoxicating drinks. Among the enactments of their National Council we find in paragraph (69), Section 57, That whenever any citizen of the Osage Nation is found in a state of drunkenness, (and) it shall be the duty of the officers of the nation to bring such person before the Supreme Judge to answer for said charge, and if it be proven that he has been drunk, it shall be the duty of the Supreme Judge to impose a fine on him of not less than ten ($10.00) dollars nor more than twenty-five ($25.00) dollars for each and every offense, and in default of said payment such person be made to serve his time in the National prison at one ($1.00) dollar per day, or be put to work on public work at one dollar and fifty cents ($1.50) per day (Sec 59.) All laws and parts of laws conflicting with the above act are hereby repealed.

The spirit and force of this law has been steadily enforced to the present time. The vigilance of the Indian Agent, Captain Frantz, and his deputies, makes the prohibition law more effective and complete than in any other section of America. Famous prohibition states, Maine and Kansas, are free license in comparison with the Osage country. Proprietary medicines containing alcohol or distilled spirits are rigidly excluded. Observing the law you dare not sell them or introduce them for your own individual or family use, nor shield others in doing so. Men, the writer is told, can't even get Hostetter's Bitters, nor the ladies Peruna. But near the lines cross over to old Oklahoma, Kansas or Indian Territory.

C. B. THOMAS' BLACKSMITH SHOP

HISTORY OF THE OSAGE NATION

Anything in the Iron and Woodwork Line. Horseshoeing a Specialty, U. S. Licensed Indian Trader.

Pawhuska has some skilled mechanics, among whom C. B. Thomas ranks high in his trade as a blacksmith of excellent ability. Two years ago he came here from Poala, Kansas. He has folowed his trade many years and has here won a wide patronage in all kinds of iron work, vehicles and farm implements. Having made a specialty of horseshoeing he gives expert service in shoeing and guarantees satisfaction to his patrons at reasonable prices. In meeting many good men in the shops, how frequently comes to our minds the poet's "Village Blacksmith," the man of iron and steel, both within and out. Some trades seems to help to make men, others to destroy them. The blacksmiths are generally high grade men, other as firm in the conviction of right as the steel they temper.

FLANNIGAN AND JAMES.
Sanitary Plumbing, Steam and Gas Fitting.

With the finding of gas and oil in this vicinity, the plumbing business was in immediate demand. Flannigan and James are a newly established firm of first class plumbers and steam fitters, and are doing a growing business. They are progressive busines men, and will do your work satisfactorily and promptly.

THE LUMBER COMPANIES.

THE SPURRIER LUMBER CO., J. T. YOUNG, MGR.

One of the first necessities of immigrants to a new field is that of material to build dwellings for themselves and barns for their stock, and other improvements. This employs an army of men to cut and saw the timber, transport it, and others to sell it to the contractors and builders; thus sustaining a great industry in every densely populated center. Pawhuska has four lumber yards, doing business in supplying these needs, as the town has doubled in size in one year, with good prospects of doubling again during the next year. Some of the largest companies are located here. Among these the Spurrier Lumber Co. with headquarters and main yard at Guthrie, O. T., have eleven yards over the two territories, and are extensive dealers in yellow pine and cypress lumber, shingles, sashes, doods, mouldings, etc. They have been in business in Pawhuska two years and are located on the east side of the Triangle under the management of Mr. J. T. Young, an experienced lumberman. Besides a full line of building material they carry also a large assortment of paints, and welcome your patronage, and furnish you estimates for building. Give them a call and meet Mr. Young, when preparing to build.

Duncan Bros., C. A. and G. H., Dealers in Yellow Pine Lumber & Hardware

They carry a full line of oak, cedar, cypress, redwood, lumber and lime, sand, brick and cement.

These young men were the first to build fine lumber sheds and office, a cut of which appears. They do an extensive business in all kinds of building material, from tin buttons for your tar paper roof, to the finest lumbers and paints for the finishing

HISTORY OF THE OSAGE NATION

touches. They contract for building for all work from the stone foundations to the hangings of the paper. They are from Winfield, Kansas, where they did a wholesale

(Photo by Hargis)

commission lumber business for years. They have one of the finest locations in Pawhuska, just in the rear of the Indian Agent's office, in the center of the business district. Mr. C. A. Duncan, the senior partner, is an active member of the Baptist church and leader of its choir. You will find them courteous gentlemen and obliging in supplying your needs.

AN ACT RELATING TO NEGROES

The Osages have always been friendly toward the whites and welcomed them to their reservation and into their families by inter-marriage. They have never been in war against the white Americans. On one occasion they were on a trip west for a hunt in western Oklahoma and were attacked and fired upon by the Kansas Militiamen who were reported to be misinformed of the Osage purpose. The braver ones who rushed to their guns but their chief and leader said, "No the soldiers are Americans, white people! You must not shoot! And the Federal Government rewarded them generously for the dead and wounded.

In all treaties with them, we find the following or similar expressions of friendship, and good will as found in a treaty concluded between William Clark, Ninian Edwards and Auguste Chouteau, with the Osages, December 26, 1815.

"Art. 2. There shall be perpetual peace and friendship between all the citizens of the United States of America, and all individuals composing the Osage tribes or Nation."

They have kept the letter and spirit of this treaty with even a self-sacrificing sincerity for which Uncle Sam has amply rewarded in money and fostering care, education, and other essential things to encourage the domestic arts and agriculture. They still welcome the whites who are honest and conduct themselves rightly.

But they seem to have an aversion for the African race and to hold proudly aloof from them, only one it is said holding the marriage relationship with one of the black race. In the constitutional law of the Osage Nation Article XII, the National Council passed an act relating to negroes.

HISTORY OF THE OSAGE NATION

(114.) Sec. 1. That from and after the passage of this act the Negroes residing within the Osage Nation shall be ordered to get out.

(115.) Sec. 2. Any citizen of the Osage Nation shall be subject to a fine of fifty dollars ($50.00) for the employment of any negro upon their reservation.

(166.) Sec. 3. The United States Indian Agent is hereby requested to take such action as is necessary to have all negroes put out of the Osage Reservation.

And as this aversion seems to continue among these people hence no inducements for the negro.

In concluding this synopsis of the Constitution and laws it is especially worthy of note that in Article VI, Section 1, the qualification of religious belief is prerequisite to office holding.

"No person who denies the being of a God, or a future state of reward and punishment, shall hold any office in the civil department in this Nation." Signed, James Bigheart, President of the National Convention, and Ne-kah-ke-pon-ah, Wat-ti-an-kah, Saucy Chief, Tah-wah-che-he, William Penn, Clamore, Two-giver, Tall Chief, Thomas Big-chief, Ne-kah-wash-she-tan-kan, Joseph Pawnee-no-pah-she, White Hair, Cyprian, Tayrian, Paul Akin, interpreter, and E. M. Mathews, secretary.

The Constitutional form of government laws were enforced up to the time the large payment of a million and a quarter dollars was made when conditions arose that caused the abolishment of the Council and other officers except the Chief and Assistant Chief and through the recommendation of Mr. Churchill, the inspector, the Secretary of the Interior ordered that a business committee of eight be appointed.

Fifteen councilmen or three from each of the five districts composed that body, as provided by the constitution and laws, and to be elected the first Monday in August. The council was partly abolished by the committee of eight, but holds is meetings for deliberation in the same manner as before.

On June 5, 1872, Congress passed an act authorizing the removal of the Great and Little Osages from their lands in Kansas, to their present reservation, bounded east by the 96th meridian, south and west by the Creek line and the Arkansas river and north by the state of Kansas. By the act of Congress July 15, 1870, the reservation for the Osages was retricted to a tract of land in compact form, equal in quantity to 160 acres for each member of said tribe, but in the early settlement of the Osages in Indian Territory, most of their valuable improvements and valuable farm lands proved by later survey to be east of the 96th meridian. Their present boundaries were fixed in this act of June 5, 1872, yet based upon the stipulations of the congressional act of 1866, section 16 of said act, so far as applicable to the reservation. The act provided that the Osages were to allow the Kansas (Kaw) Indians, to settle within their reservation, on land not to exceed 160 acres to each member of the Kaws at a price not higher than that paid by the Osages to the Cherokees for their lands.

In the Act passed March 3, 1873, provision was made for the transfer of $1,650,600, (or as much as necessary for the purchase of lands from the Cherokees, for the Osages from the Oagge trust funds) to the Cherokee credit, in conformity to an act passed June 5, 1872, entitled, "An act to confirm to the Great and Little Osage Indians a Reservation in Indian Territory. But the Osage reservation in Indian Territory was excepted from the operation of the Dawes Act (the general allotment Act of 1887,) as provided in that Act, May 2, 1892. And for civil and taxable

53

HISTORY OF THE OSAGE NATION

purposes has been attached to Pawnee and Kay counties, Oklahoma. But by the Act of June 7, 1897, only the district court should have exclusive jurisdiction of any actions in civil cases against members of the Osage and Kansas tribes residing on their reservation in Oklahoma Territory. No Justice of the Peace or Probate Court shall have jurisdiction in such cases, and at least two terms of the district court should be held, each year, at Pawhuska, on the reservation, at such times as the supreme court of Oklahoma shall fix and determine for the trial of bith civil and criminal cases.

The Beautiful Country Home of Judge J. W. Pettit, Near Pawhuska.

The taxes of the taxable property, etc., of the business men of the Osage country adjoining go to the counties, on the theory that the alien's law business, civil, and Circuit Court, be held in Pawhuska, twice each year, but the Circuit Court business in Pawhuska seems to have consisted mainly in continuances, changes of venue and adjournment.

Juries, it seems are brought from Pawnee county at great expense, while men all over the Osage, equally intelligent, and moe wealthy, and should be more competent, are excluded as jurymen. It seems to be on the verge of the colonial days, "Taxxation without Representation." A county government will soon remedy this.

An act of the 49th Congress, February 8, 1887, Section 6, makes the provisions that upon the completion of allotments and the patenting of land of allottees, each and every member of the respective bands or tribes of Indians, to whom allotments have been made, shall have the benefit of and be subject to the laws, both civil and criminal, of the state or Territory in which they may reside, etc. And every Indian born within the limits of the United States and has voluntarily taken up his residence separate and apart from any tribe of Indians therein, and has adopted the habits of civilizzed life (and every Indian in Indian Territory,) is hereby declared to be a citizen

HISTORY OF THE OSAGE NATION

of the United States and is entitled to all the rights, imparing the right of any such Indian to tribal or other property."

According to this act many of the Osage, allied families, have long been citizens of the United States and should be forthwith entitled to all the privileges of American citizens, regardless of those who do not allot, and live apart in severalty. For many of them live just as much apart in manner of life, in eating, drinking, dressing, and in finely improved homes, farms and town residence, with education and culture, as the better citizens of New England or the Pacific coast, the wealthy North, or "Proud South," and are entitled to become citizens.

By the act of March 3, 1901, provision was made for the settlement of all Osage debts due Indian Traders upon a just basis of fair profits upon the goods sold to them by the Osages. Such payments are or may be made direct from the government representatives who adjust or O. K.'s all debts contracted by the individual Indian or head of a family. But the trader is prohibited by this bill from giving credit to the Indians to an amount exceeding sixty centum of the Indian's next quarterly annuity, under the penalty of forfeitinng the right to collect any of the debt, and the trader's license shall be void, and revoked for such excess credit by the trader. This act protects the trader in credits and the Indian against consuming all his money before getting it. It is a wise provision for all classes.

DR. F. C. GALE, D. D. S.

With the advance of society and civilization there seems to be a corresponding deterioration or more rapid decay of the human teeth. Whether this be caused by less use in eating foods pulverized by artificial means, or often by inheritance, or medicines, is a question to be solved by the dental profession, or individual care. Pawhuska has three dentists, young men, among whom Dr. F. C. Gale, the brother of Miss Gale, the vocalist, has established a well furnished office in the **Old Historic Council House** since May 1905. He is a **graduate** of the **Western Dental College** of Kansas City, Mo., one of the best colleges of the "West." With the latest knowledge and experience of his profession he is doing a fine practice with satisfaction to his patients. He is an excellent young man, and adds much to to the progressive element of the Osage.

GIVE THE INDIAN A WHITE MAN'S CHANCE

(Passed in Council Assembled Dec. 5, 1905.)

"Whereas, The People of Oklahoma, and Indian Territories are greatly interested in the Statehood Bill introduced by the honorable Bird S. McGuire, Delegate for Oklahoma Territory, which provided for the admission of the aforesaid Territories into the Union as one state, and

"Whereas, The terms of said McGuire Statehood Bill have been made known by the press of the country, within the past few days, thereby giving us an opportunity to examine into the minor details of same, and

"Whereas, said Oklahoma Statehood Bill if passed, will materially effect the intterests of the Osage Tribe of Indians now living in Oklahoma Territory, and

"Whereas, we feel sure that the Honorable Bird S. McGuire and the Congress of

The Mitscher Allotment Delegation to Washington, D. C., 1904. Top Row.—Frank Corndropper, Bacon Rind, Fred Lookout, W. T. Leahy, Eaves Tall Chief, and Charles Brown. Next Row.—Charles N. Prudom, Arthur Bonnicastle, W. S. Mathews, James Bigheart, and Lawrence. Lower Row.—Brave, Heh-scah-moie, Ne-kah-wah-she-tun-kah, Back Dog, Shun-kah-mo-lah, Peter C. Bigheart. Tom Mosier, Interpreter; Oscar A. Mitscher, U. S. Indian Agent.

Cottage and Business Block of R. M. Hunt.

Mr. Hunt, whose cottage and fine business block appears herewith is an intermarried citizen of the Osage. He has lived in Pawhuska eighteen years, engaged in the blacksmithing business fourteen years of that time, and also conducted a well stocked farm and ranch 23 miles northwest of town on Beaver Creek, which his son Orial now farms. Mr. Hunt resides in Pawhuska, where he has valuable property and will soon establish himself i nbusiness here, being long a licensed Indian Trader. He married Miss Mary A. DelOrier. They have four children from three to sixteen, two boys and two girls. Orial is attending Nazareth Academy at Muskogee. He is sixteen and preparing himself for a successful business life. Mr. Hunt believes in preparing his children for the practical affairs of life and self-dependence.

(Photo by Hargis)

HISTORY OF THE OSAGE NATION

the United States has the most friendly feeling for the Osage Tribe of Indians, and would not intentionally injure them or deny them any reasonable request and

"Whereas it is proper that we make known our wishes in matters that vitally affect us to the congress of the United States and

"Whereas, the Osage Tribe of Indians now own a tract of land which they bought and paid for, and which is situated in the Territory of Oklahoma, and is known as the Osage Indian Reservation, and

"Whereas, Disposition is to be made of said Osage Indian Reservation is a matter that affects the Osages primarily, and can in no way effect the inhabitants of other sections of Oklahoma Territory. or the inhabitants of Indian Territory, and

"Whereas, The Osage Tribe of Indians now hold lands and other communal property in a different mannner from that of any other Indian tribe, or other people in either of said territories, and

"Whereas, The Osage Tribe of Indians have for a long time expected that when existing conditions changed that the Osage Reservation would remain intact, and be constituted one county, to be known as Osage colunty with Pawhuska as the county seat thereof, and

"Whereas, We are acquainted with the wishes of the Osages and the people living in the Osage Indian Reservation, and know that they are unanimous as to their wants and desires in the matter above set out and fully approve of the same.

"Therefore, Be it resolved by the Osage National Council in session assembled at Pawhuska, the Capital of the Osage Nation, this 5th day of December, 1905, that in the proposed statehood bill there be inserted a clause in effect as follows:

"That the Osage Indian Reservation in Oklahoma Territory is hereby constituted a county, to be known as Osage County, with Pawhuska as the coounty seat thereof, and that the first election of the proper officers thereof should be held at the time and place, or places, and be conducted in such manner as the Governor shall appoint and direct after at least thirty days notice to be given by proclamation, and all subsequent elections the time, place and manner of holding elections, shall be prescribed by law.

"Be it further resolved, That the main and essential provisions of the said proposed Statehood Bill for Oklahoma and Indian Territories, other than the peculiar features above referred to, as introduced in the House of Representatives by the Honorable Bird S. McGuire, meets with our hearty and unqualified approval.

"Be it further resolved, That copies of these resolutions be sent to the Honorable Bird S. McGuire, the Honorable Chairman of the Committee on Territories, in both House and Senate, the Honorable Charles Curtis, the Honorable Secretary of the Interior, the Honorable Commissioner of Indian Affairs; and that copies be furnished the five local newspapers published on the Osage Indian Reservation, and the Pawhuska Commercial Club.

"W. S. Mathews, Julian Trumbly, Francis Claremore, Tom West, Charles-Me-She-Tse-He, his x mark, O-Lo-Hal-Moie, his x mark, Me-Kah-Wah-Ti-An-Kah, his x mark. Frank Corndropper, Osage Councilors; O-Lo-Ho-Wal-La, Principal Chief; Bacon Rine, Assistant Principal Chief. professional organizations. From eighteen men, the organization has

"I hereby certify on honor, that the foregoing proceedings of the Osage Council are true and correct. A. W. HURLEY, Acting U. S. Indian Agent.

HISTORY OF THE OSAGE NATION

The Home of Wm. E. McGuire, Postmaster,—Park Row.

PAWHUSKA.

(Pa-hu-ska, the name of a chief, means White Hair, of the Bald Eagle subgens of the Tsicu Gens).

After surveying, and scanning the Osage country you can quickly see why the county seat of the reservation, Pawhuska, should be called "The Hub of the Osage," both from her central location and commercial importance. Approaching the city from the east along the Midland Valley Railroad, 209 miles from Ft. Smith, 103 from Muskogee, 49 from Tulsa, 33 from Skiatook, on the east boundary of the Osage, 23 from Tucker, 17 from Nickols, 13 from Bigheart, and 4 from Nelagony Junction, you will see beautiful, rapidly growing Pawhuska, where about 1872, "Uncle Sam" selected a most favorable site for the Guardian Home of the Osage Agency Schools, and Trading Post, which it continued to be till a year ago, when it begun to develop into the present, growing and promising city of the future country, and its prosperity seems only to have begun. Pawhuska is midway between Tulsa, partly built on the extreme southeast corner of the Osage and Arkansas City nearly touching the northwest corner of the Reservation. Equal distance from Elgin, or Chautauqua Springs, Kansas, and Cleveland, O. T., Bartlesville, on the extreme east and Ponca City, west. Train connection with Arkansas City will soon be, if not already established on the newly built Midland Valley, that follows the beautiful winding Bird Creek Valley, walled up on either side by rocky, forest-covered cliffs and hills. Along this line are some of the most sublime scenes in Oklahoma. The Rocky Cliffs just west of Skiatook are most picturesque, and "Lover's Leap," three miles west of Pawhuska overlooks the Midland Valley road. It is said by some that this high, perpedicular wall was named from the incident of an elopement, a young couple who were being closely persued by an irate father and the lovers prefered to die together by leaping over this cliff rather than be separated from each other. If this legend were true, sacred would the spot to all true lovers or those desiring to make true love, but Mr. John Florer wrecks all the love dreaming on this point by claiming that he first

HISTORY OF THE OSAGE NATION

named the high cliff in jest during a family picnic party on that point. So young lovers if the romantic inspiration of "Lover's Leap" fails you in the conflicting origin of the name, see the venerable merchant of Gray Horse, and "cheer up" for it might not be true. And the towering rocks, fertile vallies and romantic forests and groves may still lend their inspiring charms.

From the slope east of Bird Creek, looking west as seen on the title page, Pawhuska nestles in a beautiful valley basin, broken east and west by the curving stream, adroned by primitive groves of pecan, persimmon, walnut, elms, all varieties of oak and other native trees that will make an "Ideal park.

It could be made "IDEAL PARK" by linking the banks together by several light suspension foot bridges. A large steel bridge, now, connects East and West Pawhuska. In these times of hustle-tustle, hurly-burly, competitive, commercial life, and constant strain upon the physical and nervous system of the human race, no city nor town could be very scientifically plotted without such a park for leisure hours, and innocent recreation. "Tis not all of life to live in the crowded blocks of business all the seven days and nights through natural life. Everyone should once in a while get a taste of that paradise on the eternal "shores beyond." A little vestibule of Eden should be made for the city, where the adventurous hunter and the feathered, painted and bronzed race used to roam. "How sublimely the Great Father of the Pale and ruuddy races has made this spot for the abode of his children." The Paradise of a romantic love—dreamer could scarcely improve upon her site. The ancient Paradise was but a lovely scene of trees, flowers, fruits and castles. And here many beautiful trees have been reared by creative laws and many ornamental trees have been planted in the yards of the older residences of the town, part of which was built years ago, by Indian Traders, and the government. But many smaller business buildings and fine residences have gone up during two years, since the town survey and sale was assured.

Many of the native people seem to have a strog love for natural beauty and fill their yards with trees, flowers and evergreens. Mr. Simcock, on the north hill, and Mr. Wheeler on Park Row, have their yards adorned with evergreens, cedar and arbor vital. Main street, as you look east from the Midland Valley tracks is walled with beautiful trees and flowers.

As the bill which will be reprinted later in this book speaks for itself it is useless to give the town sections here. We need only say that the most of a section, 640 acres will be available for homes and business, of the most beautiful locations. Pawhuska is ideal for both business in the lowest center of the basin, easily drained to the deep broad channel of Bird Creek, residences occupying the rest of the basin and its beautiful slopes north, west and south, where the grandeur of forest covered hills overlook the center. The large creek here broadens into a small river of calm unusually clear or blue waters creeping through the town forming the letter S, reversed from west to east. This broad, deep stretch furnished boating and fine fishing nearly a mile through town. Already a steam or gasoline launch and row boats afford pleasure to the romatically inclined, while the stars, like merry twinkling fairies, or perchance the moonbeams like phantom-ghosts from far-off worlds below, peep up through the listening, clear waters at Cupid's pranks. But if others prefer a firmer foundation, terra-firma, for the culture of Cupid's Arts they may find lovely walks through "Ideal Park" that will surely be reserved along this stream.

While the town has spacious room at present, her future growth which is sure to continue might in time be cramped in the bounds of one section. But there are

HISTORY OF THE OSAGE NATION

Mr. William E. McGuire, Postmaster, Pawhuska, O. T.

In the development of any community the men in places of trust and honor can wield a mighty influence. Mr. McGuire is a brother of Representative McGuire of Oklahoma, now in Congress. He is a gentleman of broad experience, manly qualities, and obliging thoughtfulness, well fitting him for the office he fills with much satisfaction to all. He first came to Pawhuska to teach in the government schools where, after teaching one year, during Arthur's administration, in 1883, he resigned because of the change of administrations. Returning to Kansas he taught till the Cherokee strip opened up, came back to Oklahoma and became a resident of Ponca City. He raised the first tent ever placed upon that townsite, where he was a leading factor in building that city into the present business center. He served as city clerk for two years and chairman of the school board, in which office he was the main figure in having erected the first complete school house on the "Strip," only sixty days after the opening. The dedication was celebrated by 5,000 while the Ponca and other Indians slaughtered twenty head of wild Texas cattle in Indian Territory mode. In February, 1898, McGuire was appointed potsmaster at Pawhuska, where he has been a potent influence in town progress. He married Miss Virginia A. Slater of Kansas, July, 1889. She often aids him in his official duties with Miss Stoner as assistant postmaster. They have four bright children, a girl and three boys, Robert and Rolland, the youngest, and twins, appear on the porch with their pet mastiff. The volume of postoffice business has increased rapidly the past year, and will soon make a high grade office. He is reported to have sent in to the postoffice department $300 as the net proceeds of one month's business last fall. Mr. McGuire is a congenial business man, leading lodge man, a K. P., a good singer, and active Christian in the M. E. church, and anxious for the good of Pahuska, and the Osage, in short an all around clever man and devoted husband and father.

(Photo by Hargis)

Mr. P. Spirling's Orchard Park and Home.

HISTORY OF THE OSAGE NATION

Mr. P. Spirling, whose park-like cottage home in South Pawhuska, appears in cut, is from the famous state of Kansas, 18 years ago, coming here while a young man. He has long been manager of Mr. F. A. G. Morris' Meat Market, the insurance man mentioned elsewhere and the first exclusive butcher shop in Pawhuska. Mr. Spirling is a deacon in the Baptist church, and an energetic Christian, and is honored by his friends with the familiar nickname, "Musical Butcher," from his fine happy temperament and singing.

To carve your mutton, pork or steak, he rises with the lark
No foes nor care, he whistles, sings, or smiles from daylight until dark.

He married a Kansas girl, Miss Jennie E. King, in Pawhuska, in '93. They have no children but judging from his merry air they must have as happy a home as possible without them.

---

beautiful quarters that may be added as needed. The 160 acres appropriated to the St. Louis School is on the west. The elevations to the north. Mr. C. N. Prudom's fine quarter section, with beautiful, successive rises, and Mr. John P. Lynn's excellent bottom farm to the east, and the sublime views from the wooded bluffs southward will make future building sites unsurpassed in any city or section. The Creator of the great, broad world in which we live never designed that men, neither in business nor social life, be packed together like sardines in a "3x4" flat box. It is to be lamented by every lover of reedom, fresh air and sunshine, that all the resident lots in the town plats of the broad prairies were not twice as wide as they are. Hence all the more necessary that other land be added to give the porest man a better chance to own his own home and garden, with room for fruit and ornamental trees.

Pawhuska being about half way between the Great Lakes and the Gulf and the Atlantic and the Pacific coasts, has all possible advantage of passenger and freight traffic. Five great systems of railways are tapping her territory. With the Midland Valley, feeling for both coasts, southeast and northwest; the Santa Fe, north and south; the M. K. & T, and Frisco systems to all points of the compass, and the Missouri Pacific ready and negotiating to enter from the north, one can quickly see the traveling and shipping facilities so important to manufacturing, mining, fruit-growing and agricultural countries. Pawhuska is only 223 miles from Kansas City, 130 from Oklahoma City, 100 from Wichita, and 425 to St. Louis. It has between 1,500 and 2,000 population of mostly cultured, intelligent, social people from Maine to California and from Michigan to Mexico. It is, and, perhaps, will be for all time the center of Osage education and business. Great sums of money are paid out here annually to the Osage varying from $41 to $46 quarterly to each man, woman and child holding a right, and listed upon the Indian Agent's rolls. The payments are made about the first week in March, June, September and December. In addition to these payments each one receives an annual payment of royalties on mineral leases, principally from oil and gas, and pasturage, so far, amounting last year to over $350,000, paid equally per capita. The annuities vary fro year to year, and will no doubt increase as other minerals are developed. From all evidences gas and oil in large quantities. The wells can be seen north and east of Pawhuska producing volumes of gas and oil. The town is heated and lighted by these wells. One of the gas wells is said to be the second largest in the world.

HISTORY OF THE OSAGE NATION

The writer had the opportunity of watching the workmen shoot one of these wells, which is owned by some of the most financially and progressively prosperous citizens of Pawhuska. Most men come here to develop, and there is, and will be, development along all possible lines. Good shale for pressed brick is found here in abundance, an excellent opening for a brick yard, for as yet no brick have been manufactured in the Osage, but fine building stone is everywhere abundant, soft to hew, but hardening in the wall. Nearly all the government buildings are stone, and many of the farm buildings. Besides natural gas and oil, there is much wood for fuel, and streams for water power. All mercantile business is well established and professions well represented by many well equipped young men, and ladies. It is always true that many homeseekers in every newly opened country are from the more cultured classes of the older communities, seeking homes and wealth in less congested fields. Generally neither the richest nor poorest, but contented, working elements, care to migrate much. This fact is soon discovered in studying all new fields.

The Osage townsite committee was composed of Col. W. A. Miller, the government representative, and Mr. Julian Trubly, and Captain Frank Frantz, the Indian Agent for the Osage. Since the beginning of this book, and the inauguration of Frantz, governor, the lots have been sold, and the town is making rapid strides in growth, and Mr. Ret Miller appointed agent. The deeds will soon be returned from the approval of the Secretary of the Interior, who ruled that all lots built on after March 3, 1905, would have to be sold and bought at public auction. This created some agitation at first, but there was but little bidding against the owners of the improvements, and one case the bidders took up a collection to help an old lady buy her lot, she had built on, and cheered the auctioneer, Mr. Ewing when it was bid off to her at the appraised value, $20.

While the present center of the business and resident portions of Pawhuska nestles under an abrupt bluff on the north, rising near a hundred feet, and crowned with the National Osage School campus and buildings overlooking the city, it is so level that it will require skillful engineering for a fine sewerage system to the creek. The Westside is one of the most beautiful homesites. Here the most lovely, native grove of small oaks and other trees, one-half block, was recently purchased by Mr. Younger and wife, of Arkansas, a well known family, and fine people. He is a breeder of fine stock.

Pawhuska now has five large general merchandise stores, besides several smaller ones, doing a good business, four hotels, three banks, three drug stores, four meat markets, three exclusively groceries, four livery barns, three blacksmith shops, six restaurants, three barber shops, four millinery parlors, four lumber yards, three wagon yards, two photograph galleries, two bakeries, two gents' furnishing stores, two racket, and several small stores and many roomiing and boarding houses sufficient to entertain all comers till the lot sale, when the population may double in the next year. Good water, but slightly mineral is found at shallow depth all over town. The government ice and water plants supply the town with both, at contract prices. Rents are high, because of the limited number of houses, till other lots can be acquired. The sooner the lot sales occur all over the Osage the greater benefit to the towns and country. While some few might welcome delay, the vast majority would gladly see the town lots sold and towns organized under municipal control, as no one can establish a business till then without giving a $10,000 bond to observe the rulings of the Indian Department and to handle no intoxicants. This last provision is a good one,

HISTORY OF THE OSAGE NATION

Mr. Westly Dial, of Dial-King Law and Realty Company is a native of Arkansas, but came to the Osage about seventeen years ago. He has been a successful farmer, stockman, and real estate dealer for five years, having first formed the Dial and Baker Realty Company.

He is now in company with E. W. King, a lawyer of good standing, an experienced real estate dealer, and Commercial Club Secretary.

Mr. Dial married an estimable lady of the citizen family, Miss Eliza Huston, in 1879. They now own the finely improved farm of Mr. Chas. N. Prudom, just a half

(Photo by Hargis)

The Beautiful Farm Residence and Orchard of Westly M. Dial

mile east of Pawhuska. His residence appears with this article showing only part of the fine orchard and fine improvements.

His quarter section of land here is one of the most fertile in the Osage country. Between his home and town grows the most beautiful pecan grove the writer ever saw. The soil is a dark waxey loam. He has a growing real estate business and is energetic for the development of the Osage and the growth of Pawhuska.

---

as the Osage under its vigilant agent, Mr. Frank Frantz, is the most quiet, orderly section the writer ever saw.

PAWHUSKA LOT SALE

The public auction of the Pawhuska lots began January 3, 1906, and continues till all were sold. Twenty-five per cent was payable on day of sale, and balance on sanction of bid or sale by the Secretary of the Interior, and delivery of deed in fee simple, making practically a cash sale. This will be the method of sale in Hominy, Fairfax, and other sites and will tend to prevent speculation by many on a credit basis. The sales in the later places will ocur, no doubt, as early as surveyed and appraised.

The first day of sale there were more than a 1,000 visitors and purchasers from all over the Union. A cold, raw wind was blowing hard from the north, but the actioneer Mr. Amos Ewing and the bidders waided through mud to the outskirts of the town to begin the sale on a lot on the beautiful creek bank, appraised at $20, the first bid. It was knocked down to J. B. Charles of Stroud, O. T., for $100. The second appraised at $16, was purchased by Ira Stewart of Cushing, O. T., at $75. One fixed at $2, brought $55; another at $5 went to $300; and $10 lot sold for $220. People from every state flocked in; expenses ran high frim $2 to $5 per day, stages received $5 for a 5 mile ride, with seats still at a premium, all paid and smiles thrown in by the town builders who saw a great future for Pawhuska. One business lot in the center of town has since sold at private sale for over $10,000. The more than 1,200 lots sold were first estimated to bring from $25,000 to $50,000 into the Osage Treasury, but the first 100 lots sold brought over $25,000, and about $225,000 will be added to the Osage wealth, netting every man, woman and child about $100 each. Some of the full-bloods cannot fully comprehend the white man's craze for the vacant lots, and tightly wrapped in their costly blankets and shawls they look in amazement, askiing, "What for, pale faces want these lots." But when in future, they get this money for more luxuries, and sell more lots, get more money, buy more delicious chuck, get finer blankets, horses, carriages, keep heap warmer, have much fun," and villages become retiring centres, and emporiums of commerce, for their homes they will know better then. Many ladies were at the sale and bought with zeal, investing here there hard earned money, thus showing the great faith placed in the future of the Osage, and her towns. A dalyi paper is reported to have started in Pawhuska and all eagerly waiting for the return of approved deeds. It all shows how lucky these Indians are as a speculator expressed it: If an Osage was to fall into the Mississippi he would come up with his pockets filled with fish."

This book was placed on contract with printers to be ready before this sale, but owing to the utter disregard of their obligation. the writer was unable to get them before; and has only this excuse for his unavoidable delay.

Other towns, as Foraker, and Bigheart, have been set apart for sales, and will come in their order and importance.

In the development of every new country much depends upon the manufacturing industries established to use up the natural products of the soil, so far as needed, without cost of shipping both ways. It is poor economy, and worse politics to ship from St. Paul and Minneapolis or elsewhere, flour, corn meal and graham, when a surplus of grain can be grown and ground at your door with less cost. How insane to ship cattle to distant slanghters, only to skin and cut, and return the meat two-fold tougher. The home made broom can sweep as clean and cheap. The native brick may be as smooth and hard right from your shale. This mill is one of historic interest, first built smaller in 1880, by treaty with the Osages, in their new home, for whom it was

HISTORY OF THE OSAGE NATION

The Osage Roller Mills—Wholesale and Retail—Soderstrom & Selby, Props.

operated by the United States for eighteen years, then sold to John P. Soderstrom, father of Eben, one of the young men proprietors. Having burned in 1897 it was rebuilt larger in 1899, a stone building costing over $8,000, fitted up with the latest improved machinery, propelled by steam. Mr. Scarborough, president of the Bank of Commerce, first bought a half interest, which he later turned to young Mr. O. M. Selby, Eben's present partner. The mill has a capacity of 75 barrels per day. These young men are experienced millers, energetic, progressive citizens, whom you will find most congenial and obliging. **Remember the newly modeled old mill by the stream,** a land mark of Osage history.

BLUE POINT RESTAURANT.
Regular meals and short order, fine cigars and tobacco. Fish and game

Mr. Ed. Simpkins, the proprietor, a Hoosier by birth, has been in the Osage country for twenty years. He has been farming and stock-raising much of his time in the Osage but has been for two years past conducting the Blue Point Restaurant, the most popular eating resort in Pawhuska. It is in the basement of the historic Council House where most of the "Old Timers" and many of the "New Comers" life to congregate and chat over times past, present and the future prospects of the Osage. Mr. Simpkins is a citizen by marriage. His wife was Miss Mary L. Del-Orier. They have five fine children. He has a first grade farm three miles from Pawhuska, and a cottage house in town where they live. He is a sociable and popular man and is finely adapted to the restaurant business. Like many other intermarried citizens he is much interested in the progress of Pawhuska and the development of the Osage country.

HISTORY OF THE OSAGE NATION

COMMERCIAL CLUB.

The Pawhuska Commercial Club was organized in October last with nearly 100 members including most of the business and professional men of the town, and by-laws formulated to govern the workings of the club. Mr. E. M. Dempsey, (real estate) was elected president; Judge E. N. Yates vice president; Isaac D. Taylor, (law), treasurer; T. H. McLaughlin (merchant,) A. N. Ruble, (band cashier,) and W. C. Tucker, (merchant), directors. Mr. McLaughlin when called upon for a speech replied: "I have no speech to make, but I am always here and ready for work" So forceably did the crisp words, "I am always here and ready for work," impress the club, that they were voted as its motto. The important office of secretary was voted E. W. King, who is a well known lawyer, and from experience in new countries will know what is needed for the town and country. May long live the club, in its efforts to advance the town along beneficial lines, and enlist the sympathy and support of all the people. Too often what is done is borne by the few, while the whole population reaps the benefit of others expense, work and benevolence. Any of the above officers will gladly give homeseekers or investors any special information and encouragement, with reference to the town, or their section of the territory, and what manufactures should be located here. A large nursery should soon be begun to supply the demand for trees. A cotton gin and compress will soon be needed. A cotton meal oil mill, a tannery, a brick yard, a saw mill, a woolen and a cotton mill, broom factory, canning factory, a cold storage, are among the many industries that could be profitably established.

The Jet White Laundry, Wayland Wood, Mgr.

So important is cleanliness of body as well as mind that a great sage said ages ago, "Cleanliness is next to Godliness." Mr. Wood is formerly from Winfield, Kansas where he lived since 1882. He began the laundry business in Pawhuska in June, 1905, and is already doing a large business, and as fine a grade of work as can be done anywhere. Skilled help was hard to get at first but by energy and skill he has trained his employees till he now runs a first class laundry, with a growing patronage, that sustains a number of employees. Mr. Wood is a young man, and his business success is already assured if he continues his successful enterprise. He has a most amiable little wife, refined and intelligent, and ever ready to help and advise. She stands by his side amid the group in the cut. Blessed is the man whose life companion is able to advise and to sympathize with her husband in his higher aspirations of life. Mrs. Wood seems to be such a one. They have built an elegant cottage home of their own planning, and are active members of the Baptist church. The world will feel the benevolent influence of their life in other ways than snowy linen robes of "Jet White Laundry."

Sha-pa-nah-she

A deaf mute Osage of unusual intelligence, with his bright, pretty babies.

HISTORY OF THE OSAGE NATION

C. M HIRT & CO.,
Dealers in General Merchandise and U. S. Licensed Indian Traders.

Mr. Hirt, head of this firm is a Virginian by birth, and has many of the characteristics of true, blue blood Virginian. He was in the mercantile business in Franklin and Roanoke counties, the Old Dominion, before coming "West" to the Osage in 1902 where he saw an opportunity for great development and great possibilities for the man of broad experience and best business principles such as he brought with him. He had already purchased the Old Red Store and dwelling by it, one of the best business stands in the town and Osage. It is one of the oldest places in town, built of stockade logs on ends. It has associated with it years of history and will be a good card for him all through time. Mr. Hirt carries a full line of general merchandise and imployes a number of clerks, and does a constantly increasing business. He will soon have to enlarge the Historical Old Red Store and make the **Remodeled Red Store**. His property is some of the most valuable in town joining the council house yard on the west. He is an active member and deacon in the Presbyterian church which has just been organized. You will be pleased to meet him and know the higher kind of citizens that are in Pawhuska, from all parts of the world. While every Virginian loves the Old State he does not love his adopted home less.

(Photo by Hargis)

James C. Ferguson, Proprietor Osage Blacksmith Shop.

Mr. Ferguson is a native of Ohio and has blacksmithed all his life. His father was a blacksmith of the highest grade, and from the machinery and outfit in the shop, a cut of which is shown herewith. His son James inherited the faculty of working iron an wood. He was a resident of Waukomis, Okla., for six years. He then came to Pawhuska to stay and has one of the best equipped general blacksmith shops in the territory and does the highest grade work in his trade. He has a **"Barcas Horseshoeing Rack,"** that tames the wildest horse in shoeing him. Shoeing is his specialty, but he makes new wood and iron work to order, employing several assistants, and guarantees all his work. He is not only an excellent blacksmith but progressive, public spirited man and citizen.

HISTORY OF THE OSAGE NATION

THE PAWHUSKA CONCERT BAND

Until last June Pawhuska had no regularly organized band or orchestra. About the first June the Concert Band was organized and placed under the excellent guidance of Prof. Ed. F. Kreyer, a well known band instructor, who has since acted as the organization's musical director and he plays the solo cornet. Though but five months old this band is the delight of Pawhuska, and renders programs, consisting of classical and popular music with the ease, technic and execution of older and in fact professional organizations. From eighteen men, their organization has grow to twenty-eight members and weekly concerts given from the band stand in the public park. To Mr. A. W. Hurley, Chief Clerk of the Indian Agency, is largely attributed the honor of its organization, and main efforts of its maintainance. Both these men and their wives are leading spirits in music and art development, and are men of noble, congenial, progressive temperaments, and literary, dramatic and commercial powers in any community. Prof. and Mrs. Kreyer have traveled for years as artists in their line, especially fitted for the work. Mrs. Kreyer, with womanly dash, and untiring courage, inspires him to his work. Two more congenial lives are seldom seen. The instrumentation of the band are: L. M. Polson, Piccolo; Chas. Duncan, A. H. Duncan, A. H. Gibson, G. Hill, William Davies, Otis Hill, clarinet; Burt Kreyer, Peter C. Martinez, R. W. Miller, B. F. Parsons, Drenx Hurley, Don Owens, cornet; W. D. Perry, first horn; C. Wheeler, second horn; Geo. H. Beaulieu, solo alto; F. W. McKinney, first alto; R. J. Woodring, second alto; Harry Koh-pay, Mart T. Bowhan, W. M. Plake, E. B. Soderstom, trombones, A. W. Hurley, baritone; Fred Labadie, Bb Bass; T. E. Gibson EbBass; G. G. LaMotte, Eb Bass Monster; Geo. Duncan, bass drum; J. F. Anderson, snare drum and traps.

Nothing could add more to the culture of communities than fine music. Harmony is heaven's first law, yea, almost the only one; harmony with God, his laws, and each other, would make heaven anywhere it reigns.

There is also a lecture and entertainment course being conducted under the individual supervision of Prof. Davies and Mr. Campbell. Some entertaining numbers have been given at the M. E. church.

OSAGE DANCERS.

Young Osages, Walley Fish, Richard Rust, Sam Barber, in their dancing suits ready for the ballroom (Round House) Hominy.

Such suits often cost from $50 up to $200, some of silks, satins, velvet or other expensive material with costly ornaments. As among many whites, fine dancers are espeially favories. The women only look on in silence.

HISTORY OF THE OSAGE NATION

The town and farm residences and orchards of Mr. and Mrs. Jno. P. Lynn, Pawhuska.

(Photo by Hargis)

Mr. Jno. P. Lynn who owns the beautiful town and farm home on the east border of Pawhuska, was born in Independence, Ks. He has been in the Osage about 20 years, farming and stock raising, having several fine allotments for his wife and four children. Mrs. Lynn was Miss Mary Rogers, a descendant of the Canvilles of Kansas City 50 years ago, where they came from St. Louis and settled near the present site of Union Depot. Their farm joining town is one of the best improved in the Osage. His fine orchards of apples, peaches, pears, plums, grapes and small fruits as black berries, strawberries, raspberries, etc., are flourishing. Persimmons and pecans are a native and luxuriant growth on this farm. Mr. Lynn is a most energetic man in his work, of cattle dealing and feeding. His farms are mostly leased to renters, while he lives in town, and spends his time mostly in the stock business.

THE PAWHUSKA REALTY CO.

Carlton and Tolson, Managers.

With the advance of immigration on the frontier comes the Real Estate man with his inexhaustible energy. He even preceeds imigration and opens up new fields. To the real estate business can be traced the opening of much of American territory, and allotting the Indian lands. It is a most legitimate business when rightly and fairly conducted, and from which more honest money has been made than from any other business of the world. The home, and society an dall foundations of wealth are based, primarily upon the soil and its products, hence none could be more honorable. Yet 'tis the honor of the man that makes honorable the profession.

Among the several real estate men and firms in Pawhuska, Messrs. Carlton and Tolson have established a business and reputation that insures their permanent success, and increase of confidence in their patrons. Both are owners of valuable property and homes here. Mr. Carlton owning the "Carlton House." Both men are men of amiable, social and business qualities, whom it is a pleasure to meet; men of high honor and unselfish purpose to see Pawhuska grow, and the entire Osage developed. There are no better real estate men in th Osage to whom the writer could direct the reader, than to these men for your best interests in their line. If you wish further information than in this treatise, write them.

HISTORY OF THE OSAGE NATION

PAWHUSKA SCHOOL ADVANTAGES

Up to this year the whites had no public schools. Select schools had been taught by various individuals. Mrs. Laura Tucker, a cultured lady, has her own school house on the "Hill," near the National School where she has taught for years. Public schools are now taught under the direction if Mr. William McGuire, Rev. Hill, Rev. James and others, in the M. E. Baptist and Episcopal church houses, till suitable school buildings can be erected, after town corporation. The parents so far as able, pay a nominal tuition of $1 per month for each child, as a school tax. It appears that the school funds of Oklahoma do not apply to the Osage reservatin. Something seems out of joint in this particular. Why the business people of the Osage counry should have to pay tax or license to Pawnee and Kay counties, without sharing proportionately in Oklahoma school funds, of which there is near a million dollars, is a problem to which the writer has not devoted sufficient investigation to solve. Opening the reservation and allotting the land, could soon remedy the lack of publio school funds for the white residents and citizens of the Osage Nation. Many of the latter prefer to educate their children in the public or private schools, rather than in the National School, which is now attended mostly by the full-bloods. The attendance at the Sisters' schools are also largely fullbloods, the whites going to the town Parocihal school near the church, of which so far, the writer has been unabel to get a photo for a cut. Considering that the Catholic people were the first and almost only church so far to begin educating the Osages, as the work of Father Shoemaker, and treaties show, we feel constrained to dwell at some length on their work. The St. Louis and St. John's schools are stone buildings almost identical in architecture, located as above stated, St. Louis for girls, and St. John's for boys. A cut of both appears herein. The campi are now far more beautiful than the cuts show. On writing to Rev. Sister Angelica, superior of St. John's, the writer received a prompt reply and unexpected check (note) to plaoe a sketch of St. John's in this book, stating that she did not know what became of the former cut of ten years ago, for which she paid the solicitor $15, but heard nothing more of it. The cut was printed but cannot be found. Sister Angelica, you shall hear from this again. Such trust is too sacred ere to be forgot. 'Tis sweet to be trusted that the noble virtues of fidelity and honesty may show their worth. How different your spirit from that of the articles later on discussed.

 Old Socrates, with lantern torch by day,
  Still stalking through the worlds,
 May yet perchance find some honest men,
  And true, free from tricks and churls.

 One of the greatest powers of the Catholic church is her systematic business principles. When they want a school or church ereoted the means are generally ready somewhere. They have been through medieval and modern history, the foremost religious and secular trainers of children. One of their greatest scholars said: "Give me the education of a child till twelve years of age, and I will tell you his future course." And the idea was not far from fact. Everywhere they have commodious brick, stone and wood schools, academies, colleges and universities, mounments of their ideas and work. They are a people who do things, not dream alone. Many of the better educated citizens were taught in these schools or at the Osage Mission, Kansas, before coming to their present country. In gratitude for the Mission work the Osages entreated the Sisters to build similar institutions here, who were not long in finding the necessary funds. Rev. Mother Katherine Drexel of Philadelphia, erected the four story stone buildings and the Sisters, taking charge have schooled many Osage children in literature, art and music. The Catholic church formerly stood near the St. Louis school, till moved by Mr. Will Bradshaw, the house mover, across the Bird Creek, to its present location on Main Street, one block east of the "Iron Bridge," Here a school and a parsonage was erected. Many of the full bloods and allied families all over the reservation belong to this church. Hither they come from miles around to bend the knee and bow the head in prayer before the crusified Christ, the infant Jesus, and the immaculate Mother Mary. Scarcely are the straps of the papoose cradles or shawls, more commonly used, unloosed from the maternal shoulders, when many of the little bronze faces are brought before the white teachers in the Missions. Many of these little faces compare in appearance and brightness favorably with many a Caucassian mother's cherubs.

The writer observed oue face among the little girls in the National School especially worthy of note. While many of them have beautiful eyes and raven blaok hair to adorn their pretty brown faces, this one especially was most fascinating in its marvelous beauty. A natural beauty artist in all his or her idealistic fancy could scarcely improve on these more than classic features. With all the bright innocense of childhood, the mild, pensive, slightly dropping eyes gave a sweet expression to the noble, partly musical, partly classical forehead, the beautifully rounded cheeks, a nose of strength, yet affection, and generous ears, all crowned with a luxuriant growth of oily black hair on an extraordinaryily harmonious head, made a picture that night be sought in vain by the bells or beauties of Paris, London, or New York. The long lauded beauty of the Southern Creole, of her world renowned brunettes, could scarcely eclipse the face of this little Queen of the Osage. The legends of Hiawatha, or brave deeds of the first native American princess, Pocahontas, could inspire a gifted pen nor more than she. But her photo she would not give. The exquisite sensitiveness and reserve of many of the full blooded girls are among their most striking characteristics. And their modesty seems to be inherited by many of their partly white descendants.

No one can visit the Sisters Schools without being impressed with an atmosphere of refinement, and religious culture. A chapel scene at the St. Louis Sohool, the devout Sister Superior Mary Gerard, kneeling before the altar, and reminders of our Christ enforce the conviction that we ought all to be more devout in the presence of God and the crucified and thorn crowned Christ. The snow white altars, the golden candlesticks, and perfect statuettes, all make an impression upon the imagination and soul of the pensively inclined that is not easily forgotten, nor is it hard to see why children are so influenced and moulded by such teachings.

In witnessing the worshipful attitude of the Sister in the rectory of their school, iit brought vividly to the memory of the writer his experience of five weeks, some yeare ago, while a boy in the east, having been robbed of all but one penny in his pocket for good luck, and hundreds of miles from home and mother, sick and lonely, he found the kindest care and motherly kindness from the sisters, the ministering angels for the sick in a great hospital. Their sympathies and encouraging words at such a time have never ceased to sound in his soul, nor has he ever since lacked a work of praise for those who may delight to spend life in so divine a place, if it but enforces in living example, the Apostle's words: "Pure and undefiled religion before God and our Lord Jesus Christ is this; to visit the fatherless and widows in their affliction and to keep ourselves unspotted from the world."

Oh, how many times we almost envy them their calm, thrustful happiness, apart from the turmoils, excitements, the conflict, pains, sadness, and sorrow of many human hearts, that plunge deeper into the whirling stream to find an imaginary rest, to whom the Sisters are messengers of peace.

The Lesert brothers and Their families, four generations, the descendants of John Boy.—Pawa City.

THE GOVERNMENT NATIONAL SCHOOL.

Soon after removing from the Kansas lands to this reservation the government, in accordance with treaty stipulations, erected two commodious four story, stone buildings, (ref. supra), on the same campus, the southend structure for girls, the north end one for boys, and a recitation hall between; where there is co-education in the class rooms, the prevailing modern methods, of educating both sexes together, which should inspire the boys to more manly, the girls to more ladylike deportment, and greater zeal to excell in study. But whether it so results is often a question hard to answer. The equally modern spirit of liberty and freedom, as often seem to make both sexes careless, or indifferent to the presence, opinions and favorable impressions of the other sex in general. Here again comes in the personality of the instructor to make the benefits equal to the pupils opportunities. This school appears to be well conducted under a force of over twenty teachers, and other employes in all departments, including literary, musical, domestic arts for the girls, some mechanical and agricultural instruction for the boys. The teachers in these schools are often transferred by their own request, and sometimes through political tendencies, or other cause, as the service in the routine of such schools are by no means attractive to many younger teachers. Hence poor results sometimes follow. But from observations and the pleasure of personal interview with a few of the instructors in the service here, the writer may state that their work is efficient and progressive, with Prof. Wm. Davies,

HISTORY OF THE OSAGE NATION

principal, Miss Louise Wallace, music, and others whom we would gladly mention if the sketches had been sent in time, as promised. In the boys' department Mr. Louis Studer, from Rock Valley, Sioux county, Iowa, is instructor. He entered upon his work here last September as industrial teacher and disciplinarian. He is a young man of excellent bearing. He has several bright boys of Indian ancestry as his assistants. Earnest Harris and John Roy, a boy of an old and historic Indian family, are two of his deputy laborers. Indian boys and girls have the preference in employment where they are competent to fill the positions. This feature encourages them to excell.

THE SCHAEBER CLOTHING CO.
Dealers in All Kinds of Gent's Furnishings.

Already Pawhuska is taking on a metropolitan air. General stores are being supplanted by one line emporiums. This exclusive gents furnishing store was established in April 1905. They carry a fine line of **clothing, hats, shoes, trunks, valises and other gents wear. Mr. A. C. Schaeber,** a young man of culture and excellent business ability and energy is manager of the company. He is from Clay Center, Kansas, where he was head clerk of a large firm before coming here to start his **rapidly growing business.** He is from a section of country that knows now to make the most of its resources and even push its towns beyond its developed resources then to come again with strength and permanency. While there are other dealers in men's and boys' furnishings the Schaeber company is the only exclusive dealers in town. The have the commercial zeal not only to develop their own business but all interests of Pawhuska and merit your fullest patronage.

The Business Block of Percy J. Monk, Druggist, and Jeweler, and Mart T. Bowhan, and Hon. John Palmer's Home on National Heights.

HISTORY OF THE OSAGE NATION

Notwithstanding the rapid spread of Christian Science thought and teaching, magnetic healing, faith cure, and osteopath and homeopath among millions of educated thinkers of this century, pharmacies still stand numerous upon the streets of every town and city. The wonder is, who takes all these drugs? Pawhuska has already three drug stores, of which Percy J. Monk's (see cut) was the first established some ten years ago, when he first came to Pawhuska. He is doing the largest prescription drug business in town. He is also a jeweler and watch repairer to which he devotes most of his time, employing drug clerks. Born in London, England, he came to America in 1881, at 12 years of age, lived in the oil fields of Pennsylvania, then in Kansas, whence he came to Pawhuska. He owns valuable business and residence property and is a gentleman of broad experience and interest in his town.

Mart. T. Bowhan—Manufacturer of Harness and Saddles. Among the business young men of the Osage Mr. Bowhan holds a leading part. He came to Pawhuska from Kansas five years ago, and became one of the best manufacturers of the town. He married Miss Ida Trumbley of Osage descent, and an amiable young lady. He and Mr. Monk are joint owners of the business block shown in the cut. Both are progressive and estimable citizens, and doing a growing busineses in their lines. Mr. Bowhan carries a complete line of hand and ready made harness, saddles, whips, and other horse furnishings. Pay him a visit and you will be pleased.

Mr. L. J. Stratton, formerly of Massachusetts, has taught the mechanical or carpenter department for five years, and Laura Mahon, boys' matron, has been in Indian Territory work for nine years. Mrs. Lauradell Henry, small boy's matron, a native of Florida, has been in service four years. Her husband is the superintendent of the school ice and water plants, from which the town is also supplied.

Most of the industrial arts are carried on in a small scale in order to teach the children the domestic arts. But all the acquirements in this line seem to be slow and poorly acquired. The instructors all claim that it is difficult to fix these essential arts in the life of the vast majority of Indian children.

With such educational advantages the wonder to all who survey these privileges is that these primitive people have not long since been trained to self dependence in all domstic trade and arts. Perhaps it is not the fault of the sowers, nor the seen; but of the soil. But is not the primitive race of the western plains and forests susceptible of more rapid fertilization? The boys of these schools are trained in the rudiments of farming and ordinary domestic duties. But somehow this rustic educational plating does not seem to hold its polish. But whether it is the fault of the process or the metal and base, is a question to be solved in the future development of these people. That they are capable of a broad and useful cultivation is shown by the accomplishments of some who seem to improve their advantages in the Missions and schools, whose homes have the Ladies' Home Journal, farm papers and others constantly around their hearth. In general the Indians are shrewd people and had they been allotted their lands many years ago and made to rely upon their own resources and labor, they would in all probability, have been an independent, self supporting people today. This belief inculculcated more domestic pride, have settled down on some selcet spot of ground and have become independent and self-supporting so far as the neesessaries of life go.

Intermarriage with the better class of whites has done much for these people. Some of the brightest and most beautiful types of men and women are the descendants of such families. They have long since begun to realize the value of their great heritage, and manifest a plausible pride in their broad acres and individual homes. Among these indian descendants are some of the most excellent and richest people in the world, certainly in possibilities if not in real value of land and money income, if they only use and improve their possessions. The only education that the full bloods need for the growing generations is a thorough knowledge, in theory and practice, of farming, gardening, fruit growing and in building their own houses for future homes. Ten years of such training will do more for the aborigines of the plains than a century of mere primary book knowledge. The master stroke will be made when the treaty or bill is made and passed to allot their lands and open their reservation to the invincible advancement of commercial conquest and improvement. Let us protect them against the ravages of such a civilization, and the Indian's future prosperity is assured. He will soon learn what life means, and what the Great Spirit made the land and waters for. No "pale face" doubts the red man's comprehension along this line now since he views with wistful eyes the choice spots of lands and waters and timbers they select for their own. The Indian has never been convinced that the "Great God," who is no respector of persons, except through natural, economical and spiritual laws, has made all that's good for the white man, even though his white children of European origin replenish and subdue much more than his North American children of a more ruddy hue. The writer in former days, when far distant from their camping and hunting grounds, and having never seen an Indian in native garb, and wigwam, imagined, with millions of others with limited Indian lore, that the poor children of the forest and plains were badly treated, and felt the chivalrous impulse to come to their rescue; but since coming to the territories and tudying the true facts the writer feels more like calling upon the blessed and leisure—rich Red Man to come to the rescue of the poor white man. For many of those fertile plains have gone untilled fifty years too long for the good of the homeless renter, and certainly too long for the leisure loving aborigines. They have been at least weakened and impoverished by the excessive fostering care of "Uncle Sam." After many years those in authority are having this realization dawn upon them. The Indian Commissioner, W. A. Jones, in his annual report to the Secretary of the Interior, condemns the present system of Indian education as an obstacle to the progress of these people in their present domestic state, toward independence and self support. He does not condemn their education in the abstract, for its advantages are too great, nor does he criticize the management of any particul school, or schools in operation, but simply calls attention to the fact that the present Indian educational system, taken as a whole, has not and is not calculated to produce the results so earnestly claimed for it, and so hopefully anticipated, when it was begun.

  H. B. Freeman, Lieut. Col. Fifth Infantry, and acting agent of the Osage, in reporting to the Indian Department July 31, 1895, said:

  "The full bloods have theiir wants amply supplied by their annuity and have no others, make but little progress, the younger part suffer from the sins of their ancestors, are lacking in physical stamina and constantly decreasing in numbers. The pupils returning from the non-reservation schools have not the energy or ability to influence the other to fill such positions as I may give them, and sooner or later, casting aside all they may have learned sink into the common mass of ignorance and idleness in which many of the younger ones grow up, in not even having the industry

MR. FRANK TINKER.

One of the most interesting families of the Osage own and occupy this beautiful and costly cottage as shown on the preceeding page. Both Mr. and Mrs. Frank Tinker are of Osage lineage. His father Wm. Tinker, was half Osage, his mother, one-eigth Osage, and one-eigth Kaw. Frank was reared in the Osage, but is unusually energetic and progressive, a man of broad experience, thoughtful mind, and strong intelligence, and keenly discerns the true merits of men and measures, has served as Osage sheriff several times and constable one term. He is a successful farmer and stockman, owning several fine farms in the eastern part of the Osage, near Skiatook, and valuable property in Pawhuska, besides elegant home shown in cut. It is the best and most costly furinished home of its size in the Osage nation, costing about $5000, has all the modern conveniences of a city home with commodious rooms, bath, toilet, pantry, halls, all excellently furnished from kitchen to garret. The yard is a veritable flower bed and many other evidences of culture. He married Miss Louise Revard, daughter of "Uncle Joe" Revard and a woman of fine domestic talents and ability. They have seven bright children, a model Osage citizen family. Their oldest son Frank, Jr. lives near Shiatosk, in a historic house which appears under that heading. This home is one of hospitality and welcome to friends and many strangers, who could never easily forget its surroundings.

The Pawhuska Home of C. C. Gilmore.

Mr. C. C. Gilmore, whose Pawhuska cottage home appars in connection, was born and reared among the Osages, but not of Osage descent. His parents were from Tennessee, and were Indian traders in ante-bellum days. Mr. Gilmore is a successful farmer, having one of the finest farms in the Osage, located surrounding the west side of Skiatook. It contains 400 acres, on part of which the M. V. depot is located. It will make him one of the wealthiest citizens among the Osages. He married Miss Mary A. Choteau in 1875, by whom four children, James, Augustus, Johanna Coanna, and Samuel James, were born. Mr. Gilmore sepnds much of his time is one of the leading inter-married citizens and a man of fine qualities.

HISTORY OF THE OSAGE NATION

and energy acquired by the older ones under the stress of former poverty, but relying entirely upon the annuity and credit for support.

"Being eminently social they spend most of their time in camp near the reservation, or visiting. Few are found who work ten days in the year. Still through association with their white renters, their children are gaining some knowledge of agriculture, the care of stock, etc., which with what they learn at school must slowly, perhaps, but surely lead them to abandon their roaming lives and settle down.

Why does he say "with what they learn at school." Ought not these government schools to be the main educating institution to train all Indian children to independent life and self help? But says Freeman, "the schools were managed without regard to industrial education, or regular attendance," etc. If this were generally true it explains to a great extent the seeming failure practically of the system, not the theory of industrial training of these children. A system that will necessitate individual responsibility and manual effort in the support of life and happiness will, with the necessary protection against wrong, solve the problem in one generation.

"In view of this condition of affairs I regard the continuance of the undivided land and trust funds as a positive curse to these people, destructive of every impulse toward honest labor and consequent progress."

Wm. J. Pollock, Osage Indian Agent, reported from Pawhuska, August 29, 1898, referring to their wealth, makes this statement: "If an Indian and his wife have eight children, the annual cash income to the family is over $2,000. They are aristocrats, and like all wealthy people scorn to perform manual labor. "They toil not, neither do they spin." Who can blame them, and who is to blame for this state of affairs?"

These reports show what some of the agents have thought concerning the course to be pursued in educating the full bloods to self reliant and independent life, but set forth no method by which such a condition can be brought about. The Osages themselves are favorable to such an allotment and individual possession, but like all Indian people are naturally suspicious and shy of any person whomsoever, attempting to act or advise in their affairs, till he proves himself true to their interests. Then and only then will they give him a welcome or support of any kind. This takes time, tact, and patience. Their confidence once gained they are friends that stick closer than a brother, and nothing they have is too good for you, nor do they expect your best is too good for them, a very natural sequence of true friendship.

H. B. Freeman, reported in 1895 that the citizens, (part bloods) were unanimously in favor of the allotment of the lands, but that the full bloods were as unanimously opposed to it, and out-voted the former two to one, for the simple reason as they claimed, that the rolls contained a number that had no right to share in their tribal funds, and to the intense jealously between the two classes and factions.

DRAFT ALLOTMENT BILL—OSAGES APPOINT ANOTHER COMMITTEE.

Another move toward the allotment of Osage lands has been lately made by the appointment of a committee to draft a new allotment bill on which both factions of the tribe are represented. Last year both factions favored allotment, but differed on the details as to how it was to be accomplished and as a result sent two delegations to Washington who worked at cross purposes and failed to accomplish anything. They declared intentions of the interior departtment to take the matter of allotment into its own hands has caused the Osages to made an effort to adjust their differences if possible.

The committee appointed by Chief O-lo-ho-wal-la includes from his own party C. N. Prudom, W. T. Leahy, Bacon Rind, W. T. N. Mosier, Frank Corndropper and Harry Kohpay, in addition to himself; from the oppsition party James Bigheart, who is the leader of Osage opposition, Peter Bigheart, John F. Palmer, Black Dog, and Ne-kah-wah-she-tun-kah.

The Pretty Home of F.G.A. Morris, the Insurance Man.—Park Row.

Mr. Morris came to Pawhuska from Plattsburg, N. Y., in January, 1889. He served ten years as chief clerk of the Indian Agency here and at Muskogee, I. T.; but resigned to enter the mercantile business. He now conducts the oldest and most extensive Fire Insurance business on the Osage Reservation. He is a leader in the Episcopal church, and is a man of many excellent qualities in church business and family life. His beautiful home is one of the best in town. He is the only one here doing an exclusive Insurance business.

The Pretty Home of Dr. Harry Walker,—Park Row.

Dr. Walker not only excells in his profession, but is a man of refinement, modesty and culture the true characteristics of all high grade personalities. He has been schooled in some of the best medical schools and hospitals, east and west. He lived in Greely, Kansas, for eight years, and in Oklahoma City eight, and has practiced in Pawhuska since 1901, and has an extensive practice. With his wife and three children he has a model, Christian family. Such people wield a mighty influence for good in the churches and social circles of the community.

HISTORY OF THE OSAGE NATION

(Photo by Hargis)

THE GRADED PUBLIC SCHOOLS OF PAWHUSKA

The town schools are taught by four competent teachers. The writer, judging from his observation and acquaintance with these teachers, can truly say that if the directors had searched the whole country over they could not have secured four young men and women of better qualities to live among their children for instructors than the ones whose services they secured. They are all of fine temperaments, bright yet reserved, scholarly intelligent and of high ideals. It is the model you set before the child, not test books alone that mould the character. Would you make a manly boy; keep his eyes upon a noble man. To train the child into a charming, cultured girl, place before her tender impressive mind only the woman of bright inspiring life, and of sympathetis, modest mien, beautifully reserved. Tis the environment, the air in which we move, that inervates the soul or inspires a stronger life. Many a failure in education lies in the lack of an inspiring ideal in home and school. Prof. Austin, of broad training and experience, teaches the higher grades nad supervises the school. Prof. Robert R. McCreight, the next lower grades. Miss Blanc and Miss Pratt, the intermediate and primary grades. The scholars are increasing in number as the farmers move into town for the benefit of the schools. About 225 are enrolled in these schools. The National school has a capacity of about 200 with 138 enrolled. St. Louis with a capacity of nearly 150, with 75 in attendance. The Parochial school with a large capacity and a number of pupils. Mrs. Tucker about 25 and St. John's some 15 miles southwest with 150 capacity, and 70 enrolled.

We would gladly give a short personal sketch of each teacher, but have not the facts at hand to do so. Faithful teachers deserve as much credit for their work in uplifting the world as ministers of the gospel, often having more anxieties and trials.

Knowing Robt. R. McCreight, the teacher at the Episcopal church, as a roommate for a short time, we can surely say that he is an excellent type of a northern

HISTORY OF THE OSAGE NATION

young man. He is a product of the Buckeye state but expects to make Oklahoma his future home. Being born on a farm he received a common school education, attended high school, and later attended the Ohio University at Athens, Ohio. His first work as teacher was principal of Seamon, Ohio, schools, being the third man to fill that position that year.

He has been successful in his work, making raises in his salary each year. He is a Knight of Pythias and of the noblest ideals of what true men and women are or should be.

THE PRODESTANT CHURCHES OF THE TOWN.

There are four other church organizations in Pawhuska, besides the Catholic above mentioned.

During the unparalelled development of the towns of new countries, the religious denominations have been very active in meeting the moral, intellectual and spiritual needs of homeseekers and commercial classes. The transformation from the wilderness or the prairie to the present stage of civilization in the Osage nation, has been more graual than most towns, because of the long established Indian Agency. All the comforts and advantages of a small town have alreadyy been enjoyed by the Indian Traders and agency employees, when the bill passed to open the Osage townsites.

THE MISSIONARY BAPTIST CHURCH

The First Baptist Church of Pawhuska was organized with six members in 1898, by Rev. L. J. Dykr, Rev. Mr. Burnett, who is now working among the Osages, or has been it is said, to be the first Baptist to preach to these people, though Mr. Dyke previously formed the nucleus of the present congregation. Mr. Burnett was called as the first pastor, October 1, 1901, for full time. Miss Emly Cottrell, whom the writer has not yet had the pleasure of meeting, an amiable, devoted young lady from Richmond, Virginia, sent to the Osage by the Southern Baptist convention, is doing an excellent work among the full bloods for the past year. Daily she goes into their village, one mile northeast of Pawhuska to teach them. The writer cannot estimate the progress of the work, but all consecrated Christian work results in much good. A few citizens families belong to the Baptist church, who now have commodious, three division building, costing $3,000 seated with chairs, north and west divisions cut off by folding doors, when opened making a large seating capacity. Mr. H. C. Ripley, the Trade Supervisor of the Osage, and native of Main, is senior deacon, Mr. P. Spirling, junior deacon and Mrs. Laura E. Tucker, clerk. Rev. W. D. James is pastor; Mrs. Blanc, organist. They have near 50 members in regular standing, and nearly 100 enrolled in Sunday School. Rev. James is not only a fine preacher, but a broadminded practical man and has a pretty two story home two blocks east of the church house. Rev. Mr. Day and family, formerly of Marshall, O. T., are making their home here. So the Baptists have a strong working force in Pawhuska.

EPISCOPAL CHURCH

In the summer of 1895 when Rt. Rev. F. K. Brooks, Bishop of Oklahoma and Indian Territory made his first visit to Pawhuska, he found not more than three families of the Episcopal faith here. His work was the primitive mission work for the Episcopal church among the Osages. For several years there after no organization was attempted, though services were held in the Council House during this time at irregular intervals, as the Bishop found it possible to come or send some one else. By the first of the new year 1904, chiefly through the efforts of the Ladies Guild, a flourishing Sunday School had been organized and funds raised, sufficient to warrant the erection of a parish house, to be used for Sunday School purposes and for worship upon the occasion of the Bishop's visits. This building commenced in 1904, was completed in the following May, at a cost of $1,200. It is located on Osage Avenue, one block south of Main Street, and one block from the depot. The Mission as organized is known as "St. Thomas Mission." The work is under the supervision of Mr. J. H. Watts, Lay Reader, who came here from Philadelphia, Pa., October 1, 1905. Rev. Watts is from appearance and cultured manners, and English gentleman and pastor that will add much to the strength of the church and Sunday School. His vestrymen, D. H. Spruill, Geo. W. Simcock, and F. G. A. Morris, are all men of business and financial ability, and with the two vacancies to be filled, will guarantee permancy and progressive work for the parish in Pawhuska.

(Photo by Hargis)

The Pawhuska Home of Mrs. Monica Farrell.

The lady who owns this dwelling is only one-eights Osage. Her maiden name was Canville, the daughter of Andrew and Mary Louise Canville, both French, she Canadian-French. Andrew Canville could claim the distinction of building the first brick house in Kansas City, near the present old Union depot; traded with the Osages and owned much property there, but came with the Osage to their present home with nine children. Miss Monica first married Eugene Callahan. Her second husband was Moses Shaw, and after their death married John Farrell. She has eight children by her first two husbands. Her youngest daughter Ada, lately married Mr. James York, a worthy young man connected with one of the oil and gas companies with headuarters at Bartlesville. It is said that this young man captured his fair little bride of Osage descent after a romantic, brief courtship or wooing in which vocal music talent played a leading part.

THE METHODIST EPISCOPAL CHURCH

The Methodist Episcopal Church is also well established in Pawhuska, and have a good building, a cut of which appears on another page, and a medium sized pipe organ, played very melodiously by the young and beautiful little daughter of Mr. A. W. Hurley, chief clerk of the agency, Miss Catherine Hurley, who perhaps is the youngest pipe organist in Oklahoma and the United States. Mrs. F. T. Gaddis, who early taught a girl's school, seems to have been the very first Methodist Missionary among the Osages. She was sent by the Ladie's Home Mission Society of her church late in the '80's. The organization was formed in 1890 by Judge T. L. Rogers, Major Miles, who was then Indian Agent, Dr. G. W. Sutton, with a few others, and plans of a building drawn and erected and dedicated in 1891. For some years the services and work was sustained mostly by Judge Rogers and his generous wife, both of Indian lineage, and a few other adherents of the M. E. Church, and protestants of other denominations. The church whose building was erected by popular subscription, now has a good membership, and is in a prosperous condition under the strong pastoral charge of Rev. E. F. Hill, father of Chas. Hill, editor of the Pawhuska Capital, who by request of his people, was lately returned here by his conference. He is as refined and as scholarly a man as you would ever meet in large cities. With such officers and co-workers as W. E. McGuire, postmaster; Judge Rogers, W. D. Parry, A. F. Hatfield, and J. E. Johnson, trustees; the church has bright prospects of continued growth. Prof. Wm. Davies is choir leader and W. D. Parry, superintendent of their increasing Sunday School. The church is talking of selling its present location near the business center and building a fine house farther out. The "will," here as elsewhere, will effect the change, for next to the Catholic denomination, the Methodist people have the most effective, far reaching business rules in creating churches and parsonages on all new fields, and supplying them with regular preaching. Churches ought ot be the first to select their lots in every opening field. This is not far from the practice of the M. E. people for which they are commendable.

Mrs. Simpson's Town and Farm Residence and Mr. Simpson

whose farm residence appears in cut, was Miss Susan Mathews, the sister of Mm. S. Mathews, the president of the Citizens National Bank, in Pawhuska. She was born in Newton County, Missouri, in the "forties." Her motherwas half Osage, her father John Mathews, a Kentuckian. She married her husband in Kentucky, in 1870, who was a farmer and stockman. He died three years ago after an accident, leaving only his wife, never having had any children. Mrs. Simpson now lives in her Pawhuska cottage home, but loves her farm home much better, where she desires to spend the remainder of life. She is a lady of extraordinary refinement, and quiet temperament, spending her time mostly with her pet "pug" dog that has all the intelligence and devotion of a prococious child. Besides her town home she has a finely improved farm in the western part of the Osage.

HISTORY OF THE OSAGE NATION

(Photo by Hargis)

FIRST PRESBYTERIAN CHURCH

The First Presbyterian Church which Rev. J. H. Davies, a Presbyterian minister of Ralston, O. T., was the first to try to organize in Pawhuska, meets in the hall of the Council House. He came here in July, 1905, and called together the people of his church, and formed the nucleus of what promises to be a consecrated working church. They started with twenty charter members from some of the most priminent families of the community. Dr. Aaron and wife, J. C. Ferguson, W. D. Parry, Jos. B. Mitchell and wife, Mrs. Farrar, Mrs. Tucker, Mrs. Millard, Miss Hilton, Mrs. Scarborough and Mr. and Mrs. C. M. Hirt, and Judge Yates and others we are unable to name, composed the organization. Judge E. N. Yates, U. S. Commissioner of the court here is the only Ruling Elder at present, and Mr. Hirt, deacon. Rev. Brooks, a representative of the Territorial Home Mission Board, came to Pawhuska from Oklahoma City last fall on a visit to the church, preaching once while here. Rev. Davies has been called as first pastor for half-time, devoting other half to the Mission at Hominy, also started by him. He will live at Pawhuska. A number of other denominations are represented by members here, but as yet, have made no effort to organize. The Christian church people have had some preaching in the council house at times.

The Fine Residenc of Frank Revard, Pawhuska.

Frank Revard, whose beautiful cottage residence appears herewith, is a descendant of one of the oldest allied families of the Osage citizens. His father, Joseph Revard, has been among the Osage through a long life of 77 years, and is one of the oldest and best men of the citizen families. He was twice married and has nine children. Frank, a brother of Leonard Revard, is one of five boys, and a con of his father's first wife. Frank married Miss Amanda Nichols, of Chautauqua, Kansas. They have four bright children, and a happy home. He deals in musical instruments. He is a ledaing lodge man in the K. of P's, Masons and Odd Fellows; an honorable citizen, a good all-around fellow, and devoted to home and family; an energetic man knowing how to fashion his own home, and cultivate his "own vine and fig tree."

The name Revard was corrupted by mis-spelling from the French "Revor," meaning a riveter. It was first changed by a man named Bove, (or Greenwood,) to Revars, in which form it appears in treaty. The next form was given by Rev. Father Shoemaker, who spelled it Revard. Frank's great grandfather was a full-blood Osage, his great grandmother of French, and German lineage, and were married on the Mississippi River.

IN UNION THERE IS STRENGTH

What a heavenly, diving thing it would be if all denominations were united in work, love, and building one great church temple to hold all worshippers together, according to the Master's prayer. The Apostle exhorted, "Let me not say I am of Paul, another of Apolis, another of Cephas, another of Christ, or of Peter, James or John, etc.," as the case may be, but we are all of Christ,, all of God, commanded to do his will, obey his laws. Let "Christian Union" be your motto and battle cry of the twentieth century. From boyhood this has been the dream and hope of the writer, though often half suppressed. When we look back to the Messianic age of prophecy, there was but one temple, one tabernacle, one alter, golden, glorious, gracious the ornamentl crown of Jerusalem; to his people a type of heaven, harmony, oneness. Though there were many synagogues, (syn—together, and ago—to go or assemble) places to assemble they all taught and prepared only for one great gathering—in one temple, the one chorus, the one great concert of music at their yearly assembly. How much more inspiring would be the music of a hundred harmonious voices in chorus song, than choirs of a baker's dozen! How a teacher's (preacher's) heart might be thrilled, with thousands of bright inspiring eyes and a thousand brighter voices, than a hundred dull, indifferent ones, varying down to none. The difference lies in the electrical force of numbers and volume and harmony of action. "In Union there is strength," is truer of the churches in bringing wayward men into harmony with right, law, and God, than it is in the union of smaller principalities to protect themselves against the merciless conquests of tyranical empires. And none know this so well as the unchristionized individuals and nations; and the best business men are fast realizing that the time should come when their means, money, life and hearts, should be centered in a united Christian brotherhood. And the churches are fast learning that they cannot accomplish the greatest good without the sympathy and support of the business classes, and the strictest buines method in the material interest of the church. The churches have passed through their best days and won their greatest victories, till such a spirit and action prevails among the several great religious bodies.

IN HONOR PREFER ONE ANOTHER.

Christians, of the various congregations of the Osage nation, your abiding success in reaching the world and overcoming the mighty forces of evil which are sure to confront you, and contest every step of your advancement, lies in the spirit of unity. Brotherly fellowship should be manifest in all your labors. At least there should be a mutual co-operation pledged to stand as one church, and one body, from start to finish, in every effort to convert men from the errors of sin, and to advance the moral, educational and the spiritual interests of the whole community. All the followers of Christ should stand together for the advancement of God's kingdom in the world, as unbiasedly as the loyal members of a fraternal order stand by their "frater" under all circumstances. The time has come when the non-church-going and unchristian classes demand a unifying spirit, and action among the churches.

No man has the highest comprehension of his Master's life and teaching who loves his own opinions and denomination more than the general good of Christ'c cause, and the turning of men to God. The unspiritualized multitudes out of the churches can see some of the precious truths of the light and gospel of the Son of Man, but cannot conceive why it should be necessary for us who are his disciples, to be so diverse in our methods and opinions of following Him who prayed that his children might be one as He and God are one. As an army cnsecrates its several divisions to defend a common cause and common country against a common and powerful foe, so may the churches of the future consecrate their forces to win the whole world to Christ, the Son of God, and defend his kingdom against attack, invasion of decline. Stand together for the broad principles of the gospel, for their own lovliness and truth. All praise to God, that we are fast seeing that true life and love for souls are far above mere loyalty to forms and creeds, without such life and love.

The churches must have an interest in every man of every class if they accomplish the Lord's work, and the purposes of the Gospel. On the other hand, many men, though not professional followers of the "meek and lowly Christ," in any church, have a substantial or practical interest in every true Christian, and working church, for the good they bring to the world. Recognizing this mutual interest, the writer most humbly dedicates this history and biography to the homes, the Godspeed of the churches, and to the greatest prosperity of the business men pointing each one into whose hands it comes to the Golden Rule.

HISTORY OF THE OSAGE NATION

Christ: "Love they neighbor as thyself.
Interpretation: "Do unto others as you would have them do unto you."
Christ: "As ye woulld that men do unto you, do ye even so unto them."
In honor prefer another.
Aye. learn to love, not self, Oh erring, willful fellow man!
But another's life and good, God's will as best, and sure you can.
That when you come, your crown of jewels to receive above,
Not name, or wealth, or sect your plea, but how divine you loved.
—The Writed, P. J. D.

The Beautiful Cottage Home of Thomas Leahy.

Among the older prominent family of Osage citizens Mr. Thomas Leahy, familiarly called "Uncle Tom," holds a high place in the esteem of his acquaintances and friends. A native of Illinois he came to America in 1857, at eight years of age, lived first in Illinois six years, thence came to Kansas in 1863, where he resideed till 1875, then went to the broad plains ot the "Panhandle" of Texas, for eighteen months, and returned east to Joplin, Mo. for one year. He came to Elgin, Kansas, and the Osage in '77. In '68, at Osage Mission, in Neosho county, Kansas, he married, Miss Mary L. Champagne, who wass born and reared in Kansas City. She is only one-eigth Osage with French and German lineage. They have spent their married life in the Osage and eleven years in Pawhuska. They were honored with four children, three of whom, William Vava and Cora are living, and all married. Mrs. Saxon is his daughter. With his son Will, he conducts the largest livery business in town, just in the rear of his home shown in the cut. Will's beautiful cottage home is diagonally across Main Street from his father's, and Mrs. Saxon's, one block east. Both have finely improved farms adjoining Elgin, Kansas. No better people could be found

HISTORY OF THE OSAGE NATION

among the Osages or in Oklahoma than the Leahy families; well-to-do, yet unassuming, refined, social and hospitable.

TRUE POSSESSION YOURS

I own you not, I have you not,
   Tho' semmingly I own—
Until myself I have forgot
   And angel goodness shown,
No lingering claim of selfishness
   Must I keep in my breast,
If I would have the power to bless,
   And be among the blest!!

God has selected a new race—
   To crown the present man,
Within our souls is that high grace
   That perfects this grand plan:
It bids us live in love supreme,
   Thro' all the passing days,
And dream and work upon the dream
   And win this higher praise.

What was as prosy of the past,
   Must be abiding act,
The beauty in our living cast,
   Flower out in lovely fact;
For souls to souls are wed in love,
   And naught in kindness miss,
And how the angels live above,
   Becomes our human bliss.

O heart of love, I look on you,
   And feel the flush of shame.
That while I might have been so true,
   Such frailty to me came;
To love sincerely, that is wise,
   And soon would end earth's wrong;
And lovers looking from love's eyes,
   Would find their lives a song!

WILLIAM BRUNTON.

The Pretty Pawhuska Residence of Jasper Rogers.

(Photo by Hargis)

HISTORY OF THE OSAGE NATION

Mr. Jasper Rogers.

Mr. Jasper Rogers is one of the leading citizens of the Osage, only about 1-16 and shows but little, or none of their complexion, and traits. He was for some years one of the most successful farmers, but of late years has been engaged in various lines of busines in Pawhuska. He is now living in town where he has one of the most confortable, well-equipped himes. In nature and physique he is a fine specimen of wellldeveloped manhood. Few aree found to excell him as a devoted husband and faither in the love and pride of home and family. He married Miss Rose Fronkier, of Pawhuska. She shows as little of the Osage descent; and is one of the model wives and mothers among the Osage citizens. They have three children, one boy, Emmett, and two girls, Celia and Maud, all fine specimens of childhood. Mr. Rogers is much interested in the development of his town and country. He is a nephew of Judge T. L. Rogers, and a cousin of W. C. Rogers, the chief of the Cherokees, for whom he once clerked at old Skiatook. He is a lover of horses, and takes much pride in one of these pets. His wife, judging from a photo, taken at the time of marriage, was one of the most beautiful brides ever wedded among the Osage citizens, and wed a man worthy of her devotion.

(Photo by Hargis)

Wm. H. Hickerson's Residence and Shop.
(Gas Fitting and Plumbers' Supplies of All Kinds.)   U. S. Licensed Trader.

Mr. Hickerson was formerly from the Lone Star State where his father was a blacksmith, and his son, William Hays, inherited the art of working iron and steel, and grew up in the shop. He came to Pawhuska fourteen years ago after prospecting in New Mexico, and seven years in the Cherokee nation. He now runs the first established plumbing shop in the Osage country, having combines it with his blacksmithing from the first years in Pawhuska. He has a well stocked shop, ready for

HISTORY OF THE OSAGE NATION

all new or repair work, all guaranteed. His wife was Miss Fannie Chastain of Arkansas, and a very pleasant, bright lady. They have four children, one daughter Minnie, and three sons. Clarance is in an Oklahoma City business college, the other two in Pawhuska schools. Mr. Hickerson has done most of the plumbing in the Osage in the former years, and has a rapidly growing trade. He is an ardent K. of P. and lodge man, having represented the K. P's in the Grand lodge of Oklahoma, and is reported to have joined the Rathbone Sisters. He will gladly fit your gas and water systems with guaranteed work.

RESIDENCE AND SHOP OF T. M. McKINNEY and J. L. MILLER, Contractors and Builders, Manufacturers of Doors, Sash, Etc., and all Kinds of Interior Finishing.

These contractors have been partners in the business since first starting a shop, a cut of which appears in the back ground. They came to Pawhuska in 1900. Mr. Miller from Kansas, Mr. McKinney from Arkansas. They began work here with a small kit of tools and in three years have increased their business till now they have a large carpenter shop filled with machinery costing $1,500 for planing mill, sash and door making and all kinds of mill work to order. They are often overrun with orders during the rapid growth of the town. Both have fine cottage homes just east of their shop. The finest grade of work is produced here for the whole Osage country. They will soon be compelled to enlarge their shop and will become one of the largest manufacturing plants in Greater Pawhuska. They are such men as make a progressive city, and substantial citizens.

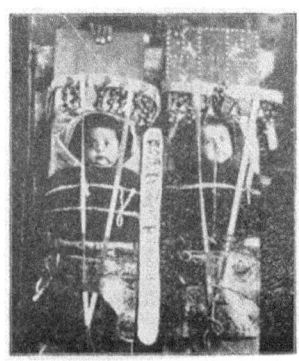

Twin Osage Papooses.
These baby twins in fancy Indian cradles are reported to be the first twins where both were allowed to live. Their ancient custom was to kill the mother and one twin, as the N-Wardarkoes and other tribes did, considering twins, for some reason, bad omens. On visiting Chief O-lo-ho-wal-la's pretty cottage home near Hominy, the writer saw a babe tightly wrapped in a similar reclining cradle. "May I see the baby?" "Yes," the little nurse smilingly replied. Beads of perspiration stood on its tiny face almost pneumatically or hermetically sealed by a heavy woolen shawl. Caucasian babes how would you like to:
    Coo and crow,
    Live and grow,
in such cradles that rock only on mama's backs, coo-ou, coo-ou, coo-ou.

The Pretty Cottage Home of Will T. Leahy, Main Street, Pawhuska... (Photo by Hargis)

MR. WILL T. LEAHY.

Mr. Will T. Leahy, the only son of Thomas Leahy, whose beautiful cottage home appears herewith, is one of the most successful men of the Reservation. Besides a most excellent farm two miles north of Pawhuska he is owner of much valuable property in town. His home is a model one, elegantly furnished, and bearing an air of refinement that impresses even the casual observer. He has held positions of honor and trust in the Osage, being two years treasurer of the Nation, and six years Councilman, and three times a delegate to Washington on tribal business. He is vice-president of the First National Bank, and a large holder in the Pawhuska Oil and Gas Co., also extensively interested in the real estate, livery, and cattle business; and ever ready to advance the interests of his town, and the Osage people. He is a man of quick perception and sound judgment, and good material for the Osage county organization. He married Miss Martha L. Rogers, one of the refined and amiable daughters of Judge Rogers, a full sketch of whose life is given on another page. They have some fine children. No parents in the Osage can feel prouder of their children and their families than Judge Thomas L. and Mrs. Rogers, and several of them are grouped in the cut of their home. No one can appreciate the finer qualities of many of the Osage citizens till he meets and knows such families as these, and sees the elegance and culture of their homes. They combine many of the better qualities of three or four nationalities, Mr. Will Leahy himself having the better blood of Osage, Irish, French and German.

The Beautiful Town Home of Leonard Revard, Just Completed.

Mr. Leonard Revard, brother of Frank, and the son of "Uncle Joseph Revard is a descendant of one of the oldest families of the Osage citizens. He spent some years farming and has some of the finest farms in the Osage, some opposite Ponca City and others scattered over the country, which he leases, but he has retired in Pawhuska and bought one of the most beautiful cottage homes in the town. He married Miss Daisy May Morris, an Arkansas City girl. They haev four of the most beautiful children among the Osages, all girls. He is only small part Osage. His mother was (nee) Miss Leanor Lessart, also of Osage descent. Their home is as beautiful within as its exterior. Who could not be happy with such a family, home, and children, needing not to think from where tomorrow's meat may come. He expects to establish a business in Pawhuska. He is a man of quiet manner and love of home and family, showing strikingly the Osage descent.

THE LADIES OF THE OSAGE COUNTRY

Perhaps the best criterion by which we may judge a people is the standard of its womanhood.

Many who know little of the advanced order of the territory think that it has lawless and bloody people, but not so. One cannot help noting the quiet and orderly conduct of the people of the Osage country. The days of the Winchester and sixshooter and the desperado have passed, as much so as in most of the states. You will meet as refined and as cultured people here as elsewhere, and many as fine models of girlhood and womanhood as modern society produces in proportion to its population. And woman is the standard by which the world today estimates the moral and spiritual degress of the home and society, and perhaps justly so, for she has in her the power to fix the pace by which the home, church and state move forward. By her pressing the button the intellectual, moral and spiritual life of man, the home, church and state, is turned on, and by her magic touch again all may become twilight or darkness and hence the old proverb, "the hand that rocks the cradle, moves the world."

might possibly be changed a little: "The hands that might or should rock the cradle still move the world." The destiny of man and home, the social world, hangs upon the aesthetic powers and virtues of the "Twentieth Century Woman." With the development of these the world rises; in their loss the homes, churches and social order is incorporated chaos. Woman is the God ordained guardian of man, his home and happiness, modern conditions reversing the old order of influence, and she is fast becoming his co-partner in the commercial arena. If man should go on an exploring expedition to the moon, the modern business woman would not be far behind him when he might make a new discovery.

The Home of Mrs. Laura Soderstrom.

Mrs. Laura Soderstrom is the widow of the late John Soderstrom, owner during his life, of the first and only flour and grist mill ever built and run in the Osage nation, first built at Pawhuska about 30 years ago by the government and sold to Soderstrom in 1894. It was the first manufacturing plant in Pawhuska. Since the death of John Soderstrom the mill was sold to his son, Ebbie A. Soderstrom, and a partner, Charles Hays, who later sold to Mr. Scarborough, the new banker of Pawhuska. The father was accidentally drowned by breaking through the ice on his pond on Bird creek. Mrs. Soderstrom's father was Coy. J. A. Coffey, the founder of Coffeyville, Kansas He was the builder of the first dwelling, store and first mill there and was first postmaster of that town, named after him. He traded much with the five civilized tribes and Osages. His son-in-law, Mr. Soderstrom, continued his trading career till death, February, 1902. He left a wife and six children in good circumstances. She occupies the beautiful cottage home shown in this cut in West Pawhuska, near the 468 foot iron bridge over Bird Creek. She is a woman of many good qualities, both domestic and business.

HISTORY OF THE OSAGE NATION

So important a part does woman play in the world's progress on the frontier, as well as in the most domesticated centers, that we cannot overlook her part and importance in its history, any less than in religion, austhetics, arts, romance, poetry, music and love, for she has gracefully combined these faculties with her business qualities, till no profession or trade, however arduous, shakes her nervves, or daunts her courage, in making a home and independence for herself, in the dawning of the twentieth century. Beauty of dress and symetrical form charm the passing glance of the aesthetic natures of men, like the swiftly passing meteor in its flash of light, or the more sublime comets, with golden trails that soon pass through the twilighted temple of the skies, charming the star gazing astrologers or astronomers. They are bright rays of nature that may soon pass from sight, but true culture of head and heart in higher accomplishments, is like the sun, moon and stars, giving constant light and life to all who behold and admire. Woman of such cultured accomplishments convinces the world of the trueness of the tribute once paid to higher womanhood by Dr. Hargraves: "A true woman is the poetry of the earth in the same sense that the stars are the poetry of heaven—bright, light-giving, charming," guiding man in his darkest hours of business, political and social life. This can be true only of the girl or woman of mind and heart culture. The ideal, twentieth century woman will be one whose head and heart is more trained than heel, and whose dignity and strength of mind is co-equal with her grace of step and beautiful symetry of form. These four qualities alone make "lovely woman."

A Quintette of Osage Bells.

May the literary, musical, and higher domestic cultures hold sway among their higher aspirations! Some in buusiness have been quite disappointed in their anticipations of what grades of millinery and ladies furnishings would be most in demand. The lower grades often have but little sale, while the most costly hats and robes have been in demand. Should you observe only the beautiful and costly hats and robes of the "fair ones" you might imagine yourself on Broadway, New York City; or Chestnut street, Philadelphia, or Indiana Avenue, Washington, and Garfield Boulevards or on the "Lake Front" of Lincoln Park, District of Chicago, or some other elite prominade.

HISTORY OF THE OSAGE NATION

Many of the wives and daughters of the Osage citizens dress as beautifully, gaudily, and as costly, as the elite promonaders of the above named boulevards; as many beautifully plumed head dresses, the rattle of silks and satins, as tastily made tailored suits, as brilliant satines and footwear a could be heard and seen in the social circles of the states. It is said that the receptions formerly given at the Indian Agency here were attended in evening opera gowns, and full dress suits. But this formality no longer prevails since the population is rapidly inceasing from the states more interested in land lots and bank acounts than social forms.

The educational advantages of the citizens and full-bloods have been as good as the government schools afford for many years. All are required to attend some school each year. Most of them while under sixteen years attend the school at Pawhuska or the Sisters St. Louis school there, or the St. John's school conducted by the Sisters on Hominy Creek, near Gray Horse, both conducted under Uuncle Sam's contract for so much per capita for the Osage children, who are compelled to board in the schools. Most of the full bloods stop with the training given in these schools, but many of both sexes go to Haskel Institute, Lawrence, Kansas, and Carlisle College, (Pa.), and some to the best schools of other states. Most all the daughters and some of the sons of the intermarried citizens go up to the best schools far and near. The girls being mostly of Catholic families, generally go to convents or academies, of the Sisters to complete their literary and musical education. Some are excellent, many fair musicians, using various instruments. Most of them are finely fitted to assume the responsibilities of home life, being kept from the contaminations of the world while in school, and most of them marry early after, or during their school days, and generally while in their teens, and some times exercising but little discrimination, as to the highest virtues essential to make true men and devoted husbands. This misfortune, or lack of judgment is perhaps partly the fault of their exclusive education, partly from home training, and indiscreet associations. But taking the average of happy marriages among blue blooded Caucasians, the Osage citizens whose sons and daughters generally wed the former, make a better showing of domestic felicity than many so-called high-bred communities. The financial independence of the girl or woman of Osage descent may make her less likely than others, to tolerate a worthless man, or one uncongenial to her nature, and be an incentive to separation and feminine liberty, but no more divorces than in the most of present-day society; and from mere observation, these women conform more happily to the highest ideals of a nineteenth century family and home than many of the finely

An Octette Drill of Osage School Girls

HISTORY OF THE OSAGE NATION

well filled with sticky dough when her husband came in, and gave her a little riddle to solve. "My dear, why is the relation of man to woman like a woman mixing dough?" (thinking she would answer: "Because she needed him"). But she studied a long time. He asked: "Will you give it up?" He thought he had the best of the joke, till she finallly replied with an independent toss of her dainty, classical little head: "Yes, I can tell you." "Let her come, then," he cried. "Because when she once gets him on her hands its so difficult to get rid of him again." His spirits fell and quiet reigned.

Mrs. Geo H. Saxon.
Mrs. Saxon's First Millinery Parlor,

Mrs. Saxon who conducts the fine millinery store, the interior of which is shown in this cut, is one of the most artistic milliners to be found anywhere, the great cities not excepted. She studied the art in New York city, then established her millinery parlor in her own home town of Pawhuska, where now she conducts the leading millinery store in the entire Osage country, both in high-grade goods and reasonable prices. She even designs some very beautiful, costly hats to be shipped by express to her old customers and acquaintancs in distant states such a her art, taste and originality in designing. She is of Irish, French and Osage descent. Her father, Thomas Leahy, stockman and liveryman, of whom a sketch is given elsewhere in this work is of Irish nationality. Her mother was Miss Mary Champagne, who was only one-eighth Osage and seven-eighth French, which fact gives the main source of her daughter's artistic taste in her millinery art, the French being world-renowned as fashion designers. Mrs. Saxon is one of the most characteristic ladies among the Osage, possessing the strongest features and complexion of the Emerald Isle lady, a fair, waxey-toned hue, light blue eyes, crispy auburn hair, all features blending to make a harmony of complexion not often seen among the fairest Americans. Among her attractive features, her unassuming, prepossessing, business-like personality are not the least. Her energy in business is not a very common trait among her sisters of Osage descent as most of them are happy only in the arena of their homes and most devoted loved of their children. But this lady is no less an ideal mother, than a lady in her business, combining all the qualifications of the love of success, progress, business frugality, social life and home. It is said of her that the cupid of wealth worshipped at the shrine of her girlhood and young womanhood, but she from all suitors selected a man of energy and good business qualities as his inheritance and store of wealth, who is now in the mercantile business at Osage Junction, but cannot prevail on his young wife to give up her millinery business that she is so excellently fitted for by natural ability and schooling under the best designers of New York City. All have the best of words for her and you only have to meet her to admire her womanly amiability and qualities. And this is said only in honor to the highest womanhood of the Osage Nation, as Mrs. Saxon is happily married, and the writer has never been able to acquire the art of flattery nor does he desire to if he could. Mrs. Saxon has contantly in her employ the most artistic help. The lady standing to the left in the cut, Mrs. Mamie Rambo, is the daughter of Rev. E. F. Hill, pastor of the M. E. church a most skillful milliner and a most amiable lady, who has been with her over a year.

HISTORY OF THE OSAGE NATION

The Elite Millinery Store of Mrs. G. H. Saxon.

Pawhuska has many cultured girls and ladies who at times entertain the public by literary and musical talent. Many are accomplished in instrumental and vocal music. Miss Gale, who has studied in the best schools under the training of the best vocal instructors, has made many successes in her musical culture entertainments.

The **"Pawhuska Dramatic Club"** was recently organized to cultivate and use home talent on the newly decorated opera house stage of Mr. Woodring. The club, under the direction of Mr. and Mrs. Ed. F. Kreyer, theatrical professionals some years, has already showed that there is comedy and dramatic ability here.

Miss May Revard.

This young lady is an amiable daughter of Mrs. Will Bradshaw, and granddaughter of "Uncle" Joe Revard. She is now taking a musical and business course in St. Joseph's Academy at Guthrie, O. T., one of the best convent schools in the territories. She comes of one of the oldest and most prominent families, and one of the fairest descendants of the Osages. Her maternal grandfather was a Papin of history.

HISTORY OF THE OSAGE NATION

This group is the bridal party of Mr. Andrew Trumbly and his new bride, Miss May Alexander, daughter of James A. Alexander, of the Osage Nation, who lives about three miles from Kaw City, O. T. They were married July 30, 1902, at Ponca City, where this group was taken on the same day. They make their new home in Ponca City but have two finely improved farms in the Osage, about 12 and 40 miles from Ponca City. Mr. Trumbly is the only son of Francis and Augustine Trumbly, both of Osage ancestry, but of French lineage on his father's side, who was only a quarter blood Osage, and his mother one-half. His father was prominent among the

AN OSAGE WEDDING PARTY

Osage people holding the place of Councilman, and was the prosecuting attornew for the Nation when he died, leaving a widow, and one son. Andrew, eight years of age, and two daughters, Rose and Ida, who married Chas. Moncravie and Martin Bowhan. Andrew was educated at Pawhuska and Fort Scott. His wife's father was of Scotch nationality, but her mother was one-quarter Osage, (nee) Miss Martha Smith. The bride in this party was educated at Pawhuska and Wichita, at Mt. Marmel Academy. Andrew is a nephew of Julian and John B. Trumbly. Julian is one of the Osage Townsite Commissioners, also a member of the council for several terms, and a representative to Washington, and John, a clerk of the Osage Supreme court. Mr. and Mrs. Trumbly are excellent types of Osage descendants, both in physique and intelligence, and highly esteemed among their many friends.

HISTORY OF THE OSAGE NATION

JUDGE J. W. PETTIT.

Judge J. W. Pettit and family are among the most prominent Osage citizen. He is descendant of the Osages and Cherokees, and his wife a descendant of the Cherokees. Miss Lorinda Hampton, whose father was from Tennessee. They were mraried in 1870, near Talequah, I. T., but she was born near old Ft. Smith. They had eight children born to them, and six still living, four sons, two at Hominy, and two at Pawhuska; and two single daughters. Judge Pettit has lived in his prsent home, three miles northeast of Pawhuska, as shown in the cut, fourteen years, but 21 years, on the same farm, being seven years in a house, first built by the government, a log house just in the rear of his present beautiful home. He held the office of Chief Justice of the Osage Nation for eleven years, and went twice to Washington, D. C., as a representative of his people. He served in the confederate army as a brave soldier in the border warfare and can relate many exciting experiences durig those years. He

Miss Nettie Pettit, the youngest and Accomplished daughter of Judge J. W. Pettit.

Miss Bell De Noya, a Daughter of Mr. Frank De Noya, Sr.

won his title of "Judge" as chief of the Oscage Supreme Court, and has rendered other services of honor and trust. He in one of the most successful farmers of the Nation, having an excellent improved farm and cultured musical family, with true Southern

HISTORY OF THE OSAGE NATION

Hospitality. He is a man of great sociability and bright intelligence and high aspirations for his family and children. Once having enjoyed the welcome of their home you could quickly realise that it is a higher type of an Osage citizen, home of unassuming but refined atmosphere. Mrs. Pettit is a fine type of the 19th century elderly, southern lady, and her children show the impression of her influence. They own some of the finest farms of the Osage country. That of Frank near Hominy, is especially beautiful, and fertile. And unlike many others of Osage descent, these young people are ambitious to excell.

THE UNITED STATES OSAGE AGENCY

Should space permit we would gladly give a sketch of the agents that have served at the post at Pawhuska, also an outline of the various reports of said agents, showing their ideas, progress and recommendations concerning the Osage nation, country and people. But so varied have these been that it would only show as many personal opinions, and very diverse figures on their terms of service. In the study of such figures the writer has never found two that gave just the same acreage and estimates of the condition of the country. For instance, one says the "Osages own 1,600,195 acres of land which they purchased at 70 cents per acre." Another gives the reservation area as 1,470,055 acres, another report has it 1,500,000 acres, still another at 1,400,000 acres, and 32,000 square miles, etc. There is as much variance as to what these people have to their credit in the national treasury, ranging from $8,584,498 down to $8,000,000 and all sums for the annual incomes from all leases not including interests, from $579,866 down, etc. Of course the population and annuities vary but not their trust fund, while the interest is paid quarterly; but there has evidently been some guessing. The most of the agency buildings are shown in the cuts. The first council house was built in the '70's, was burned down during Harrison's administration, and immediately rebuilt in its present form, where the Osage council, mostly fullbloods, nmeet every three months, or oftener if need be, in Council hall. The rest of the rooms are rented for offices. Judge Yates holds his courts here, where he offices. The agents' building is shown with the First National Bank building in cut on another page. The agents who have served are in order: Isaac T. Gibson, Syrus Beede, Labon J. Miles, (twice appointed), and furing the democratic administration Mr. Hoover, Captain Potter (U. S. A. officer), and P. Smith. Then Capt. Demsey (a U. S. A. officer), Col. H. B. Freeman, O. A. Mitscher (of the Mitscher delegation to Washington), and the present agent, Capt. Frank Frantz. During the enforcement of the Osage constitution and laws under their own officers the agent's duties were mainly to look after their financial interests, payments, education, schools etc., but since the assuming by the government of these functions, the agent has absolute authority in all matters pertaining to their control, except in cases of felonous crime, etc. To him they come with all their business and domestic troubles, like children to a father. He is looked upon as a foster father by all the Reservation Indians. To him they come with every sickness, pain or accident, every little difficulty or encroachment of the advancing "pale faces," with every broken plow, wagon, harness and tender-footed pony, like a petted child comes to a compassionate father for sympahty and succor. Nor are the disappointed, for he watches over them with all the solicitude of such a father. He is fostering their rights and protecting their lands with a plausible dignity and pride. He has not been in the Agency long, but every Osage

HISTORY OF THE OSAGE NATION

(Photo by Hargis)

Mr. and Mrs. John W. Julien's Beautiful Cottage Home.

Mr. Julien was born and reared in Ohio till 18. He lived some years in Indiana, in Kansas City about 15 years, then came to Pawhuska, Oklahoma in '95 and has resided here since, where he has clerked for the Gibson Mercantile Company. He was a miller by trade but has railroaded and been an express agent for some years. His father was of French descent as the name indicates. Julien, an ancestor escaped to America, after seeing his brother burned at the stake during the French inquisition.

Mr. Julien married Miss Maria S. Seward of Indiana, in 1889. They have no children. Mrs. Julien was also a clerk for seven years in the millinery department in the same store. They have retired to spend the rest of life in their happy Pawhuska home, in a beautiful grove of fruit and ornamental trees. They are among the first and most honored residents of the town.

---

from Arkansas River to the Kansas line knows him well. The writer had the privilege of meeting him many times. He seems to be the right man to protect his Indian wards.

The Osage Agency because of the vast sums of money disbursed here and the vast resources of the country and the advanced order of many citizen families, is the most important post in America. From $75,000 to $100,000 are spent here annually for educational purposes, and nearly a million paid through the agency in annuities to the Osage, and for the expense of the agency. It is a great responsibility on the shoulders of any man and his clerks and deputies. But the president and interior department knew a young but strong man, well fitted for the post. Capt. Frantz, who has filled the place most successfully and satisfactorily for two years, and is now advanced to the governor's chair of the greatest of all territories, Oklahoma. The people of Pawhuska endorsed his appointment by many cheers of "Hurrah for Frantz,"

HISTORY OF THE OSAGE NATION

and many demonstrations of enthusiasm, because they feel he will make as good governor as he has made an Indian Agent. Though regretting to lose his presenece in the Osage, they believe his power will still be wielded for the Osage allotment and good. It is said that he is of distant Swiss ancestry, that his father was a native of

(Photo by Hargis)

The Residence of Dr. Geo. L. Dunn, M. D., Main St.

Dr. Geo. Dunn is a graduate of the College of Physicians and Surgeous, St. Joe, Mo. He came from Nodaway county, Mo., in 1880, when a boy of 16. His father was a physician. also his other five brothers. He comes of a family of natural physicians for three generations or more. His father, Dr. Thomas J. Dunn, and uncle, Dr. Joseph B. Dunn, who is the oldest practicing physician among the Osage, came to this country in 1880, and practiced together till Dr. T. J. Dunn's death in 1900. Dr. J. B. is still in the atcive practice, though advanced in years, and very successful in his profession. Dr. Geo. Dunn has practiced medicine for 20 years in Kansas. old Oklahoma and the Osage, but mostly on the Osage reservation, where he has the marked distinction of being the most skilled in his profession. but through the unforseen forces if physically deteriorating effects that come to all at times, he has been confined to his room for 18 months, but is now growing stronger. Being constantly among the Osage citizens he naturally selected one of the fairest daughters of their descent, Miss Dora Del Orier, daughter of Antoine and Julia Del Orier. They have three fine children, two girls and a boy, Ida May, Marie Agnes, and John Timothy Dunn. Their pretty cottage home is on east Main Street. Their many friends wish him a speedy recovery.

HISTORY OF THE OSAGE NATION

Virginia and a democrat, that he ws born in Woolford county, Illinois, May 7, 1872, was educated at Eureka Christian College, (Ill.), where his brother-in-law, R. E. Hieronymus was then and is now, president. His family coming to Wellington, Kansas, Frank left college in his junior year, at 18, and came west. He made the run into the Cherokee Shrip in 1893, but later went to California, Arizona and New Mexico mining for four years. When the Spanish-American war began he left the Gold Note mine of Senator Hearst of California, joined the Rough Riders, Troop A, at Prescott, Arizona, was commissioned first lieutenant by Governor McCord, went to Cuba, under Capt. O'Neil and Col. Roosevelt. On Mr. O'Neil's death he was appointed captain of his company. All the world knows the rest. Roosevelt became president and Capt. Frantz has taken the gubernatorial reins of Oklahoma. It was said he was a democrat before the war, but never a partisan politician in any sense, and so much the better for that reason, and one in whom the people can have confidence. He is a most congenial, but frank officer and gentleman that anyone could enjoy meeting. He is as congenial, approachable and democratic in manner as he is conscious, frank and firm in the performance of official duty. And the writer, voicing the feeling of the Osage, wished him success as governor. It is said of Mr. Frantz that, while the Rough Rider Regiment, of which President Roosevelt was Colonel, was charging up San Juan Hill with a bullet torn flag in one hand a sword in the other, he, as lieutenant, was leading his company, whose captain had fallen, to "the top of the hill." His colonel, Roosevelt, riding up, asked "Where is your captain." Amid the roar of cannon and flash of musketry and glimmer of sword, the answer echoed: "Dead." "Where are you going?" "To the top of the hill!" the lieutenant replied. Heroism and patriotic courage in such men surmounted the hill, and Roosevelt and Frantz are still pushing "to the top of the hill" in their service to the nation, both unassuming and altruistically modest. But the hills of highest honor in the American nation, are now scaled by the one who beckons the other still to come, and Frantz is coming, Mr. Roosevelt, coming "to the top of the hill," of true statesmanship. He was too modest to furnish the writer his cut for this book, but can not stop a pen sketch which he deserves, and you approve. Young men of the Osage! set you goal high! Stop not short of the top of the hill. Shoot at the sun, moon and stars, and you will never hit the lower regions of the earth, though you may not be able to count all bull's eyes in your long range marksmanship. There are higher hills for every aspiring hero of industry, economy, temperance, honesty and righteous ambition. Stand by your guns, draw your swords, fixing your eyes on the topmost rampart of the highest hills, push on up its side, saying with Miller, "I'll try Sir;" with Lawrence, "Don't give up the ship," and answer Dewey, who said: "You may fire when you are ready!" We are ready to fire, ready to march and keep marching.

There are two stimuli to set before every man one, the hope of a home, wealth and independence through industry, temperance and economy, the other a physical stimulus by intemperance and prodigality in pleasure-reaping penury and commercial and social slavery as the reward. Young men, which will you choose?

Captain Frantz had an efficient corps of assistants in the following officers: A. W. Hurley, chief clerk; Ret Millard, leasing clerk; H. M. Loomer, W. M. Blake, Geo. Beauleau, Geo. LaMotte and Chas. Michelle, whose cut appears herein, assistant clerks. Harry Kohpay, interpreter, H. C. Ripley, of Maine, trade supervisor; Chas. F. Leech, engineer; Wiley G. Haines, chief of police, and J. M. Way, M. D. government physician.

HISTORY OF THE OSAGE NATION

Mr. Ret Milliard has been appointed agent to succeed Frantz. He is well acquainted with the Osage people and well fittd to direct their interests.

Incorporated—THE FIRST BANK OF SKIATOOK.—Capital $15,000.

T. E. Smiley, President; Beeks Erick, Vice-President;
Chas. H. Nash, Cashier; Gray Erick, Ass't. Cashier.

This bank was the first bank chartered for Skiatook. The president, T. E. Smiley is president of the Bank of Commerce at Tulsa, I. T. The vice-president, together with J. W. McLoud, are interested in building the Midland Valley railroad. The cashier has been in the banking business for the past six years in Oklahoma and is thoroughly conversant with the business. All the men connected with this bank are men of banking experience and their aggregate wealth if near the $100,000 mark. Mr. Nash is both a commercial club and town officer, and a man of power and push for the progress of the city. They do an extensive banking and notary, and some real estate business, and will give all homeseekers a warm welcome to Skiatook, and some man among them is a commercial must as we find the following verse quite appropriate to this fertile section on the back of their envelopes:

"Corn, cattle, hogs and hay
   Will simply take your breath away;
While plenty of gas, coal and oil
   Lies beneath our fertile soil."

Mrs. W. R. Beydler's Millinery Parlor, and the Office and Large Lumber Sheds of Dickason-Goodman Lumber Co., Skiatook, Mr. W. T. Beydler, Mgr.

Mrs. Beydler is a native of the state of Iowa, but has lived in Nebraska where she studied and followed the art of millinery for several years. She now conducts a millinery business here and draws a patronage from a long distance in the Cherokee and Osage country. She has a beautiful display of hats in her parlor, and is one of the most pleasant ladies in her home and artistic profession. Her husband conducts the **Dickason-Goodman Lumber Co. office** just next door, as shown in the cut. They lived for some time in Pawhuska where he managed the lumber lard of Dickason-Goodman Lumber Co., there before becoming their manager here. Mr. Beydler was born in Cedar county, Mo., February 18, 1872, moved to Boone county, Nebraska, in 1891; was engaged in the lumber business with the Edward and Bradford Lumber Co., in Albion, same state in 1899, since which time for the **Dickason-Goodman Lumber Co.,** who have a number of yards in the territory, with main offices at Tulsa, I. T. Mr. Beydler is an excellent young man, of good business ability and successful as a manager, a good citizen, and a happy husband of a most amiable, artistic wife. They evidently combine business with love.

SKIATOOK, I. T.
(Named from a full-blood Cherokee Chief.)

This beautiful town has lately passed her first birthday, the lots being sold on December 19th, 1904, in which the highest price paid for one lot was $300, and now worth several times that amount, for the town is fast becoming a fine trading point, for not only the rich valley or prairie surrounded it, but for a large extent of the eastern Osage. A late census showed a population of 400. It has a publc school under the efficent teaching of Mr. D. C. Quay, and C. H. Mehlhorn, with about 80 pupils. While no church house has been build, two or three denominations have held services here, and a house will soon be built. An intelligent and excellent class of people have established this town.

You can find all classes of business represented here, without going elsewhere when in need of anything. Skiatook has four general merchandise stores that would be a credit to a much larger town, besides three lumber yards, two banks, a racket store, two hardware and furniture stores, two drug stores, a meat market, livery barn, harness shop, three hotels, a bakery, two barber shops, confectionaries, blacksmith shops, feed mill, mill and elevator, two millinery stores and all other lines of business.

The town was incorporated at a cost of $100, defrayed by the Commercial Club of 50 active members, organized March 3, 1905, only three months after lot sale, with an excellent set of officers: A. E. Townsend, mayor and ex-officio Justice of the Peace; F. C. Bell, recorder; C. H. Nash treasurer; Joseph Mercer, marshal; and C. H. Cleveland, A. K. Feigley, F. Lynde, J. W. Thompson, and L. A. Tyler, aldermen. The club with Mr. Cleveland, vice president; G. M. Janeway, secretary, and A. K. Feigley, treasurer, is doing much for the trade of the town by improving the road into town, and done much for their town in various lines of inducing immigration to this point.

Main Street, Skiatook, I. T., Looking East From Midland Valley Depot.

HISTORY OF THE OSAGE NATION

They know what the best advertising ca do for a town that has her resources to place before home seekers. The writer sincerely thanks the energetic people who readily expressed their interest in this book, and regrets that owing to the need of a photographer to take the views, he cannot show many of the better buildings and surrounding rich farms, orchards, alfalfa fields, beautiful native hay meadows for which this section is noted. The fine stone farm houses and farms of Mrs. Jane Appleby, and daughter Mrs. Alph Hoots, of Tulsa, are near Skiatook. She is said to be a most intelligent and interesting old lady of Osage citizenship and the most wealthy. Along the valley of Bird Creek in the Osage nation, Mr. Jno. Lundy, Jim Perrier, Ed. Fox, Geo. Bradshaw, and Mrs. Elic Davis, and Richard Tinker, have rich farms. W. C. Rogers, chief of the Cherokees, has a most fertile and beautiful farm joining the Osage, where old Skiatook P. O., and his store was located. Mrs. Sophia Davis who lives two and one-half miles from town is the daughter of Augustus Chouteau, (French) and Roselle Lombard, who was half Osage. She married Mr. Davis of Illinois, eighteen years ago, who was for 20 years a successful farmer and stockman. She has a fine farm and orchard, but no children except an adopted daughter, Mary, bright, blond girl, who lately married Mr. Ed. Bruner. Mr and Mrs. Ed. Fox are also improving a fertile farm two miles from Skiatook. She is the daughter of Grandmother Mosier, and most hospitable people. Mr. H. C. Gilmore, of Pawhuska, owns the land surrounding the Midland Valley depot, nerly a quarter from the center of Skiatook. He has a most choice location. The Midland Valley Co. has leased considerable land for 99 years and established their material yards, and built offices, and will make a division here or at Pawhuska, which would be a boon to either place as the road has experienced progressive men to run it.

A LAND ESPECIALLY INVITING TO HIGH CLASS YOUNG PEOPLE

This section of the territories is the "Primised Land" for young people of ability, industrious, energetic habits, temperate, economical and aspiring to do and be above the ordinary. They have been settled largely by younger men and their chosen brides, who have come and are now coming to enter upon their business and professional careers, to make a mark in life, and lay the foundations of future fortunes.

The writer can fully endorse the words read from the St. Louis Mirror: "The Territory is a land which invites young men who are wide awake and ambitious; that are not afraid to work, and have a well balanced mind and heart. It is a decidedly more promising country to grow up with than far-off Manitoba or British Columbia, where winters are long and days of sunshine few in numbers." We certainly have the natural advantages of a salubrious climate combines with all the resources of soil, minerals and commercial development.

Most of the men of large business interests have come with empty hands but ready to grasp every opportunity for progress and their rapid rise to their present business standing fully coroborates the often demonstrated fact that a young man's most secure capital in beginning life's career is industry, economy, temperance and honesty; virtues, which if brought to the territory, are the only essential capital stock needed for beginning a prosperous life and beautiful homes.

THE ALLIED RACES OR INTERMARRIED FAMILIES

Many have become allied, through marriage, with the more educated, refined and thrifty sons and daughters of the natives and thus combined love with business have

HISTORY OF THE OSAGE NATION

become heirs to broad and fertile farms and herds of fat cattle. And perhaps the time will come, if not now at hand, when the Caucasian lad or lassie may be envied because they have won the hearts and full hands of the more dusky children of this lovely, fertile and sunny land. Many of the finest types of manhood and womanhood are found among the posterity of the allied pale and tinted races. The primitive families of the forests and plains have all the resources of wealth, and these, combined with the science and push of a Christian civilization, will make the Osage as a blooming garden of beautiful children, flowers and fruits.

Many of the natives have risen to political and social influence and wealth. Many of the leading families of the Osages live in Pawhuska and the other towns of the Reservation where they have beautiful, costly homes, as shown in the cuts of this book. These dwellings are often furnished elegantly, with costly pianos, fine rugs, tapestries, Axministers and best quality of ingrains and Brussels carpet, etc.

Many of them have their servants, working girls in the homes and hired men upon their farms. Many have commodious barns with fine "turnouts," costly carriages and high-bred horses. In short they are a people of wealth and many luxuries, having much money but spending it freely for whatever is desired and enjoyed, with few exceptions among the more economical classes. Some of the citizen (intermarried) people and most of the full-bloods keep but little or no money ahead, often spending it in credit before the quarterly payments, by a credit-card system, issuel them by the agent, which limits the credit, that business men of merchants may give to only 60 per cent of the next quarterly payment, about $25 to $30 credit for every man, woman and child, every ninety days, unless the merchant, as is often done credits more at his own risk. And the degree of honesty varies no more with these people, from the writer's estimate than among the most highly cultured commercial communities. Many of the full bloods are exceptionally honest, and proud of it.

It may be of interest to the reader to give here a sketch of the most peculiar, eccentric character among the full-blood Indians. John Stink, who is said to have been once, the richest Osage in ponies, formerly Indian wealth, and was looked upon with special honor because of his many ponies. The story goes that one time he died, as his friends supposed, and was buried according to Osage custom, half reclining, as if sitting back in a rocking chair, and covered with a monument of stones, around and above him, on top of the ground. But John was not dead, but in a dormant condition, a breathless trance. He soon revived and threw off his stone tomb and came back to camp; but the rest thought he had returned from the other world and would have nothing to do with him thereafter. Because of his queer actions they considered him crazy, possessed of an evil spirit, ran him off and took his ponies and all he had from him. John has never owned a pony since, nor anything else except a big knife, frying pan, tin plate, etc., for camping in the woods without tent or shelter, when not in town. He has become a swift walker quite equal to the ordinary horse, his only exercise; sometimes walking as far as Gray Horse and back to Pawhuska in a short time. McLaughlin and Farrar, old merchants here, made an greement to keep John in food, clothing (blnkets mostly), for his payments. In front of their store he sits or lies much of his time both day and night, and to all salutations simply replies in a good natured way: "Ugh!" Many times late at night the writer has found him asleep in the recess of the store room door or during warmer nights, on the sidewalk, scorning all invitations to inside lodging. Here he eats and sleeps, as happy as a fat pig; and just as contented, seemingly taking for his motto: "If ignorance and dirt is bliss, 'tis folly to be wise,"

HISTORY OF THE OSAGE NATION

Dr. Sheafe was born in Ottumwa, Iowa, December 15, 1866, and educated at the Southern Iowa Normal Bloomfield, took a medical course at the State University of Iowa, from which he graduated in 1892, then practiced medicine at Riverside, Iowa, till 1902. From there he moved to Oklahoma, then to Skiatook, March 1st, 1905. In 1905 he joined the International Medical Congress at Paris and during the same year traveled over Europe, visited Turkey, Greece Palestine and Egypt, thus adding to his broad professional culture and schooling, and all-round man, a K. P. and good physician with a growing practice.

Dr. Jos. Sheafe.

Interior View of Feigley's Department Store, A.K. Feigley and Son, (H.L.)
Mr. Feigley and son came to Skiatook from Elkhart, Ind., where they ran the Elkhart Department Store, but were formerly of Bloominngton, Nebraska, where they conducted a department store for twenty-five years. They started in business in Skiatook, February 1st, 1905, own their building of two stories and 184 fet deep. They carry a complete line of up-to-date line of merchandise to supply the

railroad, oil and farmers' trade; but carry an exceptionally fine line of shoes and gents' furnishing goods. They are excellent men to help make an ever-growing, prosperous town, broadly experienced in selling goods since 1882, and most pleasant gentlemen

HISTORY OF THE OSAGE NATION

to meet. Mr. Al Feigley is prominently connected with the town and commercial club. Meet them at the corner of Main and Broadway.

---

and clean. He is said to be so honest that these merchants often invite him in winter to sleep in their store, but –John prefers the sidewalk and natural elements. On receiving part of his payments he carries it wrapped in a bandana handkerchief. When he buys a meal or lunch to eat, he unfolds his bandana money bag and makes signs or says in Osage, as he never speaks English: "How much (cost?) Take!" He is perfectly peaceful and molests neither persons nor anything, but carries a big knife which he brings into service when harassed by another. When missed from town he is perhaps off at his forest camp-fire, eating, and after hiding or hanging up his scant outfit, returns to town, where he sits, lies or moves about in silence, having nothing to say to whites nor full-bloods, but seldom fails to recognize a greeting in his indifferent mood. By all these peculiarities he doubtless incited the epithet John Stink, but when it was first bestowed or what his name in native dialect we are unable to state. He will not allow the camera or Kodak to invade his physiogonomy, quickly snatching his blanket over his face or turning away. But by chance Mr. W. G. Hargis, having his camera ready caught him unawares, as he was exhorted to look around from the steps of Mr. Monk's drug store, where you see hin standing. His own people think him as much a freak of nature as do strangers.

But with all the peculiarities of these people they are in general a noble type of full-blood, and when allied by marriage with the better class of other races make as fine a type physically and mentally, under right education and training as you could find anywhere. In fact some of the last century claim that the highest development of the human race can only be attained by the intermarriage of the best types of all races, according to the laws of natural affinity and high intelligence. And the posterity of least diverging, allied races, seem to sustain the theory. Many of the greatest men and women of every age have been the off-spring of intermarried nationalities. It is claimed that the great Japanese generals, Oyama and Oku, eliminated, are in fact of Irish and Japanese descent; that O'Yama and O'Keough, were the first spelling of these names. Irishmen in the Elizabeth period having been shipwrecked and cast adrift in the Philippines, found their way to Japan, became military men, intermarried with natives, Patrick O'Yama handing down the lineage of Field Marshal Oyama, the Napoleon of the Japs, and the name O'Keough, being of difficult spelling was eliminated to Oku. (Note—This is given as a newspaper report). There are some fine people of Irish descent among the Osage citizens, also English, some German and other nationalities. But those of French ancestry, as the biographical sketches show, are largely in the majority.

The writer would have no one think that he is an advocate of social equality of the races under all circumstances, far from it except upon a basis of individual fitness and merit, and not extremes in color. The broadest social equality between races and families widely different in habits and life, can only be an individual matter at best. But it is not alone a question of color. The natural laws of God among a million species and retro-volution and evolution of unrecorded ages and above all, **the law of the survival and improvement of the fittest deems it so.**

Mr. James Bigheart, a former chief, while before the allotment committee in Washington, paid a high tribute to the better classes of Osage citizens when he said:

"Well, as it stands, and fro what I have observed, (etc., etc.) the most intelligent persons have the best land and most of it, wither in farming lands or pasture, and it seems to me in the case of minerals, too," etc: Of course I do not know absolutely, but I am convinced from my knowledge of the situation that these intelligent ones are

WHITNEY HOTEL, MAIN ST. AND LELAND.
Mr. G. A. Whitney, Proprietor.

There are three hotels in Skiatook, two of which are conducted by Mr. Whitney. He is an old hoted man of ten years experience. He is a native of New York state. He is well adapted to the hotel business by nature and experience. Nature does a great deal for a man when they select what they are most naturally fitted for, and here lies much of the secret of success in all professions and business. Mr. and Mrs. Whitney conduct a good **restaurant and café with the hotel, so it is both European and American plan..** They are opening another **FIRST CLASS HOTEL, THE LELAND,** just a little northeast of the depot, where they will make a specialty of the commercial trade, but will continue their $1.25 per day house and restaurant and café at the old stand on Main Street, where they now keep one of the best houses for the rate in the territory. He meets all trains and shows the traveler every necessity and congenial courtesy. **The central long distance phone is located in his office..** He formerly refited the New State Hotel in Tulsa, I. T., but came to the rapidly growing town of Skiatook, to which he adds much interest.

(Photo by Hargis)

TOWNSEND, SULLIVAN & CO., GENERAL MERCHANTS,
17 North Broadway, Skiatook.

Townsend, Sullivan & Co., a cut of whose business house appears herewith is one of the leading firms of Skiatook, doing a general mercantile business. Mr. A. E. Townsend, the senior member of the firm, is mayor of the town and one of the most public spirited men in the territory, and enthusiastic in the growth of his town. He is from Massachuusetts, and a typical New England gentleman; and has a cottage home, (see cut), and a family. His partner, Mr. H. C. Sullivan, is a native of Pennsylvania, and a young man of excellent business ability. They have done business in Ohio and Tennessee, contracting on government locks on the Cumberland river. They have been established in business here since the early part of 1905, soon after the town was built. **They deal in all kinds of produce and farm machinery, coal, etc.** They are both members of the commercial club and have an increasing trade from far into the Osage. A few such citizens can make any town prosperous and elevate its social, commercial and civil life. Mr. Townsend, by virtue of his office as mayor, holds the only court in this section at present.

THE CITY BARBER SHOP.
B. M. Daniel of N. Y., and E. H. Haddock, of the Cherokee Nation.
established a nicely-equipped, up-to-date shop in Skiatook during the summer of this year, 1905, and are doing a good business. Both are young men and will add energy to the commercial interests of the town. As in many other towns of the territory. Skiatook business is conducted largely by young men, just establishing themselves in all the trades, and professions. These young meme are highly deserving of all patronage. As the country develops they will become the leading tradesmen and professional men of the new state. Every young man should be encouraged to start in business for himself as early in life as consistent with his judgment, and such are especially deserving of our constant patronage and encouragement.

---

getting the best entries in our country, both as to farming lands and minerals. * * * The intelligent ones—I mean of course, the half-breeds—would get the best lands."

In this he expressed, perhaps unawares, the supremest law of nature, and nature's God, the Great Spirit.

"The survival of the fittest." Christ passed judgment under the same law, in solemn accents: "He that hath, to him shall be given, and he that hath not, even that which he hath shall be taken form him and given to him that hath and he shall have more abundant." And this was not spoken concerning intellectual and spiritual self-assertion and reward; but equally true of economics, temperance, and industrial development, and honest increase. In the alliance of the races lies much of the secret of the intelligence and thrift referred to by Bigheart. This law and fact will in future years raise most of the primitive American race to the class of the intelligent ones of industry, economy and progress. In being chief of the Osages he acquired much knowledge and experience by years of contact with the indomitable energy of business men and intermarried citizens. The taxable property of these men in the Osage, as assessed by Pawnee county, not including Indian property has run up to three and nearly a quarter million dollars. This law of commercial conquest is bringing the Osage millions of dollars in annuities that would never come otherwise. From a quarter to a half million dollars per year for mineral, pasture and other leases, is no mean sum for 1,900 people who have not to turn their hands, but only hold them for the golden fruits of their fields and groves to fill them full, as industrial development shakes the trees. The more broken, rocky hills may appear to the home-seeker valuable only for grazing. But the oil lessees' drill has already placed some of these next in value to those of "Spinie Top" in a stretch of Texas swamps, or Sour Lake, fed by mineral springs, in the edge of a poorly timbered forest bordering a broad expanse of desolate prairie, where land before went begging for $5 or $10 per acre, soon sold for as many thousands. The "Shoestring" district of 17 acres were drained of $75,000; another tract of 850 acres sold for $900,000 before a single hole was drilled. Cities grew to 10,000 in a short time where naught but pine or scrub oaks stood before. Of the 120,000,000 barrels of oil produced in 1904, the southwest fields supplied over half. Oil derricks mark the belt from the Mississippi clear into the foaming waters of the Pacific in Southern California. The Osage is in this belt and there are fine prospects that her stores of mineral beneath. The creative hand strikes an equilibrium of benefits, blessings and wealth everywhere.

Many of the allied families have become wealthy by farming and stock raising, making thousands of dollars from these sources besides the quarterly payments and annuities. Even the full-bloods of the most thrifty class, have good incomes from their improved or cultivated farms. It is said that one of them received $800 from the sale of one-third of the crop grown on his farm, and there are many such instances among the mixed bloods and intermarried citizens. Many of the finer farms lie along the Arkansas Valley and the streams leading into it. But all over the Reservation are many fertile and improved farms. There will be near 200 acres of excellent land for every one of those having a right, numbering about 1,900, besides 600 to 700 acres each of poorer lands, much of it being hilly and rocky. Not more so however, than many states that are considered fine agricultural states, such as Pennsylvania, West Virginia, Tennessee, Arkansas, Southern Missouri, North Carolina and others.

Wm. E. Curtis, writing of the Curtis bill, says: "Storng pressure will be brought upon congress during this session to enact a law for the allotment in severalty of the lands belonging to the Osages. Of the 1,470,055 acres in their reservation, he says, 40 per cent is timber (on bottom and hill lands) and 60 per cent prairie; and only 100,600 acres are now under cultivation or pasturage by the Osages themselves, leaving 1,370,055 leased to white ranchmen for grazing purposes." The acreage in these statements is only approximate, but near enough for practical purposes.

This country has been the cattleman's pardise and many have made small fortunes on lands leased for grazing. The winters are mostly mild and short, enabling stock to live on native grasses, bluestem and other varieties, which mostly grow in abundance in ordinary seasons. The farmers can cut plenty of hay by only leaving part of the land unplowed.

THE HARLOW LIVERY AND BOARDING BARN—SKIATOOK
John Harlow, Proprietor.

Mr. Harlow was formerly in Texas bbut has been in the Osage about 17 years, as a successful farmer and stockman, till he went into business in Skiatook, conduucting the only livery in town, where he has built a beautiful cottage home. He married Miss Fine Jim, one of the best types of part Osage lady, a half sister of Mrs. John Daniel, who is equally as comely, and lives next door in a like model of a cottage home. Mr. and Mrs. Harlow have one bright child, the pride of both. Their fine farm is located on Bull Creek, about 16 miles from town. He is a congenial, accommodating, energetic business young man, and good citizen. Mr. John Daniel, a brother-in-law, and also a leading citizen farmer and stockman, is a native of the Sunflower state but has been in the Osage about the same time as Mr. Harlow. He married in 1892 Miss Sophia Perrier, of a prominent French-citizen family, mentioned in treaties. They have four fine specimens of children and some excellent farm lands on Delaware cheek. The failure of artist to send views prevents cuts of these homes appearing herein. These men will add much to the prosperity of Skiatook, which they have chosen their home.

HISTORY OF THE OSAGE NATION

"Home, Sweet Home" of Richard Tinker and His Wife.

Richard Tinker, whose first home after his marriage is shown in this unique picture is a son of Frank Tinker, of Pawhuska. He is a young man of more than ordinary native ability. He married Miss Minnie Voila Spybuck, a young lady of the Delawares. He was schooled at St. John's Catholic school near Gray Horse. She was educated in the Friends School, or Skiatook Mission. She is a model little housekeeper, and their cozy little home is kept like a parlor. She is a high and cultured type of her race. They have lived here since their marriage, January 27, 1903. In the foreground of this antique government-built log house, is a historical well with its triangular poles for the well bucket. And in the background is one of the finest of orchards of apples, peaches, pears, and cherries of large size. This is one of the most fertile farms in Bird Creek Valley, and Mr. Tinker will soon build a fine home. His wife's parents, Henry and Mary Spybuck, were French, Delaware and Shawnee by descent. These two young people are happy in their first home, which formerly belonged to Mrs. Adline Mosier, his grandmother, who gave it to him, as a wedding gift. She is one of the most typical and honored old ladies among the Osage, and spends some of her time, with Richard and her daughter, Mrs. Ed Fox.

Besides the pasture leases which cover most all untilled land, there are mineral leases, ocvering the same lands thus giving a double income from all the lands so leased. One much discussed lease was granted by Hoke Smith, March 1896, while secretary of the Interior, to Ed. B. Foster, of New York, covering the entire reservation. For this he was to pay the Osages a royalty of 10 per cent of all oil produced and $50 pearly for each gas well utilized. Though a valuable lease, Foster did nothing with it for nearly five years. But in 1900 began to sublet it to practical oil developers who soon raised the Osage royalty to about 150,000 a year, till E. B. Foster died, and his son, F. B. Foster assigned the entire lease to the ndian Territory Illuminating Oil and Gas Co., who paid him from 16 to 17 per cent royalty; leaving him a net profit of 6 or 7 per cent, after paying the Osage 10 per cent. He made from $50,000 to $100,000 each year. Their lease expires March, 1906, but the lessees declining to renew it, besieged congress to pass a bill by which they get an extension for ten years longer, and the president to fix the terms, who after investigation issued orders for the company to pay one-eighth of the value of all oil produced and $100 per annum for each gas well in use—an increase of 2½ per cent royalty and $50 more for each gas well. Add to these the moneys coming in from railroad right of kays, the town-lot sales an dother franchises, and the reader can easily see how immensely rich per capita these people are becoming. Besides the common fund, the "more intelligent ones" have hundreds, some thousands of dollars annual income from their farms, leased to white men, while others make still more by cultivating their own selected and improved lands. One cultured lady, Mrs. awrence, who owns a beautiful farm some 20 miles west of Pawhuska, related that she had received as high as $1,200 cash rent one year and many others do as well, hence no danger of ever suffering.

Through development how different the full-blood income now from a few years ago when their lands were leased as low as from 3 to 20 cents per acre, and later from 25 to 61 cents, for the best. Scarcely one-fourth of all the tillable land is under cultivation. All the arable land well cultivated would bring in from $10 to $50 per acre, thus marvelously increasing the allottees' income. **Hence the full-bloods have much to gain and nothing to lose by alloting their lands, which should be done at once..** If the allotment bill when passed, contains a provision that all shall share in the mineral wealth for 21 or 25 years, as the first bill passed in the house, but defeated in the senate, last congress provided, then no one need fear being worsted from this proviso unless the nation as a whole should get far too little royalty to justify alien or corporation leases, which may be true or not according to the quality and quantity of mineral found. At any rate, Bigheart's "most intelligent ones" are the only parties gaining by the present condition of undivided lands. And in many instances even they may lose through the death of one who has improved lands which the less "intelligent" ones may gain by alloting. But this evil is small in comparison with the unsettled condition of the people, because of a community of possession. The former classes improve and increase in wealth and numbers, the latter decrease in numbers and increase in poverty ultimately by prodigaiity, leisure and inveterate gambling for which many full-bloods are noted. Many of them and some part-bloods, assemble in crowds in their homes, or tents as the case may be including the women, and gamble for days and nights with cards or in other ways, after each payment. They stake small sums of five and ten cents, generally, but keep at it till all is lost or won. The writer has seen squals sitting on the floor or ground in Indian Territory villages with piles of nickels or dimes in purses or laps, the smaller sums, seeming to be preferred because of the more time or games they afford for play.

The alloting of the land to the Indians and the future exchange of their tribal government to that of a state, will eventually bury the coveted traditional history of the Osage and finally extinguish the full-blood race. This is the idea that one of the oldest citizens expresses. It indicates with what adoration and unyielding tenacity the Indian races hold on to their old habits and traditions of life and fear extermination by the advance of the white race. But the higher the development of civil, and social life, the less danger of the extinction of the primitive race. They are only engrafted by the intellectually dominant progressive races.

The publisher would reprint the entire bill introduced last session of congress, but that can be gotten from congressional records. As it did not pass the senate an outline is all sufficient in this brief treatise. It provides that "each duly enrolled member of

The Elegant Country Home of Mr. George Bradshaw.

the Osage Reservation, Oklahoma, should be premitted to select a homestead of 160 acres, and that the remaining lands (except certain tracts reserved for the common use of the Indians, for townsite and school purposes) should be aloted equally to members of the tribe by a commission to be appointed in accordance with the provisions of the bill. Doubtless a similar bill will soon be introduced in the present congress, and the Indian office does not know of any strong preasure against it.

Perhaps the greatest objection that might be raised to that bill was the provision that the allotments of all these people should be inalienable for 25 years, which should apply only to those clearly incapable of conducting their own business to the good ofth emselves and posterity. There are a thousand citizens and many full-bloods among the Osage that are as capable of caring for their own interests as the senators and congressmen from the states, making such provisions as concerns them entirely unnecessary, and should have all the rights of free action accorded every other American citizen. But from another important principle this is a wise provision; for every poor man might wisely be given at least cost to the government some space of land, however small, to have and hold as a homestead inalienable, for himself and family, and be required to keep the same till exchanged for some other spot for like purpose. But these people are not poor, literally, and no prospect of ever becoming poor so long as "Uncle Sam" holds the less intelligent ones shares in money and pays

HISTORY OF THE OSAGE NATION

them 5 per cent interest quarterly. "The intelligent ones" can use their moneys with greater increase than 5 per cent. And in the words of Mr. Curtis: "There seems to be no reason why the land should not be divided and the reservation opened to settlement. It is rapidly increasing in value; so that when it is sold the wealth of the tribe will be enormously increased. Reserving for each individual man, woman and child an allotment of 160 acres, or a total of 304,000 acres for the entire tribe, 1,166,000 acres will remain to be disposed of. If they bring an average of $25 an acre the proceeds will be $25,150,000. Adding this to the $8,372,427 now to the credit of the Osages in the United States treasury, their trust will reach a total of $37,522,427, an average of nearly $20,000 for each member of the tribe, which would bear an income of the tribe, which would bear an income of $1,000 more or less, according to the interest allowed by the government. Thus a family of five wold have a permanent income of $5,000 a year and a farm of 800 acres. There is no community in the world so rich as this, and no member of the tribe will ever be compelled to work for a living unless he squanders his fortune. By the census of 1904 they numbered altogether 1,895 souls, of whom 808 were full bloods and the remainder mixed with the whites; 846 are men and 949 are women of all ages, and 910 of both sexes are under 18 years of age. The mixed and full-bloods have equal rights in the tribal property and will participate in the distribution whenever it occurs, with the following strange exceptions:

RIGHT OF INHERITANCE AS APPLIED

With all this wealth there there is a law or ruling for some years past discriminating against the children of white men married to Osage women or their descendants. The writer has not traced this ruling to its origin, except the report of others. It seems that the first act governing the rights of child-citizenship, or inheritance among some Indian tribes, perhaps, the Sioux or Omaha, was passed in 1887 declaring that the child's rights would follow the father. Another Act in 1897, construing or amending the act of 1887, decreed that children born of white fathers prior to that was to follow the mother, but made no provisions for the lineal rights of those born subsequent to that date. For some reason those Acts, first intended to meet conditions among other Indians have been applied to the Osages without tribal enactment or solicitation to enforce such a construction. Many of the children of white men intermarried prior to 1897, were for some time excluded from sharing in the tribal funds, but by legal contest was again placed upon the rolls and draw their per capita share. Their fathers, however, have no personal rights in such funds except to use them for the keeping and good of his children, born of mothers of Osage lineage. Those born of Osage mothers wed to white men since that date draw nothing except, (as is said) she be a full-blood, though the children of Caucasian mothers and 32nd degree of Osage fathers inherit a right to draw and allot.

If this be the construction and enforcement of any law, it is prima facie, a very unjust one. It partakes of medieval and ancient customs or inheritance in which woman was considerel a little above the slave, with no rights of inheritance for herself or children, except through her lord. All of equal degree of Osage ancestry should share equally in their common funds, especially so when they are resources of God-created wealth, not made by ancestral skill and labor. The ancestry on the mothers side is always absolute and certain. It cannot be equallly certain of the father's side. Hence the greater injustice of disinheriting the child of any degree of Osage mother.

HISTORY OF THE OSAGE NATION

Mr. Geo. Bradshaw.

Mr. Geo. Bradshaw, one of the most prosperous farmers in the Osage was formerly from Michigan, but lived in Kansas for some years before settling in the Osage country, about 1890. He married into one of the most prominent families of the Osage citizens. Mrs. Bradshaw was the daughter of Thos. Mosier, the national interpreter at Pawhuska. They were married in the old Catholic church, when it stood west of Bird Creek, in Pawhuska. They have seven fine children, and have selected a most excellent allotment for each of them, three boys and four girls, from one to thirteen years of age. Her mother, Mrs. Mosier, is Osage by adoption into the tribe. She was Miss Adline Perrier, of French lineage. Thomas Mosier, her husband, was only one-eighth Osage. Mr. Bradshaw has his allotment near Skiatook, and on Hominy creek. He has lately built a beautiful residence on his wife's allotment, four miles north of Skiatook, a cut of which appears on another page. The rear of the house is one of the old government hewn log houses, which still stand all over the Osage country. This home stands near the Midland Valley tracks, and is surrounded by a most fertile farm, well improved with orchards, barns, etc. This is a most excellent, hospitable family. Mr. Bradshaw is a brother of Will, of Pawhuska, and is one of the best farmers and stockmen of the Osage, an energetic business man, and a devoted husband and father, feeling great pride in his rosy children.

Beautiful Skiatook Home.

Jno. Javine's Beautiful Home.

Mr. Javine, the subject of this sketch is only part Osage, the nephew of Mrs. Adeline Mosier. He grew up among the Osage but has traveled exensively in the west. He has been a successful farmer and stockman for some years owning an excellent farm about 2½ miles west of Skiatook with a fine two story house and large orchard which along yields a profit of over $500 per year. It is claimed that this orchard produces the finest apples and peaches in the Osage. His home in Skytook is one of the most elegant in town. He was in the meat market business but has close dout in order to give more of attention to his ranch. He first married Miss Emma Haynie in 1886 who was the mother of five children, three girls and two boys, after the death of his first wife he married Mrs. Ollie McCoskey who died in 1903, without any children by her last marriage but one by her first husband. Miss May who wed Mr. James Long. They still make their home with her step father, Mr. Jovine, who is of one of the leading families of the Osafge and one of their best citizens.

GRAY HORSE.

This village, and trading point was named after an Indian. It was once an important point with some large stores doing a prosperous business in the midst of a fine agricultutral and grazing country, adorned with large dwellings. But with the coming of the iron horse to facilitate commerce and travel Gray Horse almost bodily moved to the new towns upon the railroads, even taking their store and cottage buildings to Fairfax, leaving Mr. John Florer with his store and beautiful cottage home.

To hold this once commercial stronghold. He is one of the oldest Indian traders among the Osage, living among them for nearly half a century, and most familiar with their history and life. From a short meeting Mr. Florer is a most energetic, successful business man and a congenial gentleman who will long hold the big trade he still enjoys, and keep alive the sacred memories of the former glowing dreams of Gray Horse.

Here lies the possibility of a plume in some one legal cap before allotment. It should be changed. Nor has the writer heard one Osage or citizen claim justice for the law or ruling; but many expressions against it. In the provisions lately drawn up, Feb. 6, 1906, by a committee composed of the Chief, O-lo-ho-wal-la (*), and Asistant Chief Bacon Rind (*), and Jas. Bigheart (*), Ne-kah-wah-she-tan-kah, Black Dog (*), W. T. Mosier, Frank Corndropper (*), C. N. Prudom (*), W. T. Leahy (*), Peter Bigheart, J. F. Palmer, and Tow-ah-hee, selected by chief to draft allotment resolutions unanimously adopted, 9 articles of which, the ninth contains this bighearted clause. That provision be made for the enrollment of the children of white fathers the issue of marriage, contracted since June 7, 1897, provided, their mothers are entitled to enrollment. "This is a noble and just provision that should prevail, and shows honor to many of the best mothers of the Osage people. The above men, (*), and O-lah-hah-moi, Min-ke-wah-ti-an-he, and Moh-e-kah-moi, composed the delegation of ten invited to Washington by letter from the Indian Commissioner, to look after the Osage interests and prospective allotment bill. It will neither keep an honorable, aspiring man from wedding an Osage girl or lady, for he marries for natural affinity and love. Nor will it deter a dishonorable man, and mere money seeker from so doing, as her share would be inducement enough, if she were indiscriminate enough to receive the offered hand, not heart, of such a man. Some of the best educated full-bloods, or even the least cultured might be far too good for such a one. A news paper reporting says: "Two views of Indians." A former agent describes the Osage as "a mild mannered, good humored, contented sort of a fellow, with an appetite for something good to eat and plenty of it. He has a good opinion of himself and is ever jealous of his honor and integrity. The mixed bloods predominate and some of them are shrewd and progressive: but like many of their red brothers, the appetite of some of the Osages for liquor is insatiable. Still, I do not believe that there is any more liquor drinking among them than there is among other residents of the United States, taking the population throughout."

Others not so charitable to the men as the women also say: "Everybody speaks well of the women, as being honest, industrious, modest and intelligent; and with a little training they make excellent housewives. But the men, as a rule, are lazy, drunken, stupid loafers, who are found of sport but hate work, and prefer to hire white and negro laborers to cultivate their farms, as they are perfectly able to do."

We do not think the last view as true as the first. Yet more correct perhaps of the women than the men. For the Osage women are widely praised for virtue, and their descendants, also, where not too much possessed of the modern ideas of society life. "Uncle Joseph Revard," a noble old gentleman, is authority for the statement that only one Osage girl was ever known to become a mother out of wedlock, and only one other was ever known to lead a life of public infamy, and she was banished from camp and her food carried to her at a distance, too contaminated to live in contact with other females. And men of that character were treated with greater severity before the days of their more liberal civilization. In their catalogue of sins the one most punished for disobedience against the Great Spirit was adultry on the part of the male who was administered 100 lashes. The public female was ostracised from camp and association with the virtuous of her sex, and the men known to associate with her received severe punishment. From time immemorial among them a man using force with a virtuous woman was punished by 100 lashes, equal to a death sentence. What effect would a public whiping post have on our modern, highly civilized society with her thousands of divorces primarily from such causes, and thousands of others from the curse of drunkenness, and frivolous prodigality, but only a few from natural incompatibility. The law of force is seldom applicable among the whites under present social conditions; only once in a while to negro brutes.

OSAGE NATURAL RESOURCES—RAINFALL, SOIL PRODUCTS, ETC.

Years ago when "Uncle Sam" was casting his eyes southwestward to find some last ideal section for the hunting an dcamping frounds for the Osage people, who had sucessively surrendered by treaty their plains and forests to the westward sweep of the Cauucasian treks, or trail, he rested his vigilant eyes upon forest covered hills and valleys. intersperced with fertile prairies than which none could be more ideal for the Osage hunters, then teeming with fish and wild game, a land once his own, but lost by Cherokee removal and conquest. But in peace it is bought back for the last earthly home of the once strong, stalwart tribe. To this they come to abide and make their final allotments. It is a land fair to look upon, fairer in nature, perhaps than in gold, but destined to be productive of the finest race of the Twentieth Century. It requires more than gold and grain to make men and women. Sunshine, pure air, pure sparkling waters, varied vegetation, and above all the glorious beauties of God's art galleries, of hills and hollows, rugged rocks and rushing, rollicking roaring rills, receding slopes, with fertile valleys lying between, make men, eral men. Gold alone might contract the soul, destroy, mayhaps, the mind and body, but nature's wealth, never.

No country, nor people, were ever more wealthy, naturally and financially, per capita, than the citizens of the Osage Nation, if rightly educated. But their greatest riches are manifest in the ebautiful broad, fertile prairies, extensive hard and soft wood forests, many meandering streams and rivers, beds of coal, stone and the discoveries of lead, iron, zinc, silver and gold, and the rapid development of

HISTORY OF THE OSAGE NATION

seemingly inexhaustible voluumes of oil and gas for market, manufacturing and fuel, make it one of the most promising sections in the future state of Oklahoma.

How sublimely the Great Father of the Pale and Ruddy races has made this spot for the abode of his children. The Paradise of a romantic love dreamer could scarcely improve upon the territory. The ancient Paradise was but a lovely scene of trees, flowers, fruits and castles. And here many beautiful trees have been reared by creative hand and thrifty man is planting flowers and fruits. This section of the country has proven its adaptability to all kinds of the finest fruits and vegetables, which could scarcely be excelled by the products of southern Illinois, southern Missouri, and northern Arkansas—the sections that have taken the premiums for the best large and small fruits. Unlimited wealth lies in the soil of this section of the territory, for fruit growers and gardeners. Even the roughest hilly land will grow the most perfect fruits. Irish potatoes grow 200 bushels per acre on good land, and two crops a year, but are sweet potatoes were never exceeded in size, quality and quantity. Water melons and cantaloupes and all kinds of vine products were never excelled by those of any section. Peanuts and tobacco grow as well or better than in Virginia and North Carolina. Grapes of which there are already fine vineyards, and peaches, pears, apricots, plums of every variety, and apples grow to perfection, with few failures. In fact all that grows in America except tropical fruits and products, grow here in perfection. Strawberries and all other shall fruits can be grown as well as in the small fruit or berry sections of Missouri and Arkansas; and cotton and corn together with fruits and vegetables, will be the future sources of wealth here, and upon the development of the country depends the support of the town. This part of the territory is conceded to be one of the finest farming regions and yields the largest average in grain products. As high as 100 bushels of corn per acre have, it is claimed, been gathered from one acre of the best creek bottoms, and good land averages from 40 to 60 bushels per acre. Wheat yields as high as 50 bushels, with an average ranging from 10 to 30 per acre. Oats average from 50 to 60 and sometimes 100 bushels per acre, an other cereals as well. Cotton grows to perfection and matures a fine quality of the long-fibre staple, even during the driest seasons, as cotton is considered a dry weather plant. A good yield produces from one half to one and one-half bales per acre, and sells at 2 and 3 cents in the seed and from 6 to 12 cents per pound in the line, or $30 or $40 per acre. This section of the territory produces more corn and cotton than any other products, because they grow easily and bring in more money to the farmer than other farm products.

A local paper in Oklahoma reports that Frank Kirk of Enid, O. T., mowed nine cuttings of Alfalfa from one 35 acre field and that the ninth crop was a good as the first and of fine quality. Ten acres averaging one and one-half tons per acre for each mowing produces 135 tons of alfalfa in one season, bringing $8 per ton, brough $1,080, over $125 per acre. It was done by his experiment of disk harrowing after each cutting, something after the Campbell system of waterlelss irrigation. Without authenticating the above figures the writer can state that the Osage is one of the best natural sections for alfalfa in America. Fine fields are now growing in this reservation. Many other products rightly cultivated will net as profitable results. How many men live and die upon their farms never knowing the undeveloped wealth in the soil, the main source for all wealth.

All the agricultural products cultivated between the Great Lakes and the Gulf, from Maine to California, can be grown here with profit. The climate is a pleasant

HISTORY OF THE OSAGE NATION

moderation between the extreme heat of summer to the south and the rigid cold of the north. Along the wood lines streams are some excellent sites for summer cottages and the sanitariums for health seekers.

Some who are not well versed with the climatic conditions of the territories entertain some fear of sufficient rainfall. But there is less anxiety about the rainfall here than in many parts of the territories. A few figures may be of much value to those contemplating homes or investments. There are abundant rains. It is a well settled scientific fact that where there are many streams of water there is a greater precipitation of moisture than in sections where few streams flow. And it seems a divine decree for rain to follow the plow and hoe, as the agriculturist westward wends his way.

The average temperature of the two territories since the opening of Oklahoma was 62.0 degrees in 1896, and the lowest 59.0 in 1892 and 1895. The mean temperature of the winter season is about 37 and for autumn and spring about 61. The highest degree of heat, 144 degrees, August 5th at Mangum, O. T., and the lowest degree of cold about 10 to 15 below zero at Ft. Reno, January 27. The greatest annual precipitation was 40.56 inches in 1902, and the lowest 22.78 inches in 1901. South McAlester, Indian Territory I. T., received the heaviest precipitation, 53.20 inches, and Jefferson, O. T., the least, 27.82. The abundant timberof the Osage Nation also causes a heavier rainfall. The above figures do not include the heavy rains, cold and heat of the last year which might modify them slightly.

―――――◇―――――

(Capital)   THE SKIATOOK BANK.   ($10,000.)

W. C. Rogers, President;   L. Appleby, Vice-President;   C. R. Cleveland, Cash.

The officers and stockholders of this banking institution are so well known to the people of the lacality in which they live and transact business **ers, the president,** is one of the finest specimens of Indian statesmen, and is that is seems hardly worth the space to make any introductory remarks in presenting them to the readers of this brief piece of history. **W. C. Rog-** destined to go down in history as the last of the famous red warriors that held a place of trust and honor with his people, to whom he has always been strictly loyal and whose rights and interests he is now guiding and guarding as sacredly as if they were the Golden Calf of old. Mr. Rogers is accomplishing as a statesman what his forefathers failed to maintain with their rud weapons of warfare and agriculture—providing for each and every one of his fellow citizens a good home and living in their declining days, in acting as administrator, to a certain extent, for his people, who pace implicit confidence in him. **Mr. Lou Appleby,** the first to be elected vice-president, although having passed away from the world, still lives in the minds of his friends, which means everybody, as he had no enemies. **C. H. Cleveland,** is well known throughout the two territories as a representative of two of the largest manufacturing plants in the United States, viz: The McCormack Harvesting Machine Co., and the J. I. Case Threshing Machine Co., having acted as collector and credit man for both the above firms for several years, at different times. **Mr. Geo. M. Janeway,** the ever-courteous and genteel assistant cashier, received his first and early education in the windy state, and later attended the popular college at Stillwater, Oklahoma, graduating in 1902. He then took charge of the chemical department as one of the faculty, but later resigned to accept a place in the National Bank of Commerce, Stillwater, resigned his position there for one with the Mangum National bank of Mangum; again from there to the Bank of Eldorado, and lastly casting his lot with the early business men of Skiatook, I. T., which place he now claims his home. **Clifton George and C. W. Brown,** each of whom are directors, are well known throughout the banking fraternity in the southwest, having been in the banking business for many years. This bank was organized December 14, 1904, and opened its doors for business January 26, 1905, since when it has done a fairly nice business, and fully enjoys the full confidence and support of the leading farmers and business men of the community in which it transacts business.

CLIMATE EAND HEALTHFULNESS OF THE OSAGE COUNTRY.

This climate should be a guarantee that this section is a healthful home for the prudent and wise liver. But we would have no one imagine that the country is a perfect life insurance against disease and the deteriating effects of sanitary carelessness and of old age. Plenty of busy pure air and clear, pure cold water and fine medical skill is the best she has to offer you along this line. If you wish better God's perfect moral, spiritual laws, and life insurance men are as kind here as anywhere you may go. Men may not gain herculean frame nor women find elixir of unfading, perpetual youth and beauty, unless they rightly use the elements and forces that make these idolized fortunes. Yet it is man's fault that these do not exist anywhere and everywhere.

The Osage country with central location, fine drainage, slightly sandy soil with a good clay subsoil, and mostly soft water so bountiful at a moderate depth, makes the Osage a sanitarium for all who will observe nature's laws govering the human anatomy. You sometimes hear it said in the states that this section of the territtory is not healthful. But taking all climate conditions that go to make the race healthful, viz: rolling country, bright sunshine, pure air and plenty of it, good water, excellent fruits and rich and varied flowers, this part of the territory will produce for the wise man or woman, as rosy cheeks, as bright eyes, and as vigorous physique as the mountains of Colorado and New Mexico, or the sunny tropical climes of Italy and the mountains of Switzerland. You need have no solicitation about your health here if you have learned that health and beauty of soul and body are but the first products of nature rightly venerated. The territory has not yet discovered the spring of perpetual youth, nor magic to drive all diseases away, but it is among the most sanitary sections to be found. But if you should get sick after coming to the Osage she has skilled doctors, some of whom are from the best medical schools of the country, and several dentists to pull out, fill in, or make you new "grinders." (Ecc. 12 chap.) So however ailing you may be you need have no fear of ciming here to live. And if you have worn out your body in the hustling business or disipations of life and concluded you must die, here you will find as beautiful a place to retire and lie down to rest as any spot in the world for the government cemetery is a naturally beautiful twenty acre park. And should the inevitable come to you here it would be a most beautiful place to rise in the resurrection; and many here feel like the patriotic American, taken by a loyal Italian to see the beauty and greatness of the Mediterrean Sea. "Oh," said the American, "we could dump the Rocky Mountains into thiis and fill it up in a jiffy." He was next taken to look down the burning throat of Aetna. "Uh," replied the patriot, "we could turn the Mississippi into this hole and put it out before night." Al last he was asked to come to a delectable mountain to see Rome and a sunrise equal to the resurrection morning. On arriving and beholding the subline scene he exclaimed: "The

HISTORY OF THE OSAGE NATION

resurrection morn! the resurrectiion morn! Hurrah for the resurrection morning! and young America is first in the field." Such is the feeling and pride of many in this reservation. While it is the last to be allotted and opened to general development on an individual possession basis, it may soon be the first n commercial, civil, educational, social, and Christian progress. Many of the people here look forward to wonderful progress and development when the land is alloted, and much of it sold; and have good cause to be elated over the great state of Oklahoma and the Osage country.

(Syrup)——SORGHUM FACTORY——(Sweets.)

Mr. C. N. Dugger, of the Osage, near Skiatook, is the first man that ever ran a full sorghum making plant and evaporator in the Osage country. He is from the coast country of Texas, where he manufactured the famous syrup from the ribbon cane. His plant is located two miles from Skiatook, where he made last year many barrels of the best sorghum, of the finest quality, from the Silver Drip Cane, which grows to perfection in this country. He is here to stay, and will enlarge his mill to supply all the demands. The cane produces from 120 to 160 gallons per acre and sells at 50 cents a gallon at the mill or 60 cents canned for market, making one of the most profitable farm products as it is easily cultivated and made up. He can evaporate from 60 to 75 gallons per day. **Here is money for the farmer for little work.**

Skiatook is located on the border between the Cherokee and Osage countries, 35 miles by the Midland Valley railway, southeast from Pawhuska, right down the Bird Creek Valley, down which the road runs from Pawhuska to Skiatook, where the creek wends its way eastward, and the railway south to Tulsa. The town is beautifully located in one of the most fertile, dark soil plains, and valleys, in the two territories, with Bird Creek east, and prairie stretching two miles northwest and many miles southwest to Hominy Creek Valley. It is an ideal location for an inland town. The best water is secured in the town and all over the valley, at a short depth beneath the surface. There is a fine volume of pure spring water flowing out of the hillside about three miles from and above the town, that could be easily stored in a reservoir and piped to Skiatook for a fine water supply, as the population increases. While the townsite is on the Cherokee side of the line, the Midland Valley depot being on the Osage side, the town is for all commercial purposes an Osage town, at most of its trade will be drawn from fifteen miles west where much of the best farming contry of the Osage is already being cultivated and when fully developed will sustain a good sized town without any other resources. But gas and oil have been found on all sides and within a few miles of Skiatook, and in all probabilities stands over these minerals. The Standard Oil Co. has struck oil one and one half miles from town and the oil is piped and pumped to Neodosha, Kansas. Gas is now burning on Bird Creek a few miles distant. A rig is being erected by the Prairie Oil and Gas Co., 2 miles west of town, and the Boggs Drilling Co., another two miles south of town. This whole country from its topography, will supply both oil and gas, and the more hilly districts a good quality of coal, which is already found in evidence.

If the country were thoroughly developed in agricultural and horticultural products, its prosperity and growth would be assured without other resources. These products are the primary sources of all wealth. Others are only speculative mediums and add largely to the luxuries of life. Fine fish and game are found everywhere. Excellent heavy timbers are found on the bottoms along the streams, such as oak, walnut, pecan, hickory, etc., and a more scrubby growth for fuel and fencing on the hills. Good building stone are abundant on the hills. All kinds of wild fruits and nuts, except tropical, grow here.

PECANS

The pecan industry of this section of the territory (Skiatook,) is an item of considerable commercial importance. In the yaer 1903, over 4,000 buushels of pecans were gathered and shipped besides what were hauled off in wagons. One firm shipped three carloads of 600 bushels each. They do not hit every year, as the late frosts sometimes destroys the nut in the blossom. Last year there was about one-third of a crop. The price ranges from three and one-half cents a pound up for the gatherer and perhaps double that amount in the market of Kansas City and St. Louis. The groves are most beautiful, the trees being somewhat like a walnut or hickory tree, but with smaller, helmet shaped leaves. They are fine ornamentl and shade trees when allowed to grow in plenty of space. The wood is as valuable as hickory, and more so than walnut timber and equal to or more valuable than persimmon timber of which there is so large a quantity, and equal to bodock and lignum-vatae for tool handles, planes, etc. Al lexcept the latter grow here voluntarily and most perfectly. The persimmon is also a valuable fruit to those who appreciate all fruits. It is frequently called the American date, being very similar to the date in seed, construction and delicacy. They are delicious when fully ripened by the frost and become granulated like sugar when kept till dry, and late in the winter. Pawpaws grow here in perfection. Wild grapes are found in abundance, and black haws grow in many of the valleys. All these natural wild growth of fruit. The wild plum grows in abundance in good fruit season, and as fine as may be found in the south and north central states, and as excellent a flavor for preserves and jellies. From observation Mr. Allen C. Helmick, postmaster at Skiatook, claims that when it rains on the first day of May for some unexplainable reason there are very few or no wild grapes that year, nor strawberries, and other fruits that are in bloom at that time. The scientific botanical explanation might be found in the theory that the rain about that time washes the fertilizing pollen from the blossoms, and then no fruit or offspring. For plants produce fruit by a similar process of fertilization to that of the seminal fertility in animal life in producing offspring. For all kinds of farming, gardening and fruit growing, the soil of this section can not be excelled, nor the town location.

Square, 300 miles of richest land, in every way you look,

Farming, gardening, orchard, parks on all main roads to Skiatook.

WYNONA, O. T.

Mr. Antoine Rogers, owner of the land around Wynona, names from Winona Wagon, has one of the most beautiful homes in the Osage, one mile south of the station. A very beautiful large orchard grows just east of his house, which bears the finest fruits, apples, especially peaches, plums, cherries, apricots, pears, grapes, blackberries, raspberries gooseberries and all other kinds of small fruits grow to perfection. He is part Osage, but grew up in the Cherokee, and is a first cousin of W. C. Rogers, chief of the Cherokees. He is the son of Louis Rogers, the brother of Judge T. L. Rogers of Pawhuska. He has been mainly engaged in the stock raising business for years, but at present has only about 500 head. His pastures extend for miles over the beautiful rolling prairies around Wynona, which lies on a plain, bordered by subline hills on the west, partly covered by low timber, and for some miles to the south and east line a most beautiful expanse of fertile prairie, making an ideal view.

The Country Mansion Home of Mr. Antoine Rogers—Wynona, O. T.

The railroad runs the full length of it, north and south. Mr. Rogers lives right on the same spot where he settled seventeen years ago, but first resided 30 miles ast, on Bird Creek. He married Miss Elizabeth Carpenter, and has raised a fine family of six most amiable and practical children, five girls and one boy, Kenneth. They have been eduated in some of the best schools. Only two daughters are single, one daughter, Miss May, is now taking a business course in a Kansas City business college. Mr. Rogers grows from 30 to 40 bushels of corn per acre. He has one of the finest improved homes in the Nation. He has a large stone barn, also one of the best in the territory. Ten different kinds of ornamentl trees adorn his yard, facing the south, right on the line of railway running from Parsons, Kansass to Oklahoma City. His son is married and lives on his farm a mile north, right west of Wynona Station. Mr. Arthur Rogers, a nephew, also owns a well improved farm west of the station. All are extensive stockmen and excellent citizens. Wynona is 8 miles from Nelagony Junction, where there is only a small grocery and restaurant, and section house at present, about 12 miles from Pawhuska, and 226 from Kansas City. It might appropriately be called Rogersville, as Mr. Rogers has set apart a townsite and built some business dwelling houses. He will warmly welcome any business enterprise that may seek a location here. It is far enough from Hominy 10 miles south, to make an excellent trading point surrounded for miles with the most fertile farm and fruit lands. There is not a more beautiful location for a village in the Osage. There is only one

HISTORY OF THE OSAGE NATION

small general store, since Mr. Rogers closed out his stock, but is said to be thinking of putting in another soon.

To illustrate how democratic and practical many of the better Osage citizens are with their wealth and possibilities, many of like wealth and homes in the old states would be most exxclusive and asistocratic in their social discriminations; but not so with most of these citizens. It is said that a young man who now lives in a cottage home at Wynona station first came to Wynona in charge of a cattle shipment; but possessing only his energy, industry and good character as his greatest riches. He started in as a railway secton employe, taking the first best opening for an income, but soon met and won a most amiable, and domestically inclined daughter of this excellent family, their attachment being strongly mutual from the first meeting; and being set up in house keeping by his generous father-in-law t he young people are now land lords of many broad fertile acres. And many other examples of similar nature can be found all over the Osage. It is the man, not the money, that counts with the daughters of most Osage citizens, the right ideal of selection.

HOMINY, O. T.
Hominy is 18 Miles South from Nelogany Junction.

Which like Nelagony (Ne-water, and –lagony, good; meaning in Osage Goodwater) has a suggestive name, derived from a settlement of Indians of or allied with the Cherokee, who are noted for their prevalent custom of eating hominy, a usage brought with them from North Carolina and Tennessee a hundred years ago. Hence the name of Hominy Creek and Hominy Post on its south bank, in a primitive forest grove. And new Hominy is only an extension south on the beautiful incline. Thus the term came from an article of food. In former times the Osage, like many other tribes, never used bread, as they had no way to grind corn; nor used salt, as they thought salt was not good in food, and only crushed their corn or baked it whole like mush and used mostly wild game, of which they had a bountiful supply. They had a kind of a potato they called Tes-kah, which were found along the streams and low places, and the roots of a pond lily they called Cha-wal-lah. Pumpkins, beans and Indian corn, and other vegetables they cultivated only with the hoe, as they used no other implements at first. Hominy Valley is unexcelled for her rich soil and fine farms, for which she is noted. Hominy is located in the best section of this valley. Like Wynona, she has a western background of bulwark, fortlike hills, and a beautiful border of ribbon like forest, skirting the creek banks north and east, the whole making a subline scene viewed from the "Round Top" or Castle Hill west. What has been said concerning the fertile soil and its products of grain vegetables and fruits of every variety except tropical, is equally true of Hominy section. Many fine orchards here are bearing or growin. Many of the best improved full blood farms with large dwellings are in this valley. A mile south is their village as it seems difficult for them to get out of the habit to band together in villages, living only part of the time on their farms. Each village has it "Round House" for dancing and council. Four miles northeast of town is the pink cottage of the present chief, O-lo-ho-wal-la and his wife and daughters, the latter speaking English quite well, but the chief speaks only Osage, a dignified, and honorable, intelligent full-blood Osage family. Through a bright young daughter, as interpreter, the writer got his consent to have his home and family photographed for a cut for this book, but for some unexplained reason the photographer never took or sent the view, a sore regret. **The chief also commended**

HISTORY OF THE OSAGE NATION

the industrial, scientific and litery college plan of the author and promised to consider the granting of a location before the Osage council. The grant of a section of land would be but **one-third of an acre per capita less in the allotment, and one acre per capita for the beginning of such an institution for their children would be but three sections less for 1,900 allottees. Surely they could not put each an acre to better use. It need not be all first, but second grade land, as the location is more important** than the grade of land. Yet the best land in the right location would be far more preferable. But if the generosity of the Osage people should fail to grant this amount of land for such a college site on condition that it be forever inalienable except for such school purposes, then the writer would gladly pay the government cost price, for a favorable location at $1.25 per acre for the college, as mentioned in the introduction. But he fully believes, when rightly understood, the gratis location will be readily granted, which he guarantees will never be regretted by the Osage people. For nowhere in the great world of social, civil and commercial life has a model institution ever been established either ancient or modern, to meet the main requirements of all classes, for the most sucessful life of all; so far as the writer's ideals of education and ultimate aim of life has been able to comprehend. There are several locations in the reservation that might be good for the institution. With another main line of railway running east and west through Hominy it would be favorabtle to any large enterprise. She now has a firmly established bank, four general stores, a drug store, three hotels, two liveries, two lumber yards, two restaurants, meat market, a bakery, barber shop, groceries, a hardware and furniture, telephone system, good water, two blacksmith shops and a gin. Much more cotton is grown as you go south in the Osage. The Arkansas River Valley grows the finest grade. Other lines of business, are perhaps established by this date, as the town is rapidly growing. The finest stone block in the Osage is being completed from the excellent stone found in abundancre near by. A stone school building has been erected and subscription school taught by Prof. Gill and wife, each pupil paying $1.50 per month for about 100 pupils.

As yet only one church building has been erected here but several churches hold services here. Rev. Davies, of the Presbyterian church, divides his time between this point and Pawhuska. The Holiness people have quite a membership here. Hominy has a population of over 400, intelligent, progressive people, ready for any good thing. The townsite will be in the next to be surveyed, appraised and sold, Pawhuska coming first. Homny will no doubt, be one of the three largest towns in the Osage, as she has the resources to sustain its growth when thoroughly developedd. On visiting the Osage, you should not fail to see this town and section with their large farms, fine homes and business. Gas and oil are being found near by and will be a good place to invest or begin any manufacturing business.

(Capital)—FIRST NATIONAL BANK.—($25,000.)
**Prentiss Price, Pres.; Fred Drummond, Vice Pres.; Howard M. Haner, Cash.
Other stockh'dr's, R. E. Bird, J. E. Martin, Hominy Trad. Co., A. B. Mahr.**

The First Bank of Hominy was organized December, 1903, and nationalized September, 1905. This cut shows Hominy's first stone, two-story building, 26x60 feet, and cost, with fixtures, $8,500. Mr. Price, the president, formerly of North Mississippi, came to the Osage 15 years ago as an Indian trader and has been doing business ever since in Hominy, where he is largely interested in the leading lines of

business in th town and is a most excellent young man.

The vice president is president of the Hominy Trading Company, a full sketch of whose life and home is given on other page. Howard M. Maher, cashier is a son of the widely known proprietor of the Leland Hotel, Pawhuska, and has lived in the Osage country for 18 years. These are all young men who have the energy and business sagacity to quickly see a thing of merit, and like many other Osage traders, have improved well every opportunity which assures the progress of Hominy as well as the continued prosperity of their owne enterprise. "Go west, young men!" has been well taken in their career as in all other cases of Osage capitalists.

Old Hominy Post and North Hominy.

W. R. FELLOWS' LUMBER YARD.
Dealer in Lumber, Sash and Doors, James Beebe, Manager.

Mr. Fellows himself lives at Stillwater, and is a member of the **Spurrier Lumber Co.,** but conducts in Hominy an individual lumber business, for two years, having bought out Price and Price. The yard is located opposite the Fraley Mercantile Co's., Store in what was **Old Hominy Post.** Mr. Beebe is from Stillwater, but formerly from Kansas, and has all the push and stability of the "Sunflower State."

(Photo by Hargis)

Mr. P. H. Harris and A. W. Nash, U. S. Licensed Traders.

The firm is from the Old Dominion, Virginia, with all the frank, congenial qualities characteristic of the people of that state. Mr. Harris came to the Osage in 1898, from Missouri where he had lived three years. He farmed up to two years ago, when he started the general merchandise bustness in the block shown in cut. His partner, Mr. Nash, his uncle, has been in the territory (Chickasaw) four years. They formed a partnership both in business property and merchandise, and are developing a large trade. Mr. Harris was the third score, in order of beginning in Hominy. Theu both have nice cottage homes in town and do a cash business with a full line of **dry goods and groceries, also carry a new line of Bradley implements** and deal largely in produce, for which they pay the highest price. They are interested in the growth of Hominy, being men woh help to make growing cities.

Mr. Fred Drummond, whose large, beautiful home appears in this cut, is a native of Glasgow, Scotland, but came to New York when a boy of 18 years. From there came west to St. Louis, where he was first engaged in the mercantile business, dry goods, for two years. Then he came to the Osage and settled in Pawhuska, where he clerked for Jno. R. Skinner, Indian trader. He continued with that company till he went into business under the firm name of "R. E. Bird & Co.," in the present Osage Mercantile Co's., building where he remained in business as a partner till 1903, when he recuperated after his long experience heer, on a farm a yar, then came to Hominy, where he organized the **Hominy Trading Co.,** and bought out Price & Price, and

Mr. Fred Drummond's Mansion Home.

became president of the company, and became stockholder in the **First National Bank,** of which he is vice president, and is also vice president of **Mullin's Drug Co.** He is a man of great intelligence and business ability as shown from the large stone block being erected for the Mercantile Company, and the elegant home he has erected in the north part of Hominy. He married Miss Addie Gentner, of Coffeyville, Kansas, and has four fine children, three boys and a girl. He sees a bright future for the Osage after his long experience here.

THE MERCHANTS HOTEL—(HOMINY, O. T.)
E. H. Carnett, Propietor.

Mr. Carnett is a native of Southwestern Kentucky, Perry County, but came to the Osage early in 1905. He purchased this hotel and has also farmed nearby. The Merchants is a new building and one of the firstclass dollar-rate hotels. He expects to conduct the house himself and will give every guest a warm **Kentucky welcome.** His family comes to conduct the hotel with him. **It is only one-half block from the depot and convenient for the traveling public.**

G. A. SHAFFNER & GUY BENNETT.
General Blacksmithing and Repair Work—All Work Guaranteed.

HISTORY OF THE OSAGE NATION

Mr. Shaffner is from Kansas, but lived in Lincoln county, O. T., before coming to Hominy. He grew up in the shop working both wood and iron, a wheelrght and blacksmith. **Hs father worked at the trade 45 years, and taught hs son hs own chosen trade.** Hs partner, Mr. Bennett s from Indiana, and formed a partnership one year ago. They do high class new work and repairing, all guaranteed to give **satisfaction.** Mr. Bennett's father was also a blacksmith. These men are not only high-class "village blacksmiths" but good citizens for the new town and state. Blacksmiths, in general, are sober, industrious, valuable men in any community.

A MODERN BURDEN IN DISGUISE

The author and publisher of this book has his attention called to some articles in one of the two local papers of the town, The Pawhuska Capital, of which Mr. Chas M. Hill, the son of Rev. E. F. Hill, pastor of the M. E. church isi editor, treated the writer like a gentleman, or as he would a fellow editor or publisher, for which we feel equal gratitude. All rightly edited publications, not dominated entirely by money and politics, are educational influences, to which the writer extends a fraternal hand. But the articles in the other local sheet were evidently coward;y thrusts at him because of the fact that he had been collecting material, historical, biographical and commercial for this book. With this exception, the writer has had the hearty support, or at least gentlemanly indifference of the local papers, in his publications of historical booklets on the various sections and various peoples of the territories, and has always published such pamphlets on definite written stipulations to the people, who with few exceptions, extend the most generous support, because the writer trusted them instead of asking for trust, on conditions, in which they knew there could be no fraud or even misrepresentation, just as in this case. He has a too high regard for his honor, education, and reputation and usefulness for the future to even attempt cunningry, if it should win him all the lands and millions of the Osage country, and a half dozen more like it. Who composed those articles not knowing the above facts, stabbed through his own disguise. while in blinding ignorance, avarice or jealousy, he thrusts at another. He knew nothing of the writer's life, ability, work, methods nor purpose. and therefore entirely inexcusable. But imagining that his own occupation was being infringed upon, his methods repeated, he deserves only the reply of Caesar to a traitor: "Et tu Brute!" "Thou, too, O Brutus." But were it not for the contemptible spirit, the falsity and gall, in casting false reflections on the writer's book and life before strangers who might not know better, he could pass over the articles in sheer pity for their author, who is uncertain, but they smell of a dirty, editorial garret where the responsibility lies. Their whole sum and substance was fabricated falsity, except as he had in mind some false printers or publishers who may have worked such impositions as he had in mind one of which will be mentioned later. The book, largely on the Osage country, printed at Ponca City ten years ago, was from two to four times as costly to its subscribers as this book, but that was gotten out partly by a local newspaper, and for that reason—"well, maybe so"—all right. In spite of some fakes in the business, the "Special Historical Illustrated books for advertising are becoming more frequent and easier to make all the time, for they are the most valuable and effective way if done by men of scholarship. All countries and colonization companies use them, all live towns and commercial clubs use the special "write up" methods, even when faked on the cost by some local office in printing them. Even the local newspaper can't advertise without special "write ups," but no one presumes they are literary. The writer hartily thanks he kind and generous, and long suffering men and women helping to publish the book; long-suffering because overtaxed by too temporary methods of advertising. Millions are spent annually that pass away with the click of the pringing press. Something permanent is to be sought for in all "ads" except brief specialties and drawing bargains. This is the secret of reaping from the dollars and cents you spend in "ads." Many a business man contributes to the support of local news sheets because he may be scorched or insulted if he does not "cough up," by something like the following rank editorial:

"When you hear a merchant make the remark that as long as trade is good as it is he will not advertise, you may say right there that he is unclassed, and is no benefit to the town. He expects to live along and catch what few people the other merchants don't have time to wait upon, and barely make enough to pay rent. He does not realize or does not care that it is his duty to help bring the trade to the town, the same as others. He must have a guilty conscience when he is waiting on a customer whom he knows belongs to the live, wide awake, and energetic competitors up the street. If he wants the trade tell the people so."—Exchange. (Repeated in this local paper.)

Every progressive business and professional person todoy realizes the great benefit of advertising discreetly where the population is sufficiently large and competition fierce enough to necessitate constant display of something to remind others of our wares and work, but no sensibe man is so foolish or crazy as to believe that he must make such display every day or week in some little local sheet along, to keek his brains, trade, brawn or business before an intelligent, thinking public. A well worded sign in front of his office or store, or board nailed to the corner posts at the forks of roads converging on the town, might be far more effective permanent and less costly, than daily or weekly insertions in very limited edly circulated local sheets, or two "up" as are usually found in every locality, burdening often sparcely populated communities with daily or weekly repetitions of matter, labor and expenses that ought to be saved to the people by publishing only the best in some well edited, literary, scientific, brain-born matter worth keeping in a book, or monthly magazine form, or journals, without the enormous waste of labor and money in publishing a ranch of chaff, and the consequent necessity of the reader's strong mental discrimination in sifting out a gill of wheat. What is not worth keeping in general is not worth the time and cost in publishing.

The thoughtful, most frank business men and scholars all say and the author has talked with thousands upon this subject, that there are too many local publications of little newspapers for the good, much less the necessity of society and business. One local paper for each town or county might be a benefit to the people, if edited with intelligence and economy, to the reader, who can get all but local items from a large, generally circulated merto- or cosmopolitan paper from which the local must necessarily reprint whatever world-wide news it has. In all other respects the local sheet is almost entirely composed of local advertising, or personal gossip, as Mr. Smith, Jones, Scott, or Brown goes or comes on political or commercial business, or Miss or Mrs. Smith, Jones, Scott, or Brown, has gone or comes to visit Mrs. Roe, or Miss Doe, who gives a reception, card party, progressive euchre, or high five for a prize. And some do not even stop here but pulnge into all kinds of scandal mongering and exaggerations under the term "news" but frequently serving only and to case unjust insinuations, even absurd falsities, upon some innocent, or perhaps some

The Elegant Home of Prentiss Price, Hominy, O. T.

....

MULLINS DRUG COMPANY.—(Incorporated).
Dr. Ira Mullin, Pres.; Fred Drummond, V. Pres.; Prentiss Price, Sec. Treas.
Dealers in Drugs and Drug Sundries.

Dr. Ira Mullin, B. S., M. D., the president, is one of the three physicians in Hominy. The Mullin's Drug Co., was organized by him in 1904, as **The First Drug Store** in the town and vicinity. He is a native of the Old Dominion, Virginia, from which he came to the Osage in 1902, and settled in Hominy. He was one of the first to practice here, building up a broad practice, both as a physician and surgeon. He is a graduate of the National Norman University, Lebanon, Ohio, taking his "B. S." degree and "M. C." from the University College of Medicine, Richmond, Va., also of the New York Post-Graduate Medical School and Hospital. His office is in the drug store. They are prescription druggists and carry a full line of drugs, and sundry toilet articles, and cold drinks, etc. More enterprise can not be found in the Osage as they are largely interested in all the leading business of the town and all most excellent citizens, town advancers and country developers. You will be pleased to meet them, and they will encourage any legitimate buisness locating there.

HISTORY OF THE OSAGE NATION

New Hominy (South Part), O. T.

....

A. L. HOUSTON'S
Restaurant—Short Order

Among the first class eating places in Homing Mr. Huston conducts one of the best. His eating parlor has the most inviting appearance not only to hungry men, but to those of dainty tastes. He is a man of congenial nature, well fitted him for the care business and being located only one half block east from the north end of the depot, you will find him ever ready to serve the traveling public, and home patrons. One of the most important parts of physical life is to be or have a good cook; then to eat only what you need or like best in right quantities. Anything you want of the best quality you will find at Mr. Houston's, Hominy, O. T.

---

comparatively innocent party, for the want of something better to fill up their space unoccupies by advertising. The writer once knew personally the editor of such a paper even to attack the llife, character, motives and teachings of men of high character, and higher motives because he was paid to do so by some prejudiced party and in some instances he would attack the affairs, or business of another in order to have somebody answer it in the columns of his paper simply to fill space that he was imcompetent to fill from the thoughtful product of his own mind but he soon emigrated.

OBSCENE JOURNALISM.

Mr. Jerome in prosecuting a libel case lately in New York City, said:

"For more than two weeks we have been wandering through Vanity Fair witnessing exhibitions of human weakness and folly, and in some instances of human degradation. Now let us see the character of this paper, (referring to Town Topics.) Mr. Shepard has told you that Colonel Mann has stated that it was the natural evolution of personal journalism. If that is true it ought to be applicable to more than one daily in New York whose trend is that way. There is scarcely a morning paper that does not print vile scandals and obscene matter. I don't seee what interest it conserves to publish such items. I do not see what interest such articles relating to the evil of this or that person have for you and me. Does it ever serve any useful purpose? Is it other than filth? It is put there for no other purpose than that of paying dividends to the stockholders. The average newspaper is run from the counting room standpoint.

HISTORY OF THE OSAGE NATION

Many of the advertisements are but a corruption fund to induce quiet about this, that or the other. This is not a pleasant statement to make but if you ask the average newspaper man why a certain paper let up on a certain proposition his reply will be 'Why didn't you see that advertisement of so-and-so?'"

In publishing this book the methods of unreliability among some printers have been clearly demonstrated. For nearly two months the engraving was delayed because of delay of photographs, either excusable or negligence; then some delay of engravers; then about December 15, 1905, a contract was placed with a Magazine publishing company to be out by all means, by January first, with the option of the writer taking the work elsewhere, if not rushed through the last week in December. With utter disregard of all legal or moral obligation, in the absence of the writer, the book was not touched and almost as willful neglect for six weeks after January 1st, with no reasonable excuse, except, perhaps, the hope of a bigger price to rush them, at one and one half pay for all time over eight hours per day, while the author toiled nearer sixteen hours per day to hurry the work, for six weeks, at great expense, and loss, and at last had to demand his material, partly lost, or destroyed, and do much of the mechanical work himself, in order to get the work complete in short order. All his work, not being delivered, replevey suit was entered, and the manager immediately swore to an affidavit for a continuance for 15 days, for the lack of material evidence, which could not possibly have been true, under the circumstances, and proved to be false in the trial, and after every possible manner of demand, except by physical force, for three weeks, the Justice (?) decreed that no legal demand had been made. Such is the **weakness of the 15 day law,** and, frequently the processes of the wise men of the minor courts, in facing unmistakable facts and the editors of local concerns, that sometimes dominate in court more than evidence, facts and law; as they often try the cases before the hearing. So the author was compelled to reproduce some material, and go over the whole work at great loss of time and expense. **But, maybe, such things will not always be so.** Justice, brains, and law may, perchance, prevail sometimes, somewhere.

The following are some extracts from the contract: "Oklahoma City, Dec. 18, 1905." "Said booklet is to be six by nine inches, etc," "The cover is to be a good quality of S. & S. C. cover 20x25, 50-lb stock." "The inside pages are to be printed upon Calender Book paper, etc." "Ink on entire work to be of blue black of best quality, etc." "The work is to be done in a thorough workman like manner, etc." "The work shall be done and ready for delivery during the last week of December, 1905, if same can be accomplished, (by the F. M. Co.) If that is not possible, however, it shall be ready for delivery as soon thereafter as possible." (Written at bottom), In case of unavoidable delay, the said Dickerson may withdraw from this contract and take the work elsewhere." (Signed). "The F. M. Co., by R. A. W., Business Manager." Philip J. Dickerson.

The last clause was written by demand of the author, so that he could arrange to get his books by the last week in December, 1905, if the F. M. Company did not get them out immediately after December 18, who promised to write in two or three days, which they failed to do till Dec. 29, too late for the work to be taken else where to be printed by January 1st. And after the promise to give said books the exclusive time of the shop till printed, taking a well equipped shop about five or six days to complete by linotype and hand), nothing was done for nearly four weeks, except having set most of the linotype not over four or five days work for a skillful operator, and many printers are as negligent of their promises. At last driven to despair, in failing to get the work done at reasonable rates, the writer proceeded to publish the book himself, using only linotype-set composition, in about one week, and asks the people interested in the book to excuse this unavoidable delay, in no way his fault, as he tries always, under all circumstances, to make his word as good or better than a bond. But we can still all rejoice in the birth of the New State of Oklahoma just as this comes from the press.

If the author of the article in this paper will tell thinking men why it is necessary to have two or three little local papers in a small town, often scarcely able to support one rightly, except for partisan, political reasons, he will do a benevolence to modern civilization that no other has ever done. The writer gladly notes from the "Osage Chief," (Fairfax) referring to an exceedingly partisan article in this paper, which there is no desire to reprint here. "In our opinion if there is any one thing a small town should do in organizing, it is to avoid mixing politics into municipal government. For

---

NEW COTTAGE HOME OF L. B. BODWELL, HOMINY.

Mr. Bodwell is an old resident of the Osage, where he has been interested in business, but came to Hominy early in its building, where he erected a dwelling for his family, his wife and daughter, a young lady of vivacious, bright social qualities. Mr. Frank Pettit, who lives three miles northeast of Hominy, and has one of the best

(Photo by Alva Spiers.)

improved farms, of nearly 1,000 acres, in the Osage, married a daughter of Mr. Bodwell. Frank is a son of Judge Pettit of Pawhuska, and one of the broadest minded, most energetic Osage citizens. He does much of his own farming, besides leasing many acres of his fertile land. Mr. Bodwell is improving a beautiful home and garden and is one of the most substantial men of Hominy and the Osage, ready to advance their interests.

HISTORY OF THE OSAGE NATION

THE HOMINY MEAT MARKET.
Wm. McConnell, Proprietor, Furnishes all Kinds of Fresh, Dried Meats, Oysters, and Game in Season.

Mr. McConnell is a native of Ireland, but lived for 17 years in Thyer, Kansas, spending his time in the oil business and farming. He came to Hominy in 1904, under the direction of F. D. Closser & Co., oil men. He took charge of their work and machinery here, but he is now engaged in the butcher business for himself, and has a large patronage for the size of the town and community. He also conducts the "O. K." Livery barn, doing a general livery business. He owns property in Hominy, and expects great things from the rapid development of the Osage.

THE FIRST SHOE SHOP.

Mr. C. C. Hopkins, the first shoe and boot manufacturer of Hominy, is a native of Missouri, but came to Ralston, O. T., in 1900, where he was engaged in the general merchandise business till he came to Hominy, and established a shoe shop. **He manufactures a high-class boot and shoe for the order trade,** and does all kinds of repairing at most reasonable prices. He can claim the destinction of being the only manufacturer in town, besides the bakeries and blacksmiths, and will soon have to enlarge his business, as many have their boots made to order here, regardless of cost. His wife and little daughter, Lenora, now help to do much of the facing and wife and little daughter, Lenora, now help to do much of the facing and stitching. Visit them and see how you feel standing in his shoes or boots.

THE OSAGE BLACKSMITH.

Bert Patterson one of the village blacksmiths, was born in Kansas, but has lived in the Osage from boyhood, and attended school at the Pawhuska Agency. He came with his father, who was a Government Blacksmith, and taught Bert the trade, which he has long followed with success. He has the reputation of being the best steel and tool worker in the country, also a fine shoer of horses, often fitting up the race horses for the races, frequently held here on the straight and circle tracks. He is widely acquainted, and speaks Osage. His friends say he is a brother, and most ideal man, in his busines career.

---

our part, (rantankerous Republicans as we are) we would rather see Fairfax organized with a full board of progressive, public spirited democratic town builders that an equal number of republican politicians. Let us see to it that when Fairfax is organized that only the best men whose every interest is identified with the town are elected, and will work for the best interests of the town regardless of party affiliations."

Of course every man feels a loyal interest in his party's success, and perhaps justly so, but the intelligent citizens will no doubt, give their hands, votes and moral support to the men of greater honor, efficiency, and unbiased interest in the general welfare of the city and county government irrespective of party affiliations. In national and state politics, a true man may love his party for its principles, but in local government he will love his city and county more.

The permanent development of Osage county, when organized, and Pawhuska, her judicial seat, whose present and future prospects seem crowned with a halo of growth and glory, depends largely upon the clean, pure men, and government they present to the world in the early years of county and town organization.

HISTORY OF THE OSAGE NATION

The writer of this book has no party politics, nor does he care to have except as any party may represent, ad vocate and put into effect the highest principles of international, national, state, county, township and municipal government, upon a basis of individual merit, civic economy and pure, clean methods of politics in the sense the Greeks used the work **Politas** (long a), their citizens being intelligent enough each to govern himself and people, thousands of years ago, before being corrupted by methods of so-called scientific politics.

FAIRFAX, O. T.

Considering the very fertile soil all through this section, the large extent of country from which to draw her trade, and the present size of Fairfax after one year's growth, and the many excellent people among her population of near 400, you can quickly see that Fairfax is one of the best locations for a large, growing, prosperous town. It is appropriately named from her **FAIR** prospects. Quite a number of her people came from the historic, old trading post, Gray Horse, some miles southeast, where they were in business long before the location and survey of Fairfax.

The Baptist, M. E., and Presbyterian denominations have organized, and hold services in the school building, which was erected by popular subscription. The school is conducted on the scholarship certificate plan of $2 per month, paid in advance, by cash, or negotiable notes, for seven months, thus insuring school for that length of time. Prof. C. A. Haggart, principal, is a graduate of Ann Arbor, Mich. His assistant is Mrs. Kate Bristow, both successful teachers, with about 80 pupils enrolled. Fairfax is located on Salt creek, some miles north of the Arkansas river, in the richest prairie country in the Osage. This creek is larger than most creeks, and along its course northward is found much of the best land, and most costly improved farms. It is the most beautiful stream in Oklahoma, having a broad, rocky bed, and clear, blue waters, with many fish, and much game upon its well timbered banks and bottoms.

Fairfax townsite has been surveyed, and when approved by the Secretary of the Interior, the vacant lots will soon be sold. For a town so young she had many fine buildings, some of which are shown in these cuts. No town in the Osage has a fairer prospect of growing into a city of several thousand inhabitants. Many excellent people have already located here, and others still coming. Many of the fullbloods have well improved farms around the town. The Tall Chief family, mentioned elsewhere, live near town, one joining it on the south. They are an intelligent family, especially Eves Tall Chief, educated in the best schools and reported to be writing a dictionary of Osage dialect containing only about 700 words in all, but some of the family are addicted to strong drink, being near the line of old Oklahoma, where they can step over and get anything they want, and "eat, drink and be merry."

The department has just given a decision that the opening of the townsites to business, without bond or Indian license, will not entitle any man to deal in intoxicating drinks in the Osage any more than before such opening, but the same rule shall apply—a wise provision for all concerned.

Fairfax is located on a line of railroad running from Newkirk, O. T. to Pawnee and on to Oklahoma City. It is being heavily ballasted for a through freight line leaving the main line more free for passenger traffic. All lines of business are well represented. There is one **first class hotel**, the **Ponton House**, 3 restaurants, 2 barber shops, one of which has the **distinction of a boy barber, 13 years of age, a fine shaver,** having begun **to help his father, John Sherrill,** in his shop, at the age of ten.

HISTORY OF THE OSAGE NATION

He is perhaps the youngest barber in **America**. They also run a short order in connection. There are 3 drug stores, 2 banks, 2 groceries, 2 hardware and one furniture store, 1 harness shop, 4 general merchandise stores, 2 fine liveries, a blacksmith shop, a mill and grain elevator, and one well edited newspaper, the "Osage Chief," one lumber yard, a large meat market, in short, all lines necessary to make a growing, prosperous city. With a beautifully undulating hill westward, nicely draining the town toward the creek east the location is unsurpassed for healthfulness, fine water near the surface and many square miles of rich country to draw from, you will find here an opportunity to establish manufactures, or lease the best lands, with rapid growth.

All through the Osage land can be leased for periods, from one to five years to improve the land by breaking sod, fencing, building houses, planting orchards, etc. But improved lands can be leased on similar conditions to those in the states, money rent or 1-3 of grain, in the field, and ¼ of the cotton at the gin. While cattle raising is a leading industry in this section, as the cut of Mr. Bowers' herd suggests, farming is co-equal.

To illustrate the large scale farming in the Osage Mr. Geo. Chrisman has one of the largest farm leases in the country at one time 4,000 acres, both with a co-lessee, under cultivation. Having dissolved partnership, he now has only 2,000 acres plowed and cultivated, but expects to ploy 2,000 acres more next spring. He farms out his leases to others to plant and cultivate corn at 12½ cents per bushel, estimated in the field before gathering, and much corn all through the Osage averages long and large ears. At L. A. Wismeyer's store some ears were seen measuring from 12 to 14¼ inches, grown by W. R. Farbes. Manning Bros., farming on Little Chief in 1905, grew ears of corn weighing up to 2 pound and one ounce.

For two years a wave of reform seems to be surging back and forth even in politics, and civil rules more strictly applied. Tlections for the last three years, and thep rosecution of corruption in high places, indicate, to some degree, that a tidal wave of reform sentiment and ballots may sweep politcal corruption with all of its "rooters" and "suckers" from the arena of American statesmanship. At least the omens are encouraging to all true, liberty-loving Americans who believe more in purity of principle than in petty partisanship. Then society and business will demand only one well edited newspaper in each town, county or state as the case may be. But editors are not resopnsible for the thousands of unnecessary, poorly composed sheets, they are only victims of the social and political conditions of the times. The introduction into civil service rules the requirement of examination i none other language, than English, according to England's practice, in order to bring the brightest young men into the consular service by hard study, instead of by political preferment, is another of many signs of many signs of the times that party politics must gradually give way to individual principle and merit, on which social and civil progress should

When the president of Harvard, or Yale and Prof. James, of Northwestern Unievrsity, recommends the great metropolitan daily and weekly rest in all advanced stages of civilization.
newspapers as important to the student of sociology and history, to keep in touch with current facts and history reported in their voluminous columns of political, scientific, social and current-event sections, they did not mean to sanction the existence of two to twenty small papers where one could serve all these purposes far better with a

proportionately less cost, in advertising, which generally overruns their literary columns five to one. Again the vast amount of irreliable, unauthenticated, fictitious, manufactured stuff to fill up columns is another reason for few papers, and truer, better quality of stuff. Whole pages are often manufactured from scarcely a shadow, much less skeleton of truth and fact, just to serve some purpose of its writer, or publisher. The average of human life is too short, mind too sacred, thought too valuable to be burdened or confused daily or weekly by columns of worthless distractions, mentally enervating matter. After the daily struggle for bread there is far too little time for the best, none for the worst publications. "But," say the publishers of light, chaffy, reading stuff, "people desire it. They won't read books and better literature." Then you have caused it. They won'tpzqmO dURsBkbonUNuavhUfture." Then you have caused, by your contnuously feeding them husk chop, instead of well-ground grain. Those who cannot enjoy reading and re-reading books, mazazines and phamphlets of the best matter and forms, and retain their contents, are scarcely apt to remember, and profit by a mere glance at big sheets of paper printed each day or week to b thrown away th next because another is printed in its place. Local editors and papers are all right in serving their place and purpose, but surely can't expect everybody to think they are "the only cheese," "the only pebble on the beach." This is a free country, for every man to follow honstly, by the "Golden Rule," the pursuit of life, wealth and happiness, without baseless imputations, and interference of another. The writer does not expect all men to think alike on all things or anything. That would be heaven, millenial! Some are always antagonistic to others' plans and work, no matter what, so it be competition. If heaven wereb rought to earth by some, others would hurl the angels back to worlds beyond, or jump off to Jupiter, Mars or Moon, for new fields of eclusive operations, because heaven might take "three or four hundred dollars out of their business" that might "never return." Oh, how many growl because they want to occupy the whole kennel, or be the only noses in the trough. If some should not like the method of publishing the historical facts and resources in book form, etc., method of publishing the historical facts and resources in book form, etc., it is not, perhaps the fault of the book, made on the fairest ocnditions to its generous, intelligent subscribers, but the experience of the one opposed to it. Many spurn the Bible, throw it away as worthless, but where lies the fault of thinking and action? in them, or the Bible? Some might fail to keep, or to give out to the best advantag, finely illuustrated "Souvenir" brief history, biography and commercial book of their country, but it would not necessarily signify that it is not worth keeping for generations. Should one paint the brightest scenes of human life, its resources and possibilities with pen, printer's ink, engravers styles and book papyrus, for a consideration, it is far better to scatter the rough paths of living beings with roses, than to plant thorns and thistles of envy and jealousy in the ways of life, then to place free flowers, or a costly wreath upon man's casket, both of which he paid for years before he retired to his tomb. It is far better to be "oily tongued manipulators," of even failures in trying to bear the burdens of long-suffering communities, (long-suffering because overtaxed by worthless papers, and too temporary methods of advertising), than to have the double-tongue of a venemous serpent, both hissing and poking poison at everyone and evtrything, that the coil behind, imagines to come in its way, though you have no intention of intruding on its ground. It [continued on page 142]

HISTORY OF THE OSAGE NATION

The Yearly Roundup on the Akin Ranch—Near Fairfax.

Mr. A. G. Bowers is manager of the Ed Akin ranch, two miles east of Fairfax, containing 7,000 acres of fine grass land, also an additional 3,000 of cultivated farm lands 15 miles west, which sustains about 7,000 head of cattle, about 4,000 of which have been lately purchased for their ranch. He was formerly from Texas, was raised on a ranch, handling cattle and horses all his life, hence a broad experience in this industry.

He has been five years in the Osage, first year with Roy Hoss, then with Stone Breaker's, before becoming the manager of the present large ranch on the Osage, a cut of which is given, showing a "roundup" of only a small part of the heard. As the manager he has to see that cattle are kept together, the strays brought in, the fences kept in good condition, etc. He has six men assistants, all the time busy. John Morris, formerly from Texas, but ranched in Comanche county for Bill Hall for five years, but been in the Osage about five years in the employ of various ranchmen. Sam Smith, also a Texan by birth, has been in the ranch business for fifteen years, having been manager for several "cattle camps," which term is applied to the ranches in this country. Henry Riley, is a Texas boy and has handled many cattle, in the employ of several camps, for the last 15 years. George Dunnovan is also employed by Mr. Bowers on this ranch, a Texan also, but of late coming to the **Osage**.

These boys lead a typical ranchman's life, batching, with no females in the camp, each one taking turns in the cook tent with one general dish and bottle washer, Mr. Clint Wagoner. However, many ladies, on horseback, are usually found at the "roundups" of this camp as the boys are single, generally ladies' men and have many friends among the fair sex who enjoy the ride after the large herds and the romantic life of the camp for a few days. At the last "roundup" there were 48 persons including 13 ladies, to see the immense herd brought together. The ranchman's life, they claim, is far from being one of ease, as many suppose, but is one continuous round of riding and vigilance, having but little time for sports and reading.

About the only pastime being the humor manifest when gathered around the camp fire, vieing with each other in telling the biggest story. And every morning they have a free exhibition of "rabbit twisting" (?) They frequently refer to each other by the nicknames, "Rabbit Twister," "Steeplechasers," "Cow-waddies," "Hill Billies," and such like. Mr. Bowers and his boys are typical jolly ranchmen.

HISTORY OF THE OSAGE NATION

were better to calm or lap with an oily tongue the waters of the troubled seas of human lives than to explode a gas well, then set it on fire in their midst. It is as well to bury some men alive as to try to soil their honesty by false insinuation. Yet some would bury you alive if it were commercial gain to do so. The Kaw City Star reports that the Associated Press once had Washungah, chief of the Kaws, buried, and his funeral ceremony in detail, even the number of his tribe that followed in mourning to his last resting place. It was a real Associated Press funeral story. But "Wash" appeared in town soon afterwards, and was asked why he was reported dead and buried. "Uh! uh!!" he replied, "Paper man d—n fool, he lie, lie, lie; Wash all time best—phist."

The article that forced this reference to the much abused, and much needed Journalism of today, was either hatched in ignorance or born in narrow-minded, soul contracted jealousy, or both together. It seems partly the former, but mostly the latter. When the writer begun to gather material for this book for the purpose expressed on the introductory page, called at the printing room of the managing editors, of this paper and explained his intention, and contract for the publication, and asked an estimate on the work. He was informed by one that they could not do the work at the price the writer was contracting to do it for, that there ough to have been a higher rate placed on it, and that he didn't believe in such publications, but couldn't do the work any way at the writer's rate to which he replied in a few remarks on inconsistency of such a position. The other managing editor brought out a Special Historical and Commercial Write-up, of one of the leading papers of Chickasha, I. T., where he was working at the time and informed the writer that they asked and got about $50, fifty dollars per page on $5,000 copies of a three newspaper column page special edition, scarcely longer than broad, and very ordinary printing and paper, with scattering cuts, all together at from five to ten times the cost to their patrons as the "oily tongued author solicited from from the generous, intelligent and wealthy people of the Osage, with far better form than can usually be produced in a local office. No wonder they sounded the alarm against anything that doesn't go through their hands. And no one ever had any reason to suppose this laborous undertaking was connected with their office, nor does he believe anyone ever seriously thought so. Mr. Managers you have just as good a sheet as thousands of others of its kind; perhaps better than some, but calm your agitated mind, for the writer has no desire to be connected with a little local paper, where there is more than one in a community of less than ten thousand population, unless to do the mechanical work of more permanent publications. If your paper is good, osmething better might cultivate a taste and patronage for it, both i reading and advertising. Real education does much for some things.

A true sayink:

"A little knowledge is a dangerout thing.
Drink deep or taste not the Pierian Spring."

I can forgive you for thinking that this praise for "Tom, Dick and Harry" could be destroyed before birth from the printing press. But how you erred! It came through all right and still lives to bless, we hope, the Osage people and the stranger who wants to know the real facts of history and resources from sources he can believe. They are triplets, 3,000 well formed copies, strong. Some will live and talk perhaps, when we have passed beyond, to give account of our editorials.

The method of printing this book is only a means of giving a greater number the benefit of its publication. Some may say: "Oh, t's an advertsing scheme!" So it is in part. All history, geography and biography, based upon the facts of a country and people are advertising in the broadest and best sense, whatever the object of their publication. The gray matter of brains, thinking powers may be used in advertising as literary in composition a sthe best books, magazines, and journals of modern civilization. At least this is the consenses of opinion of the best bueines and tion. At least this is the consenses of opinion of the best busness and profesional people in towns and countries everywhere, who do the most of their advertising in special editions of books, pamphlets, largely circulated magazines, in condenses form to be kept. Even the extra editions of little local papers must be printed in more condenses magazine form to be sent out broadly, if perchance they can get some failing list, well knowing that the narrow limits, of their little local papers are ineffective if not worthless for general advertising of its country's resources and advantages to hundreds or thousands of miles away. For few go beyond the country, or town, perhaps, as every town or village has her own paper, or two that serves its purpose if it discretely attends strictly to its own business, and furnishes some mental food for its reader's intelligence. A few exchanges go abroad but no papers, ever advertise, specifically, other than their own sections, without increased subscription lists or big money for their columns. The writer has seen many finely, costly illustrated books or pamphlets of towns and countries, in which the leading newspapers put full page displays of their presses, offices, etc., their intelligent editors, knowing the greater results of having some concise, illustrated book forms to set before the world the best of their town and section. And these pamphlets are usually written and published by men of experience and education, at great cost of time and expense to themselves, who have no desire to be connected with any less permanent, less literary publications. If their work is a "fake," or "representation false," and "contracted," "big circulation that never matures," it is because of the dishonesty of some individual, [continued on page 144]

VIEW OF FAIRFAX, O.T., LOOKING EAST.

HARRIS AND SAPP.
Bakery, Confectionary, Cigars, Tobacco and Groceries.

Mr. Harris was formerly from Texas, where he was engaged in the merchantile business about 15 years before coming to the Osage. He has been a licensed Indian Trader 5 years, at Pawhuska three and at Fairfax two where he soon located after Fairfax was surveyed. Mr. Sapp come to the Osage one year ago from Missouri the two formed a partnership with Mr. Harris. They are much interested in the growth of Fairfax and the opening of the Osage to the highest development. They are building up a fine, general grocery business.

HISTORY OF THE OSAGE NATION

PONTON HOUSE.
J. R. Ponton, Prop.

Mr. and Mrs. J. R. Ponton, owners and conductors, of this hotel are formerly from N. C., but lived for eighteen years near Wichita, Kansas from which place they came near Chandler, Old Oklahoma where he farmed for eight years; thence from there to Gay Horse where they entered into the mercantile business for two years. Then on the location of the townsite of Fairfax they came here and established this first class and only hotel in the town, and also the first meat market, the "Ponton Market" where they deal in the best fresh and cured meats and game and fish in season.

They are a fine family and make many friends among their guests. Their menu or bill of fare is the best the market affords with every cordial treatment to the traveling public. They have only one single child, a daughter, who is a fine horse back rider and considerable musical talent.

J. H. DULL,
The Blacksmith.

Mr. J. H. Dull the Pioneer blacksmith of Fairfax was born in Jamestown, Doniers County, Mo., in 1878. Worked as a farm hand until 12 years of age, when he located at Old Gray Horse, Osage Nation, where he did his first work in a blacksmith shop. When Fairfax was located he was one of the first on the ground with a shop and has pushed the town and his business to the front in every way possible. He makes a specialty of horse shoeing and plow work and treats all customers in a way that will make them lasting friends and guarantees satisfaction in all his work that goes out—a true "village blacksmith."

---

who perhaps, has been well tutored by the "fakerism" and false pretenses of some little editorial or publishing concerns that presume to live by such methods. The writer has formed a business acquaintance with many good men of the editorial and printing profession, but not all the "printer's devils," in the trade are by any means angels, as the intelligent thinking classes well know; and are able to decide what is best for them, and their town and country, regardless of any warning from such sources. While the wirter has often felt the sting of deception from some others, he has the conscientious, perhaps egotistical pride in the fact that he has never willfully or knowingly tried to use either of these contemptible weaknesses of human character with either man or woman. Who uses such traits to make headway is not a man, only an imitation, a mere thing; a very unnecessary thing. We will concede that there have been many fakes in "special write-ups," but certainly not more than in many local papers and other commercial lines. The writer was the first, so far as he knows, to combine many historical facts with true commercial sketches in order to make a publication worth its cost and keeping to a community. If the method, which is unequalled for giving time, cost and mental toil, for the amount received for same. The main purpose of some in life, is to give as little service as possible for value received, others as much as possible, even sepnding life in benevolence, but the former class cannot comprehend the actions of he latter, but judge them by their own narrow standard. All things can be raised to a higher degree of benefit to men by the man of ability and honor essential to lift them above the ordinary. Some would-be editors imagine they are using brain power in their compositions, and critical articles, when they taste, to others, like calve's brains, or scrambled eggs of a stale cold storage quality; brought from exchange storage, when a fresh supply fails to be inspired in the pigeon holes of their personal criticisms. Many men in local offices think they are thinkers, when they are fine typetinkers. They do not think enough to ever wear one hair off their heads, a bad temper and conscience too condemning to ever become fat or rich.

"An Embarrassed Editor was asked: "Why are all millionaires represented to be either fat or bald-headed?" asks a correspondent. "Really, this places us in rather an embarrassing position. We haven't a hair on our head and tip the scales at 225 pounds avoirdupois, so we might be called both fat and bald-headed. Your question, however, is easily answered. To be fat a man must have a clear conscience, a good digestion and an even temper. Baldness is usually caused by the gray matter of the brain circulating too rapidly and wearing off the roots of the hair. A man thus blessed by nature can not help get rich."—(Ex.)

The author of the sore-head articles has clearly lost no hair by arduous study, and thinking. If he ever gets to the heaven of knowledge, happines and wealth hem ust shed many yet. But he has only made the mistake of putting on a different colored powder than that he supposed in his haste and dim light. A girl dressing under such conditions to receive her beau, when she heard his call rushed for her powder to put on the finishing touches, then entered the parlor, looking as she thought her best, and vivaciously, but unconcious of her minstrel appearance, entertained the one before whom she should have made her best appearance, in her snow-white robes and blondine tresses. But on his adieu she returned to her boudoir, to see how pretty she had been. Discovering her mistake in using pulverized charcoal instead of cream powder, as supposed, she fell into a hysterical swoon, and the Arkansas City Traveler said "she never smiled again." Moral—Mr. Article Writer, when you get back to your editorial den, just see what kind of powder you really put on in your unwarranted haste, and darkness.

The Fairfax Home of J. B. Wilson
The Business Block of Mr. J. B. Wilson.

Mr. J. B. Wilson is a native of Missouri, but lived for fourteen years in Nebraska; afterwards moved to Texas, from whence he returned to Chautauqua county, Kansas. He came to the Osage about 1889, as a blacksmith by trade, and first conducted a shop at Gray Horse, about two years. He married Miss Mary Herridge, a daughter of Edward and Julia Herridge.

Mr. Herridge was of English nationality, his wife was Julia Lessart, of French and Osage ancestry, who has one of the most courtly homes in the Osage. Mr. Wilson

Business Block of J. B. Wilson, Dealer in General Merchandise, Dry Goods, Clothing, Groceries, Flour and Feed.

obtaining an intermarried citizen's right to broad and fertile acres of land became a successful farmer for some years. Their farm home appears in cut. They have one of the best improved farms in the Osage. They have moved to Fairfax and built a comfortable, pretty home, and fine business place, and opened a **large general merchandise business, handling dry goods, clothing, groceries, flour and feed.** They have four children, two boys, and two girls. He is a very progressive, congenial man, in his business and social life, and is fast becoming a leader in his lines. He is an active member of the Odd Fellows. His farm home is located at the head of Gray Horse creek, with 640 acres in cultivation. Few citizens have better ideas of what the Osage is becoming than Mr. Wilson, and no one can add more to the growth of Fairfax than he.

The Farm Residence of Mr. J. B. Wilson, Fairfax.

FAIRFAX GRAIN AND ELEVATOR COMPANY.
Henry McGraw, Pres. L. A. Wismeyer, Vice-president; Thomas McGraw Secy.

This elevator and feed mill in connection with a 20,000 bushels was erected upon the Santa Fe Railway. It was the first elevator built in the Osage reservation and began with a capital stock of $1,500. Last fall (1905) they were handling about 1200 bushels of grain per day. McGraw brothers are from Ponca City, O. T. and are young men of energetic business qualities, and with Mr. Wismeyer, who is mentioned with all the largest interests in Failfax, will help to make the town second to nono in the Osage.

ROSS AND HUNSAKER.
Furniture and Undertaking.

Mr. A. C. Hunsaker is from Missouri, where he followed the profession of teacher for ten years before coming to the Osage in 1900. Since coming he farmed one year, and then established a mercantile business in Ralston, carrying a line of hardware, furniture and undertaking in addition. When the Santa Fe railroad came through he moved to Fairfax where he opened the same line of business, carrying the only stock of furniture in the town to the present time. Mr. U. A. Ross was his partner in Ralston as in Fairfax. He is also a Missourian where he was reared on a large farm, and stock ranch. They have good property in the towns and are doing a thriving business and greatly interested in the growth of Fairfax.

HISTORY OF THE OSAGE NATION

The Large Business Block of L. A. Wismeyer, Fairfax.

Mr. Wismeyer has been in the Osage country since 1884, over 22 years. Having first clerked at the Indian Agency, Pawhuska, seven years, he is well versed in Osage affairs. He first established a business in Pawhuska, then at Gray Horse, for some years. But on the founding of Fairfax he moved his store building (see cut) and business to Fairfax in 1903, where he is doing one of the largest general business done by any man in the Osage Nation and has one of the finest homes ever built in this coutry, a mansion. He is interested in the Fairfax Grain and Elevator Co., the First National bank just organized, and doing the only lumber business in Fairfax. He is one of the leading spirits in every public enterprise, a man of experience, strong intelligence and indomitable business energy, employing several clerks. This cut shows only part of his lumber yard under the management of Mr. F. D. Waugh. Mr. Wismeyer is familiar with much of the history of the Osage people, and a most excellent man, and citizen to advance Fairfax to the front. Miss Wismeyer, his daughter, is a most graceful rider, being long accustomed to the saddle, and considered one of the belles of the reservation, and a fine type of the western girl. Fairfax has a quintette troop of young lady riders, of leading families, some of whose names the writer can not recall, but the fairest of Fairfax, who, while riding abreast, present an attractive military view.

Harvesting in Oklahoma.

The Elegant Home of L. A. Wismeyer, Fairfax, O. T.

THE OSAGE BANK, FAIRFAX, OKLAHOMA.

The Osage Bank of Fairfax, was the first bank in the town. It was organized in 1902, and does a general banking business, handling the accounts of business men, stockmen, farmers, and extending courteous treatment to all, have won a rightly

merited place in the confidence of its patrons. Its stockholders are: S. B. Berry, G. W. Berce, J. P. Girard, W. N. Quarles. The bank building of these gentlemen and

HISTORY OF THE OSAGE NATION

financial leaders as W. H. Todd, E. T. Quarles, J. J. Ballard, J. T. Plummer, J. H. Trimm, Quarles. The bank building of these gentlemen and financial leaders as shown in this cut is the first and only stone building so far, in the town, and a finely constructed bulding. Excellent building stone are gotten nearby and many stone buildings perhaps be erected in the future. These gentlemen will welcome you coming and extend every courtesy consistent with progress and good banking principles.

W. N. Ballard, Livery, Feed and Sale Barn.
Horses Bought and Sold.

Mr. Ballard grew up on a farm in Missouri, but came to Gray Horse in 1892, where he ran a stage route, and livery business, also dealing in horses. When Fairfax started in 1902, he moved his interests here. He was one of the first settlers, and built the first fine livery building in the Osage, as shown in cut, where he is doing a prosperous business. He has just completed a costly cottage home on part of his block west of barn. He was married to Miss Daisy Girard, a Kansas girl, at Gray Horse, in 1900. He has spent his life in the horse and livery business of which he is fond and experienced; and a congenial man to meet in business, an energetic and progressive citizen for his town and the Osage.

FIRST NATIONAL BANK OF FAIRFAX, OKLA

The personnel of this bank, which was organized in the fall of 1905, speaks much for its strength and success. A sketch of **Mr. Wismeyer** is given on another page. Mr. Woody, a native of Texas, has been in the Osage leasing and farming with success. **Mr. Pasche** is from St. Joe, Mo. He started as a huckster boy in grocery store in LaCrosse, Wisconsin, later came to Wheatland, Iowa, where he did a general merchandise business. Then came to Davenport, Ia., and started his banking career as the cashier of the Iowa National Bank of Davenpot, but afterwards accepted a better position ith the St. Joe Stock Yards bank, of which he is now president and a millionaire. Mr. Hoss came from Illinois to Oklahoma nine years ago, and was engaged in farming, stock raising and shipping both grain and cattle. He has lived at

THE FIRST NATIONAL BANK OF FAIRFAX.
L. A. Wismeyer, Pres., J. M. Woody and Chas. Pasche, Vice Prest., Raymond N. Hoss, Cash., Julius F. Rochau, Asst. Cash.

Stillwater and at Ralston, O. T. He is now farming and stock raising on a 4,000 acre ranch in West Osage with great success, but has accepted the position of cashier of this bank. Mr. Rochau, born near Redridge, Ia., raised on a farm, and entered the banking business in the same bank with Mr. Pasche in Davenport, Ia., at the age of 18, but came to Fairfax Oct., 1905, to become the assistant cashier of the First National, which will do all lines of conservative banking, but making a specialty of cattle loans.

The Fine Home of Mr. F. D. Waugh.—Fairfax.

HISTORY OF THE OSAGE NATION

F. D. Waugh whose beautiful home appears with this sketch, is the Manager of the Lumber Department of the Wismeyer General Merchandise business. He is a fine type and native of New York state from which he has just returned on a pleasant visit with kin and friends. He left there in '83, came to Oklahoma in 1892, where he has been in the lumber, cattle and farming business, near Ponca City, where he was a lucky winner in the run on the Cherokee Strip, and filed as No. 3, Soldier's Declaratory, and got a fine farm, ½ mile from Ponca station, for which he later received $6,000, and the same lately sold for $10,000. Mr. Waugh served three years as a Federal soldier in the Civil War, under Gen. Bank, 19th Army Corps. He has two daughters and one son who is now in South Texas. Mr. Waugh manages the only lumber yard in Fairfax, October, 1905). He has about 700 head of cattle in feeding, and over 8000 acres leased for their range. He is one of the many good men and citizens of this section.

The gentlemen composing this firm are C. L. Goad, N. H. Farrell and S. T. Dawson. They formed the company in August, 1905, in an equal partnership business and carry **full line of Hardware and Implements,** of Brown's **Mfg. Co., and Oliver Chilled Plows, etc..** Also a fine line of harness. Mr. Farrell is a citizen of the Osage, a son of John Farrell, of Irish nationality. His mother was Miss Mary Canville, of French and Osage ancestry. He was raised on a fertile farm on the Arkansas river. He married Miss Laura Goad, the sister of the senior member of the firm. Mr. Goad is a native of Kansas, but has been farming in the Osage about fourteen years. Mr. Dawson, the silent partner, is also a Kansan, but recently came to the Osage, and

entered this firm. These boys are building up a fine business in this line. Mr. Farrell is a fine type of the Osage descendants and one of the few young men of the citizens that have launched out in the mercantile business and **is worthy of all confidence and**

HISTORY OF THE OSAGE NATION

patronage, with his co-partners. They own valuable property in town and Mr. Farrell has a fine farm in the Arkansas valley.

Mr. H. G. Burt has one of the larger stocks of general merchandise in Fairfax. He is a native of Missouri and did a mercantile business in Kansas City prior to coming to the Osage eighteen months ago. He is well fitted by training and experience for his general business. He owns valuable property in town, including his one-half block appearing in the cut. **He carries a full line of dry goods, furnishings, groceries, produce, and provisions.** He and Mr. Jenness, his clerk, are kept busy selling goods to their growing patronage.

OSAGE JUNCTION.

Is just south of Hominy, in the Arkansas river valley. Here a branch line of the railroad runs down the rich valley to Tulsa, I. T., and to Muscogee. It is only four miles from Cleveland and has two hotels, and one general store, run by **GEO. H. SAXON & COMPANY, U. S. Indian Traders,** with a livery barn in connection. **B. M. Evans is postmaster,** and T. M. Alby, proprietor of the **Metropolitan Hotel** over the store, **The Osage Inn,** a large railroad hotel and café is under the management of Mr. A. Duke. There is also a section house and small round house, and a depot building.

The Morledge Livery, Feed and Sale Barn, as shown in the cut, is owned jointly by L. B. Morledge and W. G. Lynn, who built the barn in May, 1905, and one of the best in the Osage country. Mr. Morledge and son, W. R., now conduct the livery barn, Mr. Lynn having sold his interest in this part of the business. They are natives of Ohio, but have been in the Osage for thirteen years, in the cattle business, both of which they still conduct, with financial success. Their business place shows

pride and push for their town and section. They are enthusiastic in all public enterprises for Fairfax. Such men will ensure the growth and prosperity of the town.

HISTORY OF THE OSAGE NATION

Miss Morledge, his daughter, is one of the most graceful horesback riders among the young ladies of Fairfax.

BURBANK, O. T.

Travelig north up the beautiful valley of Salt creek (perhaps so-called because of some saline springs along it) we pass Mr. Jim George's before we reach the pretty location of Burbank Station, lying at the base of the towering hills westward and touching the rich valley, hemmed by the grovelines stream of blueish water, with crescent bend to the east, all upon the fertile farm of Mr. Anthony Carlton, who has platted a 20-acre townsite from the station west. Here Mr. McCorkle, and son, built the first dwelling and store, is postmaster and acting depot agent as no operator is here at present. There are a number of families in the village, who have built a school house where Miss Lillie Shields teaches about 30 pupils, and where different sects hold services at times. It is a fine location for a town to build rapidly in the near future. Already a large elevator is built to store and handle the large grain trade. It

A View of Burbank, Okla., Looking Northeast

appears in cut wit a mammoth pile of corn to the left, and Mr. Corkle's store between them, with Mr. Carlton's home in the distance beyond the creek. These business men will welcome any legitimate industry here, where there is a most excellent country to sustain it. As you pass up the beautiful broad creek, you can see the well improved farms, (in order), of Chas. Donovan, Stewart Mongrain, Joseph Pearson, Frank DeNoya, Jr., Tom Hall, son-in-law of Frank DeNoya, Sr., Jake DeNoya, Mr. Hickmon, also son-in-law of Mr. DeNoya, who lives just above him, Mr. Roach, Mr. Barber, Mr. Sam Roach and Geo. Carlton. all well-to-do farmers ready to make Burbank a flourishing little town, all of whom the writer would gladly give a sketch, but has not the facts at hand to do so. Write Mr. McCorkle or Mr. Carlton for any information. They will gladly serve you, and give every inducement to other industries.

HISTORY OF THE OSAGE NATION

Mr. Anthony Carlton.

Mr. Anthony Carlton, whose home appeas in connection herewith, is located just one half mile east from Burbank station, owns the land upon which the station is located, and the townsite of 20 acres which are platted, and lots being leased to any

The Home of Anthony Carlton.

desiring to locate business or homes here. Mr. Carlton is the son of Mrs. Augustine Donovan, the wife of Chas. Donovan, who was formerly Mrs. Carlton. Mr. Anthony Carlton is said to be one of the most model men among the Osage citizens, a good man, a model father and husband. He married Miss Mary Plomondon, also of Osage ancestry, the daughter of Mr. and Mrs. Moses and Clemmy Plomondon. She is a medium fair blonde and shows no characteristics of Indian ancestry of which both she and her husband are only distant descent. She is a most excellent wife, homekeeper and mother of three fair, beautiful children, all girls, Marie, Ethel and Francis. Mr. Carlton is an extensive farmer, and raises many stock. His farm lies on the Salt creek bottoms, and second bottoms, the richest land in the Osage. He has many young fruit trees growing and other good improvments. He will gladly welcome any legitimate business and industry desiring to locate at Burbank. The writer had the pleasure of the hospitality of Mr. Carlton, Donovan, and Mongrain for a night and day while seeing Burbank's beautiful and rich surroundings.

THE MERCHANTS OF BURBANK, O. T.

Ira McCorkle, the only merchant up to 1906, of Burbank, was born in Polk county, Indiana, 1861, came to Pulaski county, Mo., in 1877, was married to Miss Martha A. Sanders, Oct. 22, 1882, and had a family of seven children, six of whom are still living. Coming to Oklahoma in 1901 he first engaged as foreman during the construction of the Eastern Oklahoma R. R. till its completion, then went to merchandising at Burbank, Jan. 12, 1903, where he was the first, except Osage citizens, to make improvements in this vicinity. Then the R. R. Co. built a depot and the Kaw City Mill and Elevator Co. erected a strong 10,000 bushel capacity elevator, and 2,000 per day. Being located in the best grain producing section of the Osage, they ship more grain per capita population than any other point, as there are no full bloods here, and many of the thrifty intermarried citizens cultivate their own well improved farms. Mr. McCorkle started with little capital, but is rapidly inceasing his trade, and here is a fine opening for other enterprises to build up the town, and lease lots till Mr. Carlton can deed them some future time. Most of the Osage descendants

General Merchandise & Hardware Store of McCorkle Burbank, O. T.

are only one-eighth, or sixteenth, and mostly excellent people, rich and stylish with whom any one could associate with culture; and honorable in their dealings with each other and stranger. Mr. McCorkle and his family belong to the Christian church and gladly welcome all services here, and in the school house and church about four miles southwest, with 26 scholars, both recently built by enterprising people. Besides Mrs. Jas. George, he has two other daughters, Mrs. Nora (G. L.) Wayman, and Mrs. Dora (G. E.) Waller, both married in Pulaski county, Mo. His son, Robert, married Miss Lula Peterson of Kay county, O. T., all of whom now live at Burbank. Mr. McCorkle and his family are congenial, hospitable people, and furnish the only hotel accommodations so far, in the town, over his store and postoffice. He will gladly answer any inquiries for location at Burbank.

The Home of Mr. S. J. Mongrain.

Mr. S. J. Mongrain, a part of whose farm residence appears in this cut has a prominent historical connection with the Osage people and country. He is a decendant of one of the earliest citizen families.

His grandfather was Newell Mongrain, a Frenchman who came to the Osages among the French fur traders with the Choutean family while in Missouri, and first lived in St. Louis where he owned property. Mr. S. J. Mongrain's father came with the

Osages to Neosho county, St. Paul, or the Old Osage Missions where he died. He was married three times. He was one-half Osage, his mother being a full blood. He was United States Governmental Interpreter from sixteen years of age till he lied in 1865. The man of this sketch is one of four living children. He was schooled in the Osage

Mission in Kansas. came here two years after this section was set apart for the Osage and lived on Big Caney for seven years, then came to his present location and kept batch for five years as a ranchman, but at last concluded that life would be more delightful on the ranch with acompanion and sought and wed the heart and hand of Miss Cornelia Means of Pawhuska, a full white girl, and has three children. He had two fine, fertile farms joining on Salt Creek with good improvements in houses, farms and orchards of all varieties of fruits. He has about 700 acres of land in cultivation and keeps two hundred head of cattle and about one hundred horses. He is a pleasant hospitable man to be and converse with. His family spends much time at Olathe Kansas to school their children.

THE FIRST VILLAGE BLACKSMITH, R. C. NORRIS, the first and only blacksmith in the vicinity, at Burbank, is a native of Kentucky. He has been blacksmithing about 45 years, beginning when a small boy, even beginning to shoe horses at nine years of age in Cumberlad county, Kentucky. His father was a blacksmith. He came to the "Five Civilized Tribes" 28 years ago' and wielded his trade at various places in the Territory. He made the run in the first opening of old Oklahoma, where he got a claim 12½ miles from Oklahoma City. But during the three dry years he abandoned it, thinking it worthless, allowing another to take possession. But six months afterwards was offered $5,000 if he would prove up on it and sell it. Now it is worth many thousands of dollars. He came to the Osage in 1905 from Mokamah, I. T., and is doing a good blacksmithing business.

He lost his wife in 1895, but has five children with him to make his home a bright and happy one.

"Be it ever so humble, there's no place like home."
By courtesy of Mr. Chas. Donovan, of Burbank, Oklahoma Territory.

The Evolution or four stages of an Osage citizen's Home. First.—The log cabin, at left, built in the '70's. Second.—Enlarged. Third.—The Large Barn. Fourth.—The Mansion Home of Sylvester J. Soldani, one of the First Families of the Osages.

Mr. Chas. Donovan, who lives one mile above Burbank Station, was formerly from Illinois, but lived some years in southern Nebraska. He came to the Osage country about '86; and soon won a most amiable and intelligent lady, Mrs. Augustine Carlton, the mother of Anthony Carlton. She has the reputation of being one of the most cultured women, and fluent conversationalists among the Osage citizens. Mr. Donovan won a prize in winning the hand and help of such a lady. He is one of the most congenial gentlemen in the Osage, and a most successful farmer and stockman, farming some of the most fertile valley land of Salt Creek. He has only two children, both boys, Charley and Jesse. Mr. Donovan is one of the men in the Osage country who had an exciting experience with the notorious trio, Doolin, Wilson and Star, who attempted to hold up a Santa Fe train at White Eagle, but failed by information being given to the crew, who opened the throttle and ran past the gang. They then made their escape by taking two black cavalry horses from the regular soldiers stationed at Ponca City. They came east, stopping on the farm of Mr. Donovan to change horses leaving him an exhausted bay pony, but only after a fierce battle in which about forty shots were fired, 20 apiece. When ordered by Mr. Donovan to leave his horse they began firing. He rushing into his house, seized his rifle and taking his stand upon his porch fired as long as they were in sight, wounding one, and perhaps two, while he narrowly escaped the well aimed shots of the desperadoes, halted at 800 yards distance, by watching the smoke of their guns and quickly jumping from side to side. The bullet holes still show in his front porch, and three in and around a window where they supposed he was first taking aim, and two within a few inches of where he was standing near a side door. Historians herald the brave deeds of generals and men in battle, with comrades on each side, but few excel the heroism of Mr. D. standng along in the defense of his home and horses.

OSAGE TOWNSITE BILL.
Passed, as an Amendment to Indian Appropriation Bill, March 3, 1905.

That there shall be created an Osage Townsite Commission consisting of three members, one of whom shall be the United States Indian Agent at the Osage Agency, one to be appointed by the chief executive of the Osage tribe and one by the Secretary of the Interior, who shall receive such compensation as the Secretary of the Interior may prscribe to be paid out of the proceeds of the sale of lots sold under this act.

That the Secretary of the Interior shall reserve from selection and allotment the south half of section four and north half of section nine, township twenty-five north, range nine east, of the Idian Meridian, Mississippi including the town of Pawhuska, which, except the land occupied by the Indian school buildings, the agency reservoir, the agent's office, the Council building and the residences of agency employees, and a twenty-acre tract of land including the Pawhuska cemetery shall be surveyed, apprised and laid off into lots, blocks, street and alleys by the Townsite Commision, under rules and regulations prescribef by the Secretary of the Interior, business lots to be twenty-five feet wide and residence lots fifty and sold at public auction, after due advertisement, to the highest bidder by said Townsite Commission under such rules and regulations as may be prescribed by the Secretary of the Interior, and the proceeds of such sale to be placed to the credit of the Osage tribe of Indians: Provided, that said lots shall be appraised at their real value exclusive of improvements thereon or adjacent thereto, and the improvements appraised separately. And provided, further, that any person, church, school or other association in possession of any of said lots and having permanent improvements thereon, shall have a preference right to purchase the same at the appraised value, but in the case the owner of the improvements refuses or neglects to purchase the same. Then such lots shall be sold at public auction at not less than the appraised value, the purchaser at such sale to have the right to take possession of the same upon paying the occupant the appraised value of the improvements. There shall in like manner be reserved from selection and allotment one hundred and sixty acres of land, to conform to the public surveys, including the buildings now used by the licensed traders and others, for a townsite at the town of Hominy; and the south half of the northwest quarter and the north half of the southwest quarter of section seven, township twenty-four north, range six east, for a townsite at the town of Fairfax, and the northeast corner, section thirteen, township twenty-four, range five east, consisting of ten acres, to be used for cemetery purposes; and two townsies of one hundred and sixty acres each on the line of the Midland Valley Railroad Company adjacent to stations on said line, not less than ten miles from Pawhuska. And the town lots at said towns of Fairfax and Hominy and at said townsites on the line of the Midland Valley Railroad shall be surveyed, appraised and sold the same as provided for town lots in the town of Pawhuska.

**Mr. and Mrs. James B. George with
Their Six Fine Sons and Daughters**

He has a fine ordchard of apples, peaches, plums cherries, grapes etc., surrounding the house. He has one of the oldest large barns, built of palisades and logs of large size, but has erected another of large dimensions with cribs or bins holding about 10,000 bushels all full this year. His corn crop of 300 acres will yield about 40 bushels to the acre or nearly 10,000 bushels and his two sons will have about 8000 bushels more. He also keeps a herd of 400 or 500 cattle and about 100 head of horses and mules. With their sons and daughters near them it is an ideal country home and happy family where hospitality and congeniality are apples of gold painted in silver frames. Only James M. is married. He wed Miss Roxanna, October 1, 1903, the amiable daughter of Mr. McCorkle, the merchant of Burbank and took her to his cosy cottage on his fine farm by the old home, and baby James (grand jr.) George adds another link in the family lineage since October last. Mr. George is of Ossage decent but of so advanced degree that he inherits but little Osage blood and a most excellent progressive young man. His kodak took the Burbank views.

Mr. George, who lives about half way between Remington and Burbank is one of the most prominent farmers in this section. He first married Miss Marguerite Carlton of Osage ancestry by whom he had four children, two boys and two girls, James, Jr., Sylvestea, Mary and Ruby. After her death he married Mrs. Mary Mongrain, the widow of James Mongrain who had three children, Edith, Rose and Louis, a boy who died while a baby. The accompanying cut shows Mr. and Mrs. George with his two sons and daughters, Ruby and Mamie and his wife's two daughters, Edith and Rose Mongrain, party taken at Mr. Carmel Academy at Wichita, where the three young ladies are now attending school.

Mr. and Mrs. James George, Jr.

The Mongrain family is one of the noted families of the Osage citizens frequently mentioned in their treaties and laws. Miss Edith a most lovely character died while attending North Missouri Academy at Salsberry Mo. Mr. Gongres's two sons are still with him. James, Jr., married a Miss Roxie McCorkle, of Burbank, and lives near his father, 2 miles from the station.

Mr. George has one of the best improved farms an the reservation on Salt Creek.

The beautiful home of Mr. and Mrs. James George.

HISTORY OF THE OSAGE NATION

CLEVELAND Just Across the Arkansas River from the Osage, Which Will Equal This in Oil and Gas.

REMINGTON, O. T.

In proceeding north on the railroad up Salt Creek valley, about 8 or 10 miles from Fairfax, we reach Remington station, where the **COUNTRY MANSION HOME of Louis Leonard DeNoya** is located, one-quarter mile from the station. His place is known as the X-Bar, (X with a bar under it) ranch. He is the son of Frank and Martha DeNoya, the latter still living at Bartlesville, I. T. His home built here four years ago is one of the finest country dwellings in the western states, costing over $9,000.

The fine double-deck verandas all around the outside cost alone nearly $2,000, an adeal country dwelling.

It has 18 large, beautiful rooms, elegantly furnished at some thousands of dollars' cost. Moquette and Axminster rugs, Brussels and other fine carpets cover the hard, smooth floors. A Steinway piano and Pianola costing $1,000, for his parlor, besides another fine piano for the sitting room, and children's practice; a Regina Music Cabinet, costing $250 in the reception room and a $100 solid brass bedstead in one room with finest make of mahogany and oak furniture for other rooms show the elegance of his home. Each of his children, Frederick, Clement (nicknamed Budge), Josephine and Ruby each have a room with their names printed on the doors. Four more beautiful and bright children could nowhere be found in one home. Their mother, who was Miss Josephine Revard before marriage, and a handsome, bright, devoted mother, was lost by a sad accident from a runaway team, near her home, one year ago. Mr. DeNoya has lived here nine years, and runs a general store and postoffice. He is just completing a department store, and bank building, and three pretty cottages for employes. He has a private school in books and music for his children under the instruction of Miss Mable Herriman of Pawnee.

The large east room, first floor, is the billiard room with table, cues, etc., for friends who enjoy this game. Would that all games could be confined to the home for innocent recreation with select friends, then all gambling might soon cease. 'Tis not games, but the wrong use that makes greedy gamesters. Not the feet keeping time to merry music in the winding, wheeling, whirling waltz, two-step and schotische, but in excess, and public promiscuous, "sporty" associations, within the embrace of many twining, oft-polluted arms, pressing each to heart, that tune human nerves to many discordant strains that surely follow. Unwise is the man of today that opposes any innocent recreation, because unwisely or badly abused by some. Let us rather raise all rights to ideals that know no wrong by early teaching of the youth.

Here you see immense bins for grain, filled from the rich prairie and valley surrounding X-Ranch, or DeNoya villa. He once owned 7,000 head of cattle, but now has only 4,300; but is still one of the largest dealers and shippers of cattle in the Osage. This is a great grain section; seventy bushels of corn have been produced per acre on X-Ranch bottoms. Mr. DeNoya has erected an 18,000 capacity elevator and grist mill at the station, and last fall received more than they could easily handle. Remington is only a flag station now as no agent is kept in the depot. When looking over western Osage don't fail to see X-Bar Ranch and its hospitable proprietor. The memory of a pleasant entertainment here will long linger with the writer. For the lack of photographer, to take views we regret that cuts do not appear to show the idealiy of this country villa and fine orchards.

ALL HAIL TO OKLAHOMA STATE

The greatest territory, including Indian Territory, that ever knocked at the congressional door for addmission to statehood, after years of seeking admission, are, at last, seemingly about to be admitted. The bill as passed unanimously by the senate, with amendments; one to allow the people of the "Twin Territories," and New Mexico and Arizona, to vote on affairs of most concern to their people, as the capital location of Great Oklahoma, an amendment by Mr. Teller, and carried by 31 to 39; and for N. M. and Ari. to decide each as to whether they desire joint statehood, is a wise piece of national legislation, as only the people of these sections should have a right to decide for their best future course. For Oklahoma and I. T. have, still, great resources to develop, and N. M. and Ari. have only begun good. The motion of Mr. Burrows to separate the interests of the southwest territories was the part of a true statesman, but lost on the first vote of 35 to 36. Mr. Foraker's amendment to give N. M. and Ari. opportunity to vote on joint, or separate, statehood, was as magnamanious. The writer is for all effective temperance measure, but believes the "Prohibition" (?) clause should apply to both eastern and western Oklahoma alike, or neither. The appropriation of $5,000,000 for educational interests is O. K., and the provisions to set aside sections 16 and 36 in each township of land in Okla. for public sale is to be commended, for several reasons. It is to hoped political contentions in the house will not longer delay the bill. Upon the fine prospect of the "fair" bride or "ship of state," coming in a few days, this history closes with congratulations for Oklahoma and her young Governor in the following dedicatory verses:

HISTORY OF THE OSAGE NATION

Mr. James Bigheart, ex-chief of the Osages, after whom Bigheart Townsite is named.

TRUE FRIENDSHIP.
Dedicated to the Osage, and Oklahoma, January, 1906, New Bride of State.

True friendship is our golden chain and charm,
    So bards in romance often sing,
In life's onward rush a mighty arm
    To man's success in life, home, ere love, or anything.

In confidence, companions sought a bond most sweet,
    Without her fostering, tender care
Our pleasures, joys, wealth, are fleet,
    Our fame and genius weak, and victories most rate.

Then while your pen may dry, oft silent be,
    Mine in friendship's realms, shall roam;
Back, back again, fair one! to thee—
    If but for one reply: "I'll meet you in my home."

Though every straw in Osage fields of grain
    Were pens, streams Homa's showers of ink,
Seas of snowy cotton, parchment, he'd ne'er complain,
    Of unquilled sounds, while of him you think.

For written works may be but broken wings,
    Tho' beautiful as Birds of Paradise expressed,
And sweeter far on tongue that sings,
    You may return, in thought and memory you'll rest.

                —Phil Dickerson.

HISTORY OF THE OSAGE NATION

BUSINESS DIRECTORY OF THE OSAGE COUNTRY UP TO OCT. 30, '05.

(P)—Pawhuska; (S)—Skiatook; (H)—Hominy; (F)—Fairfax; (B)—Burbank.

Banks—(P). First National, Citizens National, and B. of Commerce. (S).—Skiatook B., B. of Skiatook. (H.)—Hominy First National. (F.)—Osage B., and First National. Bank of Remington, (O. T.)

Builders & Contractors.—(P.) A. V. Linscott, A. H. Hunt and Mr. Beck.

Blacksmiths.—(P.) C. B. Thomas, J. C. Ferguson, Main St. Shop. (S.) V. F. Pinson. (H.) Shaffner & Bennett, A. B. Patterson. (F.) J. H. Dull. (B.) R. C. Norris.

Barbers.—O. S. Shop, E. F. Kreyer, Mgr., and J. R. Kreyer and Jno. Vandervert, assts; Blue Point. R. D. Blanc, Mgr.; A. M.Goltra shop; T. T. Roberts, H. A. Gosney, W. W. Martin, assts. (S.) C. G. Tinklepaugh. (H.) J. G. Eversole. (F.) Jno. Sherrill & Son.

Bakeries, Confectionaries, etc.—Curtis Bros., Enterprise, Arthur O'Dell & M. O. Stephenson, Oscar Ade, Bonton, B. F. Parsons. (S.) C. F. Rogers (C); H. D. Swearinger, (E.)—(H.) Butternut B., H. L. Geeno & J. B. Meadows, Prs.

Doctors, M. D's.—(P.) J. M. Way, Government Physician; Jos. Dunn, Harry Walker, Geo. Dunn, W. H. Aaron, R. L. Hall, E. A. Jones, J. A. Speck, Mr. and Mrs. E. G. Barton, (D. O.). Geo. H. Grady (V. S.). Mr. White, (V. S.). (S) Jos Sheafe, L. A. O'Brien, J. M. Poindexter, J. C. Nickols (Hillside, I. T.). (H.) Dr. Mullins, Dr. Fraley, Dr. Spiers.

Dentists.—(P.) F. C. Gale, J. B. Talbutt, J. L. Hamilton.

Druggists and Jewelers.—(P.) Percy J. Monk, Osage Drug Co., E. E. Patterson, Mgr.,A. E Patterson, clk., I. F. Anderson, pr., Jerry L. Hartanbower, clk. Skiatook Drug Co., Fr O'Brien Ch ke Drug Co., J. Noble Thompson and T. F. McVay. (H.) Mullins Drug Co. (F.) Carl H. Hudson.

Furniture.—Baker-Cerney Co., Johnson & Fowler, Eureka 2nd H. Store. (S.) C. C. Nickles (& Undtg.) (H.) Jas. West & C. L. Kelly.

General Merchandise.—Old Red Store, C. M. Hirt & Co., Osage Mercantile Co., W. C. Tucker, Mgr., Geo. Pratt's Price Store, & W. A. Day; Racket, Mrs. M. C. Hardwick, pro., L. W. N. H. clk; McLaughlin & Farrar, (T. H. & F. W.),—W. D. Parry, H. R. Sargent, Miss Mary Loeb, W. W. Mathews, (D. G. clks.)—C. C. Garlinghouse (furniture).—H. W. McLaughlin, N. F. Overfield, J. R. Tolley & C. I. Calhahan, (Gro. clks.)—W. A. Daniels, Donal Farrar, (clo. clks.);—Roy Tolley, Frank Foote, Arthur Hunt, Elex Roberts, (Lbr Yard). G. J. Wilkinson B'k'. Miss Grace Luppy cashier;—Midland Valley Mer. Co., Leonard Polson, Mgr., A. Y. Shaw, V. V. Campbell, (clks.); J. W. Parson's (Notions & Racket).

Citizens Tradi g Co.—A. H. Gibson, Mgr. Emory Gibson, (fullblood), James Bigheart, J. H. Bartles, and Mrs. Nona P. Barndollar, stockholders, Oscar Burdette, W. J. Boone, Miss Annie Wheeler, (clks). J. H. Comer (b'k'r.), W. E. Hewitt & Son, Skiatook,—W. C. Rogers, Chas. Strange, A. B. Parks, (clks.). J. H. Craig & W. C. Webb. Feighly & Son; A. E. Townsend & Co.; L. A. Tyler, Master T. O. Jameson. Hominy Trading Co.; Fred Wood; M. F. Fraley, Harris & Nash, (Osage Jnc.) Saxon & Co. Fairfax—J. L. Van Sant (Mil. D. G. & Ladies Furnishings), L. A. Wismeyer, J. B. Wilson; H. G. Burt. Remington—L. L. DeNoya, J. R. Foote, clks. Burbank, Ira McCorcle & Son.

Groceries—(P.) Hunter Bros. J. A. & W. D.; C. B. Peters (Flour & Feed), Frank Jay (Geo. Stacy, clk.). J. W. Edwards (Hay & F.). Mr. Younger. (F.), Harris & Sapp.

Hotels—Pawhuska House; Midland, Leland, J. B. Maker, Pr.; Carlton House, J. J. Rhodes Pr.; Watkins Bdg. House, Skiatook, Whitney & Leland, G. A. Whitney, pr. Commercial & Cafe, O. E. Mason, Pr.—(H.) Commercial H. M. Westbrook, Pr.; Chautauqua, W. H. Stout, Pr.; Merchants, E. N. Carnett, Pr.; Osage Jnn. (Jnc.) A. Duke, Pr. Metropolitan, T. M. Alby, Pr. (F.) Ponton House.

Hardware—(P.) Baker-Cerney Co. (& furniture.) Hays Hickerson, Plumber; Flannagan & James plumbing. (S.) Fred Lynde Plummer and Machinist; C. C. Nickles. (H.) J. H. Stumpff, Jr., Jno. & C. L. Kelley. (F.) Ross & Hunsaker, (& Furn. & Undtg.) Goad, Farrell & Co. (Hard. & Har.).

HISTORY OF THE OSAGE NATION

Liveries, Feed and Wagon Yards.—(P.) Thos. Leahy & Son, (Will.) Stone Barn, C. L. Harris & Son (S. T.); Leland Barn, D. B. Maher Pr.; Chris Hansen; W. R. Wells; Bird Creek Yard, Davis & Hall. Red Store Yard, C. R. Hare; and Dr. Grady (V. S.) Osage Jnc. Saxon & Co. (S.) John Harlow, (& sale barn). (H.) L. H. & Bert Westbrook's L. Barn. (F.) Morledge & Son. W. N. Ballard.

Lumber Co's.—(P.) Spurrier, Duncan Bros., Dickason-Goodman & Co., W. R. Beydler, Mgr.; Cragin Lbr. Co., L. C. Snodgrass, Mgr.; Minnetonka Lbr. Co., F. C. Bell Mgr. (H.) W. J. R. Fellows, Jas. Beebe, Mgr.; Hominy Lbr. Co. (F.) L. A. Wismeyer Lbr. Yd., F. D. Waugh, Mgr.

Laundry—Jet White, Wayland Wood Pr.

Mill & Elevator Co's.—(P.) Osage M. & E. Co. (S.) Cherokee M. & E. Co., S. M. Patterson, Mgr. Fairfax Grain & E. Co., McGraw Bros., Mgrs.

Law.—(P.) J. N. Coulter, Jno. T. Leahy. E. F. Scott. Hardin Ebey, Isaac D. Taylor, E. W. King, (notary). Judge E. N. Yates, (U. S. Com. Hargis Bros., H. C. & Wrightman, Fulton & John Palmer, C. S. McDonald, J. D. Mitchell; P. A. Shinn. (S.) C. N. Cleveland (N. P.), Chas. H. Nash, (N. P.).

Millinery.—(P.) Mrs. G. H. Saxon; Famous, Leona Jarrell; J. F. Berryhill & Sister (Mable); Mrs. Ollie Crabbe; Mrs. J. W. Parsons. (S.) Mrs. W. R. Beydler; Misses Dora & Rose Miller. (F.) J. L.Van Sant.

Meat Markets—(S.) Curtis Bros. (F.) G. A. Morris Market. P. Spirling, Mgr.; Jesse Givens, A. N. Hinkle. (S.) City M. M., G. C. Smyth, Pr., J. W. Stewart, Mgr. (H.) W. H. McConnell; Palace, T. P. Countryman, Pr. (F.) M. E. Ponton's Market.

Men's Clothing Tailoring—Schaeber C. Co.; B. Liebenheim. (S.) R. F. Sunday, Shoes, C. & Racket.

Real Estate—Pawhuska Realty Co.; Carlton & Tolson, E. M. Demsey; Steffen & Smith; W. M. Dial & E. W. King; Geo. B. Mellotte (R. & Ins.) Ewing F. G. A. Morris (Insur.); Mr. Baker; C. N. Prudom. (S.) C. H. Cleveland; Chas. H. Nash. (F.) Wm. Bennett.

Restaurants—(P.) Blue Point, Ed Simpkins, Will Hall, Fred Cross; Home, G. O. Williams, Pr.; Gem, H. W. Kuhlman, Pr.; Main St. Res.; Moss Cafe, Mr. & Mrs. C. A. Moss, prs; Chilli, Joe Lenaris, Juan Rodrige. S.) Whitney Cafe, Jonathan Carr. (H.) A. L. Henston. (F.) H. R. Patton, (S. O.) City Res't., W. H. Palmer, Pr.; Barney Gibbs.

Photographers—(P.) Mrs. Gladys Hargis, and Geo. W. Hargis; G. W. Parsons; (H.) Mrs. Alma Spiers, Mr. Cavner, Ralston.

Painters, Paper Hangers—(P.) Chester Yake; E. R. Larey; Henry Barnes, (Bug. & Car. P.). (S.) C. H. Keller.

Miscellaneous—(P.) J. C. Pollard's Bottling Works.—J. C. Mendenhall, (Singer Co.); Osage Roller Mills; Wm. Kelley, boot and shoe maker; Osage Tel. Co.; P. S. Harris, Mgr.—J. W. Bradshaw, house mover—McKinny & Miller, carp. shop. W. E. McGuire, postmaster.—Rink Opera House, Mr. Woodring Mgr.—(S.) A. B. Morris, Billiard Hall. (H.) C. C. Hopkins shoe & Boot Mfgr., Martin Tel. System. (F.) Kaw City Tel. Co., R. L. Bristo, Pr. P. M. Osage Jc'n.

FRATERNAL SOCIETIES.

A. F. & A. M.—Saturday in or before the full moon of each month and two weeks afterwards at 7:30. J. W. Franks, W. N.; J. H. Comer, Sec.

Eastern Star—The 1st & 2nd Tuesdays in each month at 4:00 p. m. P. J. Monk, W. P.; Mrs. E. M. Campbell, W. M.

I. O. O. F.—Every Monday evening at 7:30 p. m. Ed. McMahon, Sec.; Chas. F. Leech, N. G.

K. of P.—Every Wednesday evening 7:30 p. m. Wm. Kelly, Rec.; E. Wheeler, C. C.

Modern Woodmen—Every first and third Friday evening 7:30. W. A. Daniels, Clerk; P. Spirling, V. C.

Juanita Camp No. 2593 Royal Neighbors of America—Meets 2nd and 4th Fridays of each month. M's. Jennie Spirling, Oracle; Mrs. Linda C. Daniels, Recorder.

(COPYRIGHTED FEBRUARY 1906.)
by Philip J. Dickerson.

**SONG OF THE TRAVELER
GOING AND COMING
ON
THE MUSICAL TIME
"THE METEOR."**

For as straight a line as the buzzing bees fly,
Carrying their honey to their distant hive,
More direct and rapid than the beautiful dove,
So silently fleet as carrier pigeons move,
Returning, afar, from strange lands, home,
Your latest of messages from friends long gone,
Ere your loved ones themselves as all go and come,
To or from Splendid Trains of easy sitting chairs,
In Pullmans, or sleepers, or diners, who cares,
Not alone by day in tourist-sightseeing cars;
On! as well by night, under moonlight and stars,

Speeds

"THE METEOR"

of the

To and from all points of the compass,
Through
The Great Osage Reservation Dispatch to all Frisco Terminals,
"THE METEOR."

FROM HERE TO THERE.

On a gun line
From
Chicago to Quanah, Texas,
From
Kansas City to Ft. Worth & San Antonio,
From
St. Louis to Oklahoma City and Guthrie, ,)
From
Evansville, (Ind.) and Springfield, to Enid, Oklahoma.
From
Eureka Springs ' Anthony, (Kansas).
From
Memphis to Wichita,
From
Ellsworth, Kan., to Hope, Ark.,
From
Joppa, (Egypt, Ill.) to Avard, Oklahoma.
From
Birmingham to Denver and Colorado Springs, and each taps the
Osage Country as the center of.

MAP OF MIDLAND VALLEY RAILROAD AND CONNECTIONS.

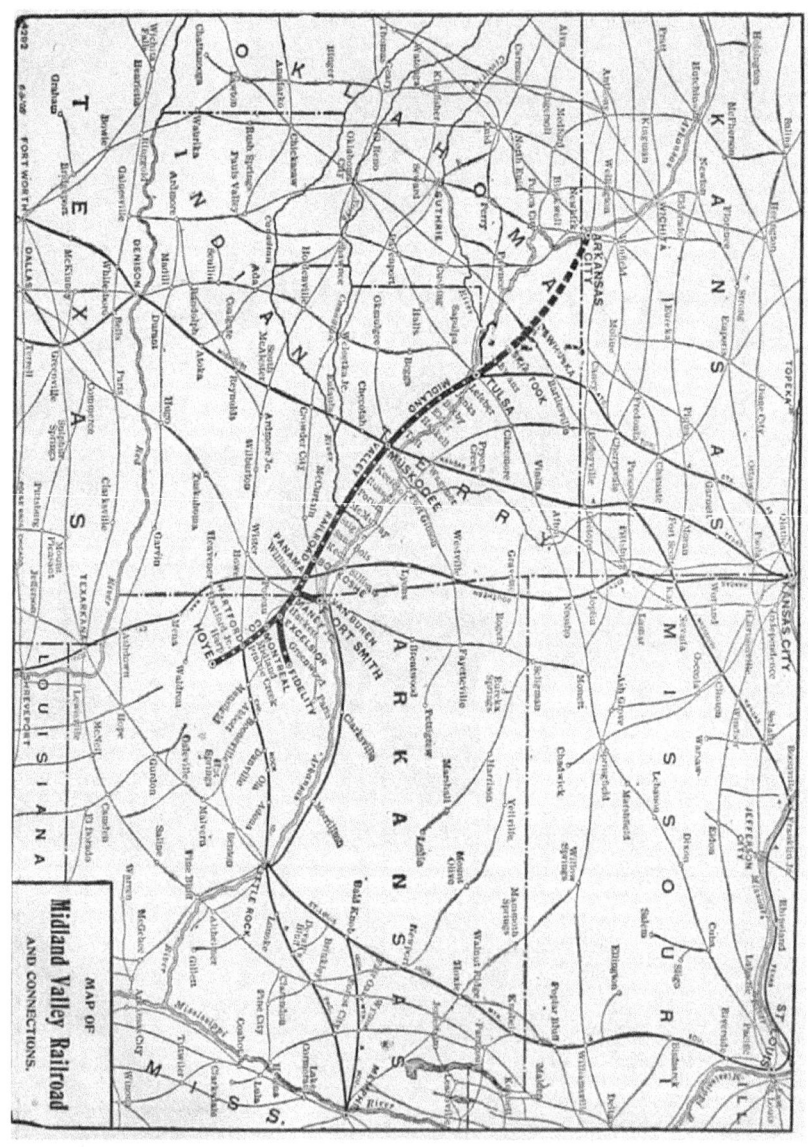

(1) Osage (fullblood) village and round house, oil and gas wells in the background.
(2) Osage national government schools, from cupola of the Agent's dwelling. First building, girls' dormitory; second, reception hall; third, boys' dormitory, and farm in the background.

Index

"BIG WOMAN" 38
"KIHEKAH-TUN-KAH" 38
"UNCLE JIMMY" 23
"UNCLE TOM" 87
(APACHE WOMAN) 27
(ISLAND MAN) 27

AARON
   Dr 84
ADA 82
A'DATE
   Chief 27
AKERS
   Mr N K 41
AKIN
   Ed 141
   Paul 53
ALBY
   T M 153
ALEXANDER
   James A 98
   Miss May 98
ALLEN
   Ethan 12
ANDERSON
   J F 69
ANGIE P 24,26
APOLIS 85
APPLEBY
   L 121
   Lou 121
   Mrs Jane 106
ARBUCKLE
   General 31
ARBUCLE
   Brig Gen M 37
A-SAH-A-WA 29
A-SAH-A-WAH 29
AUSTIN
   Prof 80
   Prof Robt E 34
AWRENCE
   Mrs 114

BABCOCK
   Gen 9
BACK DOG 56
BACON RIND 18,56,79

Asistant Chief 118
BAKER
   Mr 50
   Mr O M 49
BALLARD
   J J 150
   W N 150
BARBER
   Mr 154
   Sam 69
BAYARD
   Judge 17
BEAULEAU
   Geo 103
BEAULIEU
   Geo H 69
BECK AND HUNT
   Messrs 11,22,23
BEEBE
   James 129
BEEDE
   Syrus 100
BELL
   F C 105
BELLEIU
   Ora 22
   Steve 22
   Thomas 22
BENNETT
   Guy 131
BERCE
   G W 149
BERRY
   S B 149
BEYDLER
   Mr 105
   Mr W T 104
   Mrs W R 104
BIG HILL BANDS 40
BIG KNIFE CHIEF 35
BIG-CHIEF
   Thomas 53
BIGHEART 111,114
   James 52,56,79,110,164
   Jas 118
   Peter 79,118
   Peter C 56
BILL NIX 16

Index

BIRD
   R E 127
BLACK DOG 79,118
BLAKE
   W M 103
BLANC
   Miss 30,80
   Mr 18
   Mrs 81
BODWELL
   L B 136
BOGGS DRILLING CO 123
BOLTWOOD
   Robert 33
BONNICASTLE
   Arthur 56
BOUNICASTLE
   Arthur 8
BOVE 85
BOWERS
   Mr 139
   Mr A G 141
BOWHAN
   Mart T 69,74,75
   Martin 98
BRADSHAW
   Geo 106,117
   George 115
   Mr 25
   Mr J W 25
   Mrs 25,117
   Mrs Will 97
   Will 25,72,117
BRADSHAY
   Mr & Mrs 25
BRAVE 56
BRENNER
   Mr 11
BRISTOW
   Mrs Kate 138
BROOKS
   Rev 84
   Rt Rev F K 81
BROWN 132
   C W 122
   Charles 56
   Miss Or Mrs 132
BROWN'S MFG CO 152

BRUNER
   Ed 106
BRUNT
   Gen 33
BRUNTON
   William 88
BURNETT
   Rev Mr 81
BURROWS
   Mr 163
BURT
   Mr H G 153
CAESAR 131
CALLAHAN
   Eugene 82
CAMPBELL
   Mr 69
CANVILLE 70
   Andrew 82
   A B 40
   Mary Louise 82
   Miss Mary 152
   Monica 82
CARLTON
   Anthony 154,155,158
   Ethel 155
   Francis 155
   Geo 154
   Marie 155
   Miss Marguerite 160
   Mr 70,155,156
   Mrs 155
   Mrs Anthony 22
   Mrs Augustine 158
CARLTON AND TOLSON
   Messrs 70
CARNETT
   Mr E H 130
CARPENTER
   Miss 22
   Miss Elizabeth 125
CEPHAS 85
CERNEY
   Adolph 49
   Mr 50
CHAMPAGNE
   Miss Mary 96

Index

Miss Mary L 87
CHARLES
J B 64
CHASTAIN
Miss Fannie 90
CHIEF A'DATE 28
CHOTEAU 6
Miss Mary A 77
Peter 37
CHOUTEAU
Auguste 52
Augustus 106
Gasso 15
A P 39
CHOUTEAUS 38
CHRISMAN
Geo 139
CHRIST 21,85,86,87,111
CHURCHILL
Mr 53
CLAIRMOT-LESSART 7
CLAMORE 53
CLAREMORE 38
Francis 57
Madame 38
CLARK
William 52
CLERMONT
Chief 28
CLEVELAND
C H 105,121
C R 121
COFFEY
Coy J A 93
James N 40
CONWAY
Claud 43
John 49
COODY
Miss 34
CORNDROPPER
Frank 56,57,79,118
COTTRELL
Miss Emly 81
COTTRELLE
Miss Emily 23
COULTER
Hon J N 48

Mr J N 18
CROGHAN 5
CURTIS
C W 45
H K 45
Mr 116
Wm E 112
CUSTER 9
CYPRIAN 53

DANIEL
B M 111
John 112
Mrs John 112
DAVID 21
DAVIES
Prof 69
Prof Wm 73,83
Rev 84,127
Rev J H 84
William 69
DAVIS
A M 41
Mr 106
Mrs Elic 106
Mrs Sophia 106
DAWSON
S T 152
DAY
Rev Mr 81
DE SOTA 5
DEL ORIER 7
Julia 102
Miss Dora 102
DEL-ORIER
Miss Mary L 65
DELORIER
Mary A 56
DEMPSEY
Mr E M 66
DEMSEY
Capt 100
DENOYA
Clement (Budge) 162
Clemont 22
Francis 21
Frank 22,162
Frank, Jr 154

Index

Frank, Sr 99,154
Frederick 162
Jake 154
Josephine 162
Lewis 22
Louis Leonard 162
Martha 22,162
Mary 22
Miss Bell 99
Miss Rosa 36
Mr 163
Rosa 22
Ruby 162
DENOYAS 7
DEWEY 103
DIAL 63
W M 18
Westly M 63
DICKASON-GOODMAN ... 104,105
DICKERSON
Phil 164
Philip 1,3
Philip J 135
DODGE
Col 28
DOE
Miss 132
DONOVAN
Charley 158
Chas 154,155,158
Jesse 158
Mr 155
Mrs Augustine 155
DOOLIN, WILSON AND STAR ....
.... 158
DORA
Miss 16
DORSEY 10
Rev J Owen 6,16
DOUNCE
Mr 23
DRAKE
Frances S 14
DREXEL
Kathrine 7
Rev Mother Katherine 72
DRUMMOND
Fred 127,129,130,133

DUGGER
Mr C N 123
DUKE
Mr A 153
DULL
Mr J H 144
DUNCAN
C A 51
Chas 69
G H 51
Geo 69
A H 69
Mr C A 52
DUNHAM
Martha 21
Mrs 22
Mrs Martha 19
DUNN
Dr Geo L 102
Dr Joseph B 102
Dr T J 102
Dr Thomas J 102
Ida 102
John Timothy 102
Marie Agnes 102
May 102
DUNNOVAN
George 141
DURHAM
Martha 21
DUTCH 31
DYKE
Rev L J 81

EBEY
Hardin 36
Hon Hardin 37
Judge Hardin 37
EDWARD & BRADFORD 105
EDWARDS
Ninian 52
EHE-SAH-PE (BLACKBEARD) 34
ERICK
Beeks 104
Grau 104
EVANS
B M 153
EWING 64

Index

Mr 62
F D CLOSSER & CO 137
FARBES
  W R 139
FARRAR
  Mrs 84
FARRELL
  John 152
  Mr 153
  Mrs Monica 82
  N H 152
FEIGLEY
  H L 108
  A K 105,108
  Mr Al 109
FELLOWS
  W R 129
FENTON
  Ebert 25
  Lou Hayes 25
FERGUSON
  J C 84
  James C 68
FISH
  Walley 69
FLANNIGAN & JAMES 51
FLORER
  John 58
  Mr 118
FORAKER
  Mr 163
FOSTER
  E B 114
  Ed B 114
  F B 114
FOX
  Ed 106
  Mr & Mrs Ed 106
  Mrs Ed 113
FRALEY MERCANTILE CO ...129
FRANTZ 104
  Capt 101,103
  Capt Frank 100
  Captain 50,103
  Captain Frank 62
  Frank 63
  Mr 103
FREEMAN 78

Col H B 100
H B 42,76,78
FRONKIER
  Arthur 15
  David 22
  Miss Rose 89
  Mr & Mrs David 15
  Rose 15
GADDIS
  Mrs F T 83
GALE
  Dr F C 18,55
  Miss 55,97
GARRETT
  M O 12
GENTNER
  Miss Addie 130
GEORGE
  Clifton 12,122
  James M 160
  James, Jr 160
  Jim 154
  Mamie 160
  Mary 160
  Mr & Mrs James 161
  Mr & Mrs James B 160
  Mr & Mrs James, Jr 161
  Mrs Jas 156
  Ruby 160
  Sylvestea 160
GERARD
  Sister Mary 6
  Sister Superior Mary 72
GIBSON
  A H 69
  Isaac T 100
  T E 11,69
GILL
  Prof 127
GILMORE
  Augustus 77
  James 77
  Johanna Coanna 77
  Mr C C 77
  Mr H C 106
  Samuel James 77
GIRARD

Index

J P 149
  Miss Daisy 150
GOAD
  C L 152
  Miss Laura 152
GOD 19,69,72,85,86,87,88,
....93,109,119
GONGRES
  James, Jr....................................... 161
  Mr 161
GOOD VOICE 16
GRADY
  Dr Geo H...................................... 41
GRAHAM
  Richard.. 37
GREAT FATHER..................... 120
GREAT GOD 76
GREAT SPIRIT 17,23,76
GREENWOOD 85
GRIGNON
  Augustin.. 26

HADDOCK
  E H 111
HAGGART
  Prof C A 138
HAINES
  Wiley G.. 103
HALL
  Bill 141
  Tom 154
HAMPTON
  Miss Lorinda 99
HANER
  Howard M 127
HARE
  C R 41
HARGIS 5,13,15,18,19,22,23,
  25,27,30,34,49,56,60,63,68,80,84,88
  D C 39
  Geo W 39
  Mr 22
  Mr W G 109
  Mrs Gladys................................... 39
HARGIS & HARGIS................ 39
HARGRAVES
  Dr 94
HARLOW

John 112
  Mr & Mrs 112
HARRIS
  Earnest.. 74
  Mr 143
  Mr P H 129
  Mr R S 15,16
HARRIS AND SAPP 143
HARRISON 100
  William Henry 37
HATFIELD
  A F 83
HAYNIE
  Miss Emma................................ 118
HAYS
  Charles... 93
HEARST
  Senator.. 103
HEH-SCAH-MOIE 56
HELMICK
  Allen C 124
HENRY
  Mrs Lauradell 75
HERRARD
  Miss Tina.................................... 43
HERRIDGE
  Edward 146
  Julia 146
  Miss Mary 146
HERRIMAN
  Miss Mable............................... 162
HIAWATHA 72
HICKERSON
  Clarance...................................... 90
  Minnie 90
  William Hayes........................... 89
  Wm H 89
HICKMON
  Mr 154
HIERONYMUS
  R E 103
HILL
  Chas 83
  Chas M 131
  G 69
  Otis 69
  Rev 71
  Rev E F................................ 83,131

Index

Rev E G 96
HILTON
  Miss 21,26,84
HIRT
  C M 68
  Mr 68,84
  Mr & Mrs C M 84
HOOTS
  Mrs Alph 106
HOOVER
  Mr 100
HOPKINS
  Lenora 137
  Mr C C 137
HOSS
  Mr 151
  Raymond N 151
  Roy 141
HOUSTON
  Mr A L 134
HUNSAKER
  Mr A C 147
HUNT
  Orial 56
  R M 56
HURLEY
  Drenx 69
  Miss Catherine 83
  Mr A W 69,83
  A W 57,69,103
HUSTON
  Miss Eliza 63

J I CASE THRESHING MACHINE CO ... 121
JAKE
  Chester 35
JAMES
  Prof 85
  Prof 139
  Rev 71
  Rev W D 81
JANEWAY
  G M 105
  Geo M 122
JAVINE
  Jno 117
JEFFERSON
  Thomas 6

JENNESS
  Mr 153
JEROME
  Mr 134
JESUS 17,72
JIM
  Miss Fine 112
JOHN 85
JOHNSON
  J E 83
  Miss 44
JONES
  Miss Or Mrs 132
  Mr 132
  W A 76
JOVINE
  Mr 118
JULIEN
  Mr & Mrs John W 101
KALHIRISE
  Walter 7
KIND
  E W 18
KING
  E W 63,66
  Miss Jennie E 61
KIRK
  Frank 120
KOH-PAY
  Harry 69
KOHPAY
  Harry 79,103
KREYER
  Burt 69
  Mr & Mrs Ed F 97
  Mrs 69
  Prof Ed F 69

L M 23
LABADIE
  Fred 69
LAMOTTE
  G G 69
  Geo 103
LARSON
  Miss Jennie 13,23
LAWRENCE 56,103

Index

LEAHY 88
  Cora 87
  Edward 44
  H T 45
  Hon John T 44
  Mr J T 44
  Mr W T 11
  Mrs Will 44
  Thomas 33,44,87,91,96
  Vava 87
  W T 56,79,118
  Will 87,91
  Will T 91
  William 87
LEAHY & HARRIS 16
LEAHY & SCOTT 44
LEAKY
  Hon Jno T 47
LEECH
  Chas 45
  Chas F 103
LESSARGE 39
LESSART 7,39,73
  Benjamin 38
  Charley 38
  Clemont 19,21
  Edward 38
  Frank 38
  Julia 38,146
  Julia Roy 39
  Madame 38
  Miss Leanor 92
  Monsieur 7
  Mrs Laura 38,39
  Sir 38
  Susan 38
LEWIS
  Wm 22
LEWIS & CLARK 5
LINSCOTT
  Mr A V 45
  A V 23
LITTLE AZA 27
LOMBARD
  Roselle 106
LONG
  James 118
  Miss Mary 22

LOOKOUT
  Fred 56
LOOMER
  H M 103
LORD 86
LORD JESUS CHRIST 72
LUNDY
  Mr Jno 106
LYNDE
  F 105
LYNN
  Jno P 70
  John P 61
  Mr & Mrs 70
  Mr W G 153
  Mrs 70

MCCLUSKY 29
MCCONNELL
  Wm 137
MCCORD
  Gocernor 103
MCCORKLE
  Ira 155
  Miss Roxanna 160
  Miss Roxie 161
  Mr 154,156
  Robert 156
MCCORMACK HARVESTING MACHINE CO 121
MCCOSKEY
  Mrs Ollie 118
MCCOY
  Mr 50
  Mr A W 50
MCCREIGHT
  Prof Robert R 27,80
  Robt R 80
MCGEE
  W J 10
MCGRAW
  Henry 147
  Thomas 147
MCGUIRE
  Bird S 55,57
  Robert 60
  Rolland 60
  W E 83

Index

William 71
William E 60
Wm E 58
MCKINNEY
  F W 69
  T M 90
MCLAUGHLIN
  T H 66
MCLAUGHLIN AND FARRAR ....
.... 107
MCLOUD
  J W 104

MAHER
  Howard M 128
MAHON
  E H 43
  Laura 75
MAHR
  A B 127
MANN
  Colonel 134
MANNING BROS 139
MARTIN
  Bertha 34
  Ellen 34
  J E 127
  Judge John 33
  Martha 33,34
MARTINEZ
  Peter C 69
MARY 106
MATHEWS 47
  E M 53
  John 83
  Miss Susan 83
  Mm S 83
  Mr W S 11
  W S 13,56,57
MATTHEWS
  Wm P 16
MAY
  Miss 118,125
MEANS
  Miss Cornelia 157
MEHLHORN
  C H 105
ME-KAH-WAH-TI-AN-KAH 57

MELLOTTE
  Geo B 18
MERCER
  Joseph 105
MERIAM 21
ME-SHE-TSE-HE
  Charles 57
MICHELLE
  Charles S 32
  Chas 103
MILES
  Laban J 30
  Labon J 100
  Major 83
MILLARD
  Mrs 84
  Ret 103
MILLER 103
  Col W A 62
  Governor 31
  J L 90
  R W 69
  Ret 62
MILLIARD
  Ret 104
MIN-KE-WAH-TI-AN-HE 118
MITCHELL
  Jos B 18,84
MITSCHER
  O A 100
  Oscar A 56
MOH-E-KAH-MOI 118
MON CRAVIE 7
MONCRAVIE
  Chas 98
MONGRAIN 7
  Edith 160,161
  James 160
  Louis 160
  Mr 155
  Mr S J 156
  Mrs Mary 160
  Newell 156
  Rose 160
  Stewart 154
MONGRAM
  Charles 40
MONK

Index

Mr 109
Percy J 74,75
MOONEY
   James 9
   Mr 18
MORLEDGE
   Miss 154
   W R 153
MORLEDGE LIVERY, FEED AND
   SALE BARN 153
MORRIS
   F G A 79,82
   John 141
   Miss Daisy May 92
   Mr F A G 61
MOSES
   Mr 21
MOSIER
   Grandmother 106
   Mrs 117
   Mrs Adeline 117
   Mrs Adline 113
   Thomas 46,117
   Thos 117
   Tom 56
   W T 118
   W T M 79
MOTHER MARY 72
MOTLEDGE
   L B 153
MULLIN
   Dr Ira 133
MULLIN'S DRUG CO 130
MULLINS DRUG COMPANY .. 133

NAPOLEON 109
NASH
   C H 105
   Chas H 104
   Mr A W 129
NE-KAH-KE-PON-AH 53
NE-KAH-WAH-SHE-TAN-KAH ...
.... 118
NE-KAH-WAH-SHE-TUN-KAH
.... 56,79
NE-KAH-WASH-SHE-TAN-KAN .
.... 53
NELLIE 29

NICHOLS
   Miss Amanda 84
NORRIS
   R C 157
O'KEOUGH
   General 109
O-KE-SAH 33
OKU
   General 109
O-LAH-HAH-MOI 118
OLIVER CHILLED PLOWS 152
O-LO-HAL-MOIE 57
O-LO-HO-WAL-LA 18,57,126
   Chief 79,90,118
O'NEIL
   Capt 103
OWENS
   Don 69
O'YAMA
   General 109
   Patrick 109
OYAMA
   Field Marshal 109
   General 109

PA-HU-SKA 58
PALMER
   Hon Jno 45
   Hon John 22,47,74
   J F 118
   John F 79
   Miss Mabel 22
   Mrs John 22
PAPIN 97
PAPPAN 7
PAPPIN 7,25
PARRY
   W D 83,84
PARSONS
   B F 69
PASCHE
   Chas 151
   Mr 150
PATTERSON
   Bert 137
PAUL 85
PAWNEE-NO-PAH-SHE 53

Index

PAYNE
Miss Helen 35
PEARSON
Joseph 22,154
Mr & Mrs J R 36
Mr J R 36
October 36
PENN
William 53
PERRIER 7
Jim 106
Miss Adline 117
Miss Sophia 112
PERRY
W D 69
PETER 85
PETERSON
Miss Lula 156
PETTIT
Frank 136
Judge 136
Judge J W 47,54,99
Miss Nettie 99
Mrs 100
PICKARD
Jay E. 17
PLAKE
W M 69
PLOMONDON 7
Agnes 22
Barney 22
Clement 22
Clementine 22
Clemmy 155
Dan 22
Frances 22
Frank 22
Louis 22
Louise 22
Martha 22
Mary 22
Miss Mary 155
Moses 22,155
Mrs Clementine 21
Rosa 22
Stella 22
PLUMMER
J T 150

POCAHONTAS 72
POLLOCK
Wm J 78
POLSON
L M 69
PO-NE-NO-PAH-SHE 40
PONTON
Mr & Mrs J R 144
POTTER
Captain 100
POWELL
J W 9
PRATT
Miss 30,80
PRICE
Mr 128
Prentis 127
Prentiss 133
PRICE AND PRICE 129
PRINCE ALBERT 8
PROCTER 5
PRUDHOMME 7
PRUDOM
C N 47,79,118
Charles N 56
Chas N 63
Mr C N 61
PRUE 39

QUARLES
E T 150
W N 149
QUAY
Mr D C 105

R E BIRD & CO 130
RAMBO
Mrs Mamie 96
RAVELETT 7
REV SISTER ANGELICA 71
REVARD
"Uncle Joe" 25,77
"Uncle" Joe 97
Carl 25
Elnora 25
Frank 84,85,92
Joseph 49,84
Joseph, Jr 25

181

Index

Josephine 22
Kert 25
Leonard 84,92
Margurite 25
May 25
Miss 49
Miss Josephine 162
Miss Louise 77
Miss May 97
Mrs Zoah 25
Odel 25
Uncle Joseph 92,119
REVARDS 7
REVARS 7,85
REVELLETTE 39
RILEY
   Henry 141
RINE
   Bacon 57
RIPLEY
   H C 103
   Mr H C 81
RIVARDS 38
ROACH
   Mr 154
   Mr Sam 154
ROCHAU
   Julius F 151
RODGERS
   Judge 33
ROE
   Mrs 132
ROGERS
   Antoine 124
   Arthur 34,125
   Celia 89
   Darius 40
   Emmett 89
   Jasper 15,88
   Judge 33,34,83
   Judge T L 44,47,83,89,125
   Judge Thomas L 91
   Judge Thomas Louis 33
   Kenneth 125
   Lewis 34
   Louis 125
   Maud 89
   Miss Bertha 44
   Miss Martha L 91
   Miss Mary 70
   Mr 126
   Mr Jasper 89
   Mrs 91
   Rose 15
   T L, Sr 33
   W C 89,106,121,125
ROOSEVELT
   Col 103
   Colonel 103
   President 103
ROSS
   Miss Emma 22
   Mr U A 147
ROSS AND HUNSAKER 147
ROY 7,39
   John 74
   Julia 19,21,38,39,73
   Miss Julia 38
RUBLE
   A N 66
   A W 11
RUST
   Richard 69
SANDERS
   Miss Martha A 155
SANDS
   Mr A S 50
SAPP
   Mr 143
SAUCY CHIEF 7,12,16,29,30,
..................................38,53
SAXON
   Geo 45
   Geo H 153
   Mrs 87
   Mrs Geo H 96
SCARBOROUGH
   J D 12
   Mr 65,93
   Mrs 84
SCHAEBER
   Mr A C 74
SCHOOLCRAFT 5
SCOTHORN
   Jno H 17

Index

SCOTT
  Miss Or Mrs 132
  Mr 132
  Mr E F 44
SELBY
  Mr O M 65
SEMATMA 27
SEWARD
  Miss Maria S 101
SHAFFNER
  Mr G A 131
SHA-PA-NAH-SHE 67
SHAW
  Frank 19,22
  Moses 19,22,82
  Mrs Frank 22
  Rosa 19,22
SHEAFE
  Dr 108
SHEPARD
  Mr 134
SHERRILL
  John 138
SHIELDS
  Miss Lillie 154
SHOEMAKER
  Father 8,71
  John 42
  Rev Father 85
SHUN-KAH-MO-LAH 56
SIMCIX
  Mr 45
SIMCOCK
  Geo W 82
  Mr 59
SIMPKINS 65
SIMPSON
  Mr 83
  Mrs 83
SISTER ANGELICA 71
SKINNER
  Jno R 130
SLATER
  Miss Virginia A 60
SMILEY
  T E 104
SMITH
  Hoke 114

Miss Martha 98
Miss Or Mrs 132
Mr 132
P 100
Sam 141
SODERSTOM
  E B 69
SODERSTROM
  Ebbie A 93
  Eben 65
  John 93
  John P 65
  Mrs Laura 93
SOLDANI 7
  Sylvester J 158
SPEED
  Horace 17
SPIRLING
  Mr P 60,61,81
SPRUILL
  D H 13,82
  Mr D H 11
SPYBUCK
  Henry 113
  Mary 113
  Miss Minnie Voila 113
STINK
  John 107,109
STOKES
  Mr 39
STONER
  Miss 60
STRATTON
  Mr L J 75
STUDER
  Louis 74
SULLIVAN
  Mr H C 111
SUTTON
  Dr G W 83

TAH-WAH-CHE-HE 53
TALL CHIEF 6,53
  Eaves 56
  Elex 6
  Eves 138
TAVIBO 19
TAYLOR

Bayard 19
Isaac D 66
TAYRIAN 7,53
TELLER
Mr 163
THOMAS
C B 50,51
Mrs 44
THOMPSON
J W 105
TINKER
Frank 23,45,77,113
Frank, Jr 77
Mrs Frank 77
Richard 106,113
Wm 77
TODD
W J 150
TOHABEE (TATSI) 31
TOW-AH-HEE 118
TOWNSEND
A C 105
Mr 111
Mr A E 110
TOWNSEND, SULLIVAN & CO...
....110
TRAMMEL
R E 13
TRAMMELL
Mr R E 11
TRIMM
J H 150
TRUBLY
Julian 62
TRUMBLEY
Miss Ida 75
TRUMBLY
Andrew 98
Augustine 98
Francis 98
Ida 98
J W 47
John B 98
Julian 57,98
Miss 36
Mr & Mrs 98
Rose 98
TSA-MAH-HAH 33

TUCKER
Mrs 80,84
Mrs Laura 71
Mrs Laura E 81
W C 66
TWO-GIVER 53
TYLER
L A 105

UNCLE SAM 6,9,24,37,40,58,
.... 76,116,119

WAGONER
Mr Clint 141
WAH-DAH-NE-GAH 40
WALKER
Dr Harry 79
WALLACE
Miss Louise 74
WALLER
Mrs Dora (G E) 156
WATIE
Col Stand 33
Stand 31
WAT-TI-AN-KAH 53
WATTS
Mr J H 82
Rev 82
WAUGH
F D 152
Mr F D 148,151
WAY
J M, M D 103
WAYMAN
Mrs Nora (G L) 156
WEST
Tom 57
WHEELER
C 69
Mr 59
WHILE HAIR 16
WHITE HAIR 38,40,53,58
WHITNEY
Mr & Mrs 110
Mr G A 110
WILSON
Mr J B 145,146
Mrs Jane 49

WISEMEYER
   Mr 6
WISMEYER
   L A 139,147,148,149,151
   Miss 148
   Mr 150
WISMEYER GENERAL
   MERCHANDISE 152
WOOD
   Mr 67
   Mrs 67
   Wayland 66
WOODRING
   Mr 97
   R J 43,69
WOODY
   J M 151
   Mr 150
WOVOKA 19

YAKE
   Mr 35
YATES
   Judge 100
   Judge E N 17,18,66,84
   Mrs Mary B 17
YOACUM
   Miss 16
YORK
   James 82
YOUNG
   J T 51
YOUNGER
   Mr 62

www.ingramcontent.com/pod-product-compliance
Lightning Source LLC
Chambersburg PA
CBHW031151020426
42333CB00013B/607